SWIFT'S *DISCOURSE*

A DISCOURSE

of the Contests and Dissentions Between the Nobles and the Commons in Athens and Rome

With the Consequences they had upon both those States

By

JONATHAN SWIFT

Edited with an Introduction and Notes Textual, Critical, and Historical by

FRANK H. ELLIS

OXFORD
AT THE CLARENDON PRESS
1967

Oxford University Press, Ely House, London W. 1

GLASGOW NEW YORK TORONTO MELBOURNE WELLINGTON
CAPE TOWN SALISBURY IBADAN NAIROBI LUSAKA ADDIS ABABA
BOMBAY CALCUTTA MADRAS KARACHI LAHORE DACCA
KUALA LUMPUR HONG KONG TOKYO

PRINTED IN GREAT BRITAIN

PREFACE

SWIFT's first book, with its portentous title, *A Discourse of the Contests and Dissentions between the Nobles and the Commons in Athens and Rome, with the Consequences they had upon both those States*, has been so little regarded that not even its date of publication has been properly fixed. This failure has led to some remarkable anachronisms in existing discussion of the work. It has been variously supposed that the *Discourse* 'may have contributed to bring about the acquittal of Somers', that 'it brought [Swift] an audience with the king', and that it determined the Earl of Berkeley 'to get rid of so untractable a dependent, by gratifying him with a living'. But none of these suppositions, unfortunately, is true. Impeachment charges against Somers were dismissed four months *before* the *Discourse* was published. William III and Swift were never in England at the same time *after* the *Discourse* was published. And Thomas Roscoe made the last claim about *The Discovery* (1699), not about the *Discourse*, as Émile Pons supposed.

Critical judgement of the work has been equally unreliable. John Forster found that it contains 'nothing that calls for detailed remark', and Sir Henry Craik complained that it lacks 'the force and humour with which Swift usually invests the dry bones of a forgotten dispute'. A more recent critic has even denied that the work is satiric. But the exact opposite of these remarks seems closer to the truth. Written at the same time as *A Tale of a Tub*, when Swift had all that genius which he later was to exclaim about, with '*his Invention at the Height, and his Reading fresh in his Head*', the *Discourse* is an unusually well-constructed, bold, and sophisticated political satire.

One difficulty is that the *Discourse* is minutely topical. This is suggested even in the work itself. The first sentence in Chapter V explains that it was 'Some Reflections upon the late publick Proceedings among us, and that Variety of Factions into which we are still so intricatly engaged, [that] gave Occasion to this Discourse'. The 'force and humour' which have been denied to the work derive in fact from the crazy light which it picks up and throws back on obscure details of political history at the turn of the eighteenth century.

That the *Discourse* is an allegory presents another difficulty. Satire on 'the late publick Proceedings' of the Tory majority in the 4th and 5th Parliaments of William III is managed wholly in terms of Greek and Roman analogues. That this was something of a *tour de force* was recognized even by the angry Jacobites who wrote replies to the work. But it also makes the *Discourse* almost unintelligible today.

To make the *Discourse* intelligible, therefore, a good deal of 'detailed remark' is called for. This is supplied primarily in the form of footnotes to the text. While it is true that 'the comments often enough merely express the commentator's bewilderment', it was felt that in some cases even a guess is better than a hiatus.

The text itself is reprinted from the first edition, corrected by and collated with all later editions of any importance. A few problems are also treated more fully in the discussion which follows the text. By these means it is hoped that 'the judicious Reader' (whom Swift addresses in *The Mechanical Operation of the Spirit*) 'may without much straining, make his Applications as often as he shall think fit'. This, in turn, should enable him to understand what Roscoe *did* say about the *Discourse*: he called it 'correct and luminous'.

Charles J. Hill, Bernard M. W. Knox, and Robert Walcott have read parts of this book at various stages of its production, and it is a pleasure, at last, to be able to thank them for the assistance which they so generously provided. David F. Foxon, formerly Assistant Keeper, the British Museum, F. J. E. Hurst, Librarian, Trinity College, Dublin, and Stephen Schneiderman, Classics Department, Smith College, have also helped in ways too various to mention, but for which I am equally grateful.

CONTENTS

ILLUSTRATIONS

ABBREVIATIONS

(*Note:* Unless otherwise stated, all works are cited in the first edition, and the place of publication is London)

Allen	Robert J. Allen, 'Swift's earliest political tract and Sir William Temple's essays', *Harvard Studies and Notes in Philology and Literature*, xix (1937), 3–12.
Burnet	Gilbert Burnet, *History of My Own Time*, 2 vols., 1723 and 1734.
Corr.	*The Correspondence of Jonathan Swift*, ed. F. Elrington Ball, 6 vols., 1910–14.
Coxe	*Correspondence of Charles Talbot, Duke of Shrewsbury*, ed. William Coxe, 1821.
D.N.B.	*Dictionary of National Biography*, ed. Leslie Stephen and Sidney Lee, 22 vols., New York and London, 1885–1901.
Hawkesworth	*The Works of Jonathan Swift, D.D., Dean of St. Patrick's Dublin, Accurately Revised*, 8°, ed. John Hawkesworth, 12 vols., 1754–5.
H.M.C. Charlemont MSS.	*The Manuscripts and Correspondence of James, First Earl of Charlemont*, Historical Manuscripts Commission, 2 vols., 1891–4.
H.M.C. Cowper MSS.	*The Manuscripts of the Earl Cowper*, Historical Manuscripts Commission, 3 vols., 1888–9.
H.M.C. Downshire MSS.	*Report on the Manuscripts of the Marquess of Downshire*, Historical Manuscripts Commission, 4 vols. in 5, 1924–40.
H.M.C. Lords MSS.	*The Manuscripts of the House of Lords*, Historical Manuscripts Commission, 15 vols. (1–4 Old Series, 1–11, New Series), 1887–1962.
H.M.C. Portland MSS.	*The Manuscripts of His Grace the Duke of Portland*, Historical Manuscripts Commission, 10 vols., 1891–1931.
Nichols, *Anecdotes*	John Nichols, *Literary Anecdotes of the Eighteenth Century*, 9 vols., 1812–15.

Nichols, *Illustrations*	John Nichols, *Illustrations of the Literary History of the Eighteenth Century*, 8 vols., 1817–58.
Ogg	David Ogg, *England in the Reigns of James II and William III*, 2nd ed., Oxford, 1957.
Parl. Hist.	William Cobbett, *The Parliamentary History of England*, 12 vols., 1806–12.
Poems	*The Poems of Jonathan Swift*, ed. Harold Williams, 3 vols., Oxford, 1937.
Prose	*The Prose Writings of Jonathan Swift*, ed. Herbert Davis, 14 vols., Oxford 1939–63.
Ralph	[James Ralph,] *The History of England: During the Reigns of King William, Queen Anne, and King George the First*, 2 vols., 1744 and 1746.
Scott	*The Works of Jonathan Swift*, ed. Walter Scott, 19 vols., Edinburgh, 1814.
Teerink	Herman Teerink, *A Bibliography of the Writings in Prose and Verse of Jonathan Swift*, The Hague, 1937; 2nd ed., ed. Arthur H. Scouten, Philadelphia, 1963.
TT	*A Tale of a Tub. To which is added The Battle of the Books and the Mechanical Operation of the Spirit. By Jonathan Swift*, ed. A. C. Guthkelch and D. Nichol Smith, Oxford, 1920.
Tindal	Nicholas Tindal, *The History of England, By Mr. Rapin de Thoyras. Continued from the Revolution to the Accession of George II*, 13 vols., 8°, 1744–7.
Vernon	*Letters Illustrative of the Reign of William III. From 1696 to 1708. Addressed to The Duke of Shrewsbury, by James Vernon Esq., Secretary of State*, ed. George P. R. James, 3 vols., 1841.
Williams	Sir Harold Williams, *The Text of 'Gulliver's Travels'*, Cambridge, 1952.

1. BACKGROUND

Ground Rules for the Paper War of 1697–1702

A DISCOURSE of the Contests and Dissentions is an incident in what James Ralph called '*the Paper-War* in England'.[1] This was a literary civil war which raged during the interval of peace between the Treaty of Ryswick which ended King William's War in September 1697 and the outbreak of the War of the Spanish Succession in May 1702. During this time 'whole vollyes of *Grenadoes* . . . called Pamphlets' were discharged at targets of opportunity by two categories of troops: mercenary and volunteer. Swift, of course, began as a volunteer, but he hoped thereby to promote himself to a bishopric.

The Paper War of 1697–1702 was simply an intensification of a partisan discussion of political differences which began in England in the 1640's and which continues today in a somewhat politer form. But the violence of the controversy and the enormous volume of publication in 1697–1702 remain to be accounted for. These were largely the result of three closely related developments: the emergence of public opinion as a political force, the evolution of family 'interests' into political parties, and the absence of censorship. The Paper War itself provides the context in which Swift's first published satire was written. And since these three contemporary developments also define the conditions under which all satire was written in 1701, something may be said about each of them.

Public opinion was created as a political force in England when parliament began to appeal to it for support.

[1] Ralph, ii. 997.

Since debates in parliament were privileged, and no account of them could be published, they were inaccessible as propaganda. But the resolutions, messages, and addresses of either House could be ordered to be published by the House itself. The first time this was done, in April 1700, it was deplored as a demagogic trick, a kind of 'cringing to the Populacy'. But since it was effective, it was used again and again.[1]

When the King prorogued that 'never-to-be-forgotten Parliament, in the year 1701', in which a rampant Tory majority in the House of Commons was prevented by an equally stubborn Whig majority in the House of Lords from impeaching the Whig ministers of the preceding administration, both Houses ordered their proceedings to be published. André Louis Frédéric Bonet de St. Germain, the London resident of the Elector of Brandenburg, who had just been crowned Frederick I of Prussia, observed: 'Il parut en general que les Chefs de partis des deux côtés crurent devoir plutot faire leur Cour au Peuple, qu'au Roy.'[2] And an anonymous Whig pamphleteer tried to explain this extraordinary procedure to his readers: 'We conceive both Houses ordering their Proceedings to be printed, to be as it were appealing to the Judgment of the People, touching the Matters in dispute between them.'[3] A few months before, Bonet had tactfully reminded his master of the importance of maintaining his *reputation* among the English as defender of the Protestant faith: 'Votre Excellence sait si c'est de l'interet de S.M. [Frederick I] qu'un Peuple, qui jettera peut étre un jour ses vuës sur l'auguste Maison de Brandenbourg pour s'y choisir un Roy, soit dans des prejugés de cette Nature.'[4] Although parliament, in this

[1] *C.J.* xiii. 318–19; B.M. Add. MSS. 17677UU, f. 208; 30000D, ff. 353–353v; Ogg, pp. 451, 465.

[2] *A Letter to a New Member of the Honourable House of Commons, touching the Rise of all the Imbezzlements*, Amsterdam, 1710, p. 6; B.M. Add. MS. 30000E, f. 172v.

[3] *A Letter from Some Electors, to One of their Representatives in Parliament*, [August ?] 1701, p. 5.

[4] B.M. Add. MS. 30000E, f. 86.

very session, cast its glances upon the House of Hanover instead of the House of Brandenburg, it is evident from these passages that the world's great age of publicity, propaganda, and projection of public image had clearly begun. It was a time when 'a club of Novelists' was not a literary circle but a gang of intelligence fabricators, and when the 'popular Arts' were not square-dancing and basket-weaving but the arts of demagoguery.

Charles Davenant, the leading Tory writer in the Paper War and Swift's main antagonist in the *Discourse*, showed that he understood this when he complained that 'A Lye shall reach to forty thousand Persons, of which not the twentieth part come in a long time to be put right'. On the other side, the greatest of the Whig election managers, Thomas Wharton, 1st Marquis of Wharton, boasted that 'a lie well believed is as good as if it were true'. Both Davenant's uneasiness and Wharton's cynicism testify to a growing awareness that 'Opinion is the principal Support of Power'.[1]

The emergent force of public opinion found its natural vehicle in 'the intestine shocke And furious cloze' of party politics. Political parties in 1697–1702 were not so much in existence as in the violent process of formation. Since there were no party platforms, there was only a struggle for power—and irreconcilable differences of opinion on every conceivable subject, from the trading status of the New East India Company to the guilt of Captain Kidd. Parties sought not merely to succeed each other in power, but to destroy each other. On 10 April 1700, in the heat of the crisis over the Resumption Bill, Sir Christopher Musgrave's motion to address the King to remove the Lord Chancellor, Lord Somers, from his presence and Council forever was defeated by only 61 votes. Two months later, after Somers had been forced to resign,

1 [Charles Davenant,] *Tom Double Return'd out of the Country*, 2d ed., [January] 1702, p. 13; cf. 'a malicious Lye is more heeded, and propagated, than any true Vindication' (J. F., *A Letter from the Grecian Coffee House*, [October] 1701, p. 6); *D.N.B.* xx. 1333; [Charles Davenant,] *Essays Upon I. The Ballance of Power*, [March] 1701, p. 31.

Robert Harley, the new Tory leader in the Commons, was still 'exasperated against my Lord Somers' and threatening to fall upon him at the next session. Failure to impeach Somers during this session only made the Tories more vindictive. Sunderland warned the King in September 1701 that 'the Tories will not be satisfied without ruining my Lord Somers', and James Vernon, the Whig Secretary of State, added that 'nothing would satisfy [them] but the utter subduing of those whom they have sett themselves against'. Vernon had made it perfectly clear what the Tories meant by 'subduing': 'excluding those [Whigs] from ever coming into power again'.[1] In the following month, while Swift was hoping 'to damp their Warmth in such Pursuits' with the publication of the *Discourse*, young Henry St. John was receiving assurances from Harley that he would soon witness 'the strong convulsions of a dying party and . . . the last efforts made to finish the great work of their destruction'.[2]

In these circumstances it is not difficult to understand why Whig and Tory, who concurred in nothing else, did agree that the very existence of parties was a national scandal. Demands to abolish the 'damn'd Names and Distinctions of Parties' were made on both sides, but, short of reverting to absolute monarchy, no one could devise a way to do without them. It was only very slowly that the existence of parties came to be accepted as a necessary consequence of the constitutional monarchy which had been established willy-nilly in 1689–90. By 1698 the words 'Whig' and 'Tory' had already found their way into dictionaries—with their pejorative origins still clinging about them:

Tories, Zealous Sticklers for the Prerogative and Rights of the Crown, in behalf of the Monarchy; also Irish-thieves, or *Rapparies*.

Whigs, the Republicans or Common-wealths-men, under the

[1] Vernon, iii. 88; *Miscellaneous State Papers*, [ed. Philip Yorke Hardwicke,] 2 vols., 1778, ii. 446; B.M. Add. MS. 40775, vol. 5, f. 116; Vernon, iii. 144.

[2] H.M.C. Downshire MSS. I. ii. 810.

Name of Patriots, and Lovers of Property; originally the Field-conventiclers in the West of *Scotland.*

However unexceptionable these definitions may appear to be, they are a totally unreliable index to the opposed factions in the Paper War, in which John Trenchard, John Tutchin, and John Toland were all enlisted as Tories.[1]

The difficulty was that in 1697–1702 the parties had momentarily reversed their traditional roles, so that it became possible to say that 'the Dissenters [are] the Tories of this Reign' and 'Tories [are become] down-right Republicans'. It is confusing to find Tories celebrating 'Parliament, by whom Kings reign, and from whom proceed all legal Rights of crowned Heads', and Whigs defending 'the *Jure Divino* Right of our Kings'; Tories insisting that 'the supreme Authority of this Kingdom [lies] in a Parliament', and Whigs arguing that 'the House of Commons is *not* the whole People of England's Representatives'. But 'this strange Metamorphosis of Principles' was widely recognized at the time. Daniel Defoe, for example, called attention to the fact that 'the People's Right to make Kings . . . is what these [Tory] Gentlemen are so fond of'. And the Tories themselves referred to William III as 'our King by Modern Contract'.[2]

This reversal of principles also helps explain why Swift began his political career as 'A Whig and one that wears a Gown'—a High-Church Whig, 'a political character', as Sir Walter Scott remarked, 'of which all parties refused to recognize the existence'.[3] When the parties resumed

[1] *Division our Destruction: Or, A Short History of the French Faction in England,* [February ?] 1702, p. 16; B. E., *A New Dictionary of the Terms Ancient and Modern of the Canting Crew, In Its Several Tribes of Gypsies, Beggers, Thieves, Cheats, &c.,* [1699].

[2] [John Toland,] *The Art of Governing by Parties,* [February] 1701, p. 28; [John Somers,] *Jura Populi Anglicani: Or The Subject's Right of Petitioning,* [August] 1701, pp. xii, vii; *Remarks Upon a Late Pamphlet Intitul'd, The Two Great Questions Consider'd,* [November] 1700, p. 11; *A Letter to a Modern Dissenting Whig,* [September] 1701, p. 25; [Daniel Defoe,] *The Two Great Questions Further Considered,* [December] 1700, p. 12; *Gloria Cambriae,* 1702, p. 9.

[3] *Poems,* p. 121; Scott, i. 94.

their more normal principles and practices in 1709–10, Swift could claim quite plausibly that it was the Whigs who had changed, not he.

Despite this reversal of roles, however, the party conflict in 1697–1702 was so pervasive that it became almost impossible to discuss anything without being partisan, or even 'without some Sting of Satyr'. One Englishman with no interest in party politics observed in July 1701 that 'Every Cause of almost every sort is now become a Party-cause'. Even Bonet, the most astute of the diplomatic residents in London, confessed that he was unable to be impartial: 'Quoy que je tache d'eviter avec soin d'embrasser aucun partis, ce qui arrive souvent sans qu'on s'en aperçoive, je ne peux m'empécher de reconnoitre dans le partis Whigs plus de candeur, plus de bonnes bources, et plus de pouvoir et de credit dans le Pays. Et beaucoup plus d'habilité et de meilleures tétes parmi les Tories.'[1]

The words 'Whig' and 'Tory' are not even mentioned in the *Discourse*. Many years later Swift claimed that when he wrote the work he was still ignorant of 'the difference between the principles of Whig and Tory'.[2] Within the work itself Swift adopts a pose of almost pedantic impartiality. But despite all this, the *Discourse* is as Whiggish a work as *The Public Spirit of the Whigs* is Tory.

Since every cause was a party cause, it was almost impossible to be non-partisan. Robert Harley, for example, professed to disbelieve in the whole scheme of party, but still insisted that every justice of the peace throughout England should be a Tory. For James Vernon, in June 1700, non-partisanship was simply unimaginable: 'Mr. Harley professes himself to be of no party, and yet finds fault with the new reform of the Commissions of Peace, as if it were done by halves. What this third invisible power should be, I can't imagine.'[3]

[1] Charles Leigh, *A Reply to John Colebatch*, 1698, sig. A2r; William P[udse]y, *The Constitution and Laws of England Consider'd*, [July] 1701, p. 99; B.M. Add. MS. 30000E, f. 396v.

[2] *Prose*, viii. 120.

[3] Vernon, iii. 91.

The third of the rules of land warfare by which the Paper War of 1697–1702 was conducted, the absence of government censorship, came about almost by accident. Freedom of the press was not one of 'the Rights and Liberties of the Subject' which were reaffirmed by the Convention Parliament in 1689. On the contrary, it was felt that political controversy should be limited to the privileged sanctuaries of St. Stephen's Chapel and the House of Lords. And as if to confirm this tradition, the Convention Parliament, after declaring (against all the facts) that James II had 'abdicated', went on to renew the very Licensing Act by which Sir Roger L'Estrange had maintained an effective censorship of all opposition to the policies and actions of James II.

In April 1695, however, the Licensing Act was omitted from a routine bill for continuing certain acts, which the Commons sent up to the House of Lords. The Lords restored the Licensing Act to the list but subsequently yielded to the reasons which the Commons supplied for the omission. It is surprising to learn what the reasons were. The Commons desired the Licensing Act to expire, not because freedom of the press was desirable, but 'Because that Act prohibits printing any thing before Entry thereof in the Register of the Company of Stationers . . . whereby *both Houses of Parliament are disabled to order any thing to be printed*'. Before the Commons returned its answer to the Lords, John Locke had been asked to provide reasons why the Licensing Act should be terminated. Among the arguments which Locke produced is the following: 'I know not why a man should not have liberty to print whatever he would speak; and to be answerable for the one, just as he is for the other, if he transgresses the law in either. But gagging a man for fear he should talk heresy or sedition, has no other ground than such as will make gyves necessary, for fear a man should use violence if his hands were free.' These brave words, however, were omitted from the Commons' message. But in any case on 3 May 1695 was ended 'the

Discipline of the last Reigns, when *Scribere* was *Agere*, and Thinking was Treason'.[1]

Expiration of the Licensing Act created one of the conditions which made possible the enormous volume of publication in the Paper War, but it is no longer believed to be 'the emancipation of our literature' that Macaulay proclaimed. Statute and common law against blasphemy, libel, and sedition remained in full force and were applied much more rigorously than they are today. In the years immediately following the expiration of the Licensing Act Robert Crosfeild was committed to the Poultry Compter for six weeks by a justice of the peace for 'a Seditious and Scandalous Libel' which he swore under oath he had not written. The Irish House of Commons ordered John Toland's *Christianity not Mysterious* to be burnt by the common hangman and the author arrested and prosecuted for blasphemy. John Tutchin was taken into custody, under a warrant signed by the Secretary of State, for his poem *The Foreigners*. And one paragraph of Davenant's *Essays Upon I. The Ballance of Power* was immediately declared 'a PUBLICK SCANDAL' by the Convocation then sitting in the Jerusalem Chamber of Westminster Abbey.[2]

These were hazards to which no writer in his right mind—and particularly no unknown clergyman—would wish to expose himself. At the height of his career, when he was *chef de propagande* in the Harley ministry of 1710–14, Swift wrote a famous paragraph on how to write libel without incurring the penalties of the law. It began: 'First, we are careful never to print a Man's Name out at length; but as I do that of Mr. *St—le*: So that although every

[1] *C.J.* xi. 305–6; *L.J.* xv. 545 (italics added); Peter King, Lord King, *The Life of John Locke*, 2d ed., 2 vols., 1830, i. 375–87; [Charles Montagu ?] *The Present Disposition of England Considered*, [January] 1701, p. 7.

[2] Laurence Hanson, *Government and the Press 1695–1763*, 1936, pp. 14, 36–43; Luttrell, iv. 130; Robert Crosfeild, *Corrupt Ministers the Cause of Publick Calamities*, [February] 1701, pp. 12–13; [Pierre Des Maizeaux,] *A Collection of Several Pieces of Mr. John Toland*, 2 vols., 1726, I. xxiii–xxv; Luttrell, iv. 676; [White Kennet,] *The History of the Convocation*, 1702, pp. 75–76.

Body alive knows whom I mean, the Plaintiff can have no Redress in any Court of Justice.' But in 1701 Swift had no such confidence—or daring. The truth of his witticism, however, is confirmed by the Tutchin case in 1700. Tutchin's poem, *The Foreigners*, is a particularly nasty attack on Hans Willem Bentinck, Earl of Portland, and Arnold Joost van Keppel, Earl of Albemarle, 'disguised' as 'Bentir' and 'Keppech'. But the Attorney General, Sir Thomas Trevor, advised the Government that since Tutchin had used 'covert names' no action could be taken against him. In *A Discourse of the Contests and Dissentions* the unknown clergyman adopted an even more secure method, the 'way of Allegory'. And these facts, incidentally, help to explain the popularity of allegory in the political satire of the Augustan age.[1]

There was still violent disagreement in England as to whether liberty of the press was desirable at all. Neither Swift nor Defoe thought that it was. As party writers in the Paper War grew bolder, cries that this was 'not Liberty but Licentiousness' grew louder. A Tory pamphlet of July 1701 proclaimed that this 'Currency and Superabundance of *Libels* is a sign of a sickly State'. James Drake, who wrote one of the replies to the *Discourse*, feared that freedom of the press might destroy the State. The foreigner, Bonet, had also been shocked at the freedom writers enjoyed to destroy the reputations of public figures. But he came finally to the very opposite conclusion from that of Drake. It is important enough to be quoted at length:

> Mais quand on ballance tout, il semble que ces reproches mutuels caracterisent plus les partis et les particuliers; qu' ils ne menacent ou indiquent la ruine de cet Etat; bien loin de là, ils sont un frein l'un a l'autre; Et si quelcun a recours a quelque voye indirecte, il ne peut la menager longtems avec succes, comme il a paru en ceux qui ont receu de l'argent de là France, et qu'on designe à present par nom et surnom; y ayant toujours quelque faux frere parmi eux qui revele les mysteres. . . .

[1] *Prose*, viii. 14–15; B.M. Add. MS. 30000D, f. 253v.

Rien ne repand un plus grand jour sur les affaires de ce Pays, que ces combats à coups de plume. . . . On ne peut pas aussi disconvenir que ces reproches n'ayent été des freins aux partis; et ne les ayent obligé à marcher droit, ou à faire moins de mal.[1]

It seems fairly certain that the literary campaigns of the Paper War were managed, however haphazardly, by the political leaders behind the scenes. Everyone thought so at the time, and although there is no direct evidence of the kind afforded by Swift's *Journal to Stella* for the period 1710–13, the indirect evidence indicates that the Tory campaign was managed by Robert Harley and the Whig by John Somers.

The field marshal of the Tory forces, however, was Charles Davenant, a self-styled doctor of laws, M.P. for Great Bedwin, and a learned economist. The most able Tory skirmishers were Anthony Hammond, James Drake, Sir Humphrey Mackworth, and (much to Davenant's embarrassment) the deist, John Toland.

The real hero of the Paper War, however, was Daniel Defoe, who poured out at least twenty-eight publications in verse and prose in support of the King and the Whig junto between 1697 and 1702. Skirmishers on the Whig side, mercenary and volunteer, included Sir Richard Blackmore, George Stepney, Nahum Tate, Elkanah Settle, and Luke Milbourne—a strange company of dunces and near-dunces for the future dedicatee of *The Dunciad*.

Almost all of the works published on both sides were

[1] [John Toland], *The Art of Governing by Parties*, [February] 1701, p. 27; cf. 'Is this the Liberty of Writing and Speaking he [Davenant] challenges as his Right? If so, 'tis *Licensiousness* with a Vengeance, not Liberty' (*Animadversions on a late Factious Book, Entitled, Essays upon I. The Ballance of Power*, [May] 1701, p. 45); *England's Enemies Exposed, and its True Friends and Patriots Defended*, [2d ed.] 1701, p. 25; [James Drake], *Mercurius Politicus*, No. 1, 12, June 1705: 'to have the most weighty and important Affairs, and the Conduct of the great Council of the Nation canvass'd in this publick manner, is an Invasion of the Prerogatives of the Crown, and the Authority of Parliaments, which may in time prove fatal to 'em both'; B.M. Add. MSS, 30000D, f. 253v; 30000E, ff. 326, 339; cf. 'The liberty of the Press must keep a Ministry within some tolerable Bounds, by exposing their ill Designs to the People' ([Matthew Tindal], *Reasons against Restraining the Press*, 1704, p. 13).

anonymous and the authors of many of them may remain for ever unidentified. There are even works described in the documents of which no copy can now be found.[1] Among these *ephemeridae* the *Discourse* stands out as a major work of literature. Even in the canon of Swift's work, it is certainly one of the two or three most effective of his political pamphlets. Swift himself tended to depreciate these works, calling them 'temporary occasional things, that dye naturally with the Change of times'.[2] But reasons are given below (Section 4) for thinking that it is probably the only work of real literary value among the hundreds published in the Paper War of 1697–1702.

The political history of 1697–1702 has been described by a whole succession of distinguished historians from Macaulay to David Ogg,[3] but the literary history of the period is a major *desideratum*. Apart from a few pages in James Ralph's *History of England*, published in 1744–6, and a few articles in the learned journals, there is practically nothing. Nor does the brilliance of the political histories make up for this deficiency, for literary studies require an entirely different *kind* of history.

The political historian struggles to be objective, to see both sides of the question, and to trace existing institutions and practices to their origins. The political satirist, on the other hand, makes no attempt to be objective or to see both sides of the question. In so far as he does, he ceases to be effective. His art requires him to adopt 'some partial

[1] One of these is a Whig pamphlet of March 1700 entitled *Vox Populi*, described both by L'Hermitage and Bonet (B.M. Add. MSS. 17677UU, f. 180ᵛ; 30000D, ff. 86ᵛ–87); another '(apparently by Lord Somers himself)' is 'a Folio-Sheet of Observations' (Ralph, ii. 997).

[2] *The Letters of Jonathan Swift to Charles Ford*, ed. David Nichol Smith, Oxford, 1935, p. 163.

[3] Thomas Babington Macaulay, *The History of England from the Accession of James the Second*, ed. C. H. Firth, 1914–15, vi. 2940–79; Leopold von Ranke, *A History of England, Principally in the Seventeenth Century*, Oxford, 1875, v. 235–69; A. S. Turberville, *The House of Lords in the Reign of William III* (Oxford Historical and Literary Studies, vol. iii), Oxford, 1913, pp. 196–224; Keith Feiling, *A History of the Tory Party 1640–1714*; Oxford, 1924, pp. 330–59; David Ogg, *England in the Reigns of James II and William III*, Oxford, 1955, pp. 459–509.

narrow' view and to hold up to contempt any deviation from this view. His success depends upon the singleness, and the assuredness, of his vision. This is not a new discovery, of course, and the anonymous critic of 1701 who described 'the *Assurance* and *self-perswasion* and *concern*, which becomes a Satyrist' would undoubtedly have agreed that these qualities do *not* become the historian.[1]

Despite his calculated pose of aloofness from party issues, Swift does not present both sides of the question in the *Discourse*. He takes the Whig side and makes 'the late publick Proceedings' of the Tories appear to be corrupt, villainous, and potentially dangerous. Similarly, in 'the Great Quarrel between the Houses', Swift takes the side of the House of Lords, for it must have been as obvious to him as it was to another anonymous pamphleteer that 'in all Points in Dispute between the two Houses, one of them must be more in the right than the other'.[2] For describing the background of the *Discourse*, therefore, objective political history is misleading.[3] What

[1] *The Present State of Physick & Surgery in London*, 1701, p. 11.

[2] *Some Remarks on the Bill for Taking, Examining and Stating the Publick Accounts of the Kingdom: And on the Proceedings thereon in both Houses, the last Session*, 1702, p. 3.

[3] A good example is J. D. Simms, *The Williamite Confiscation in Ireland 1690–1703*, 1957. This excellent book devotes four chapters to the resumption of William's grants of forfeited Irish estates, which, as Simms says, 'provided material for the first of Swift's political writings'. This is as objective an account of the matter as it would seeem possible to produce, but it provides only one incidental detail which helps to explain the *Discourse*. This is the surmise that Swift's opinion, that the King was 'hardly used' in this matter, seems 'to have been more prevalent among Irish Protestants than in England' (p. 113). Simms indeed records that 'The Act of Resumption constituted a humiliating setback for the king and an assertion of parliamentary authority in a field in which the royal prerogative had appeared to be firmly established' (p. 82). But he also calls Davenant's *Discourse upon Grants and Resumptions* 'an able statement, fortified with many historical precedents', and quotes Burnet's complaint that William's grants 'could hardly be excused, much less justified' (p. 111). If the reader were told nothing about the Act of Resumption but the last two facts, he could not understand Swift's *Discourse*. Furthermore, Simms does *not* quote either Methuen's letter to Harley or any of the numerous pamphlets objecting to the Act. John Methuen was Lord Chancellor of Ireland and a friend of Harley. Harley, of course, was the manager of the Resumption Bill in the House of Commons. Methuen confessed to Harley that 'the English here are in very ill humour and

I. The Four Lords Partitioners

is needed, is illustration of what Swift saw in 'the late publick Proceedings among us'. If Macaulay had lived to complete his *History* beyond 11 April 1700, it is possible that no further account of the Paper War would be necessary.

But even this is doubtful. Macaulay was looking back on the fitful and unresolved struggles of the late seventeenth century in full knowledge of what these controversies had produced by the mid nineteenth century. Literary studies, on the other hand, require history without benefit of hindsight. For the literary student, intent only upon understanding how the events of the past were precipitated into literature, the evolutionary bias of the historian can also be misleading. A few examples may help to illustrate this point.

In 1701 the Tory pamphleteers were demanding that all appointments to the chief offices of state should be made by the House of Commons. Since this has in effect come about, it now seems right. But in 1701 it seemed absolutely wrong; it seemed to be another invasion of the prerogatives of the King which could only lead to a serious imbalance of power. More particularly, on 16 April 1701 the House of Commons, having voted to impeach the four 'Lords Partitioners', as they were called [Fig. 1], moved an address to the King to remove the four lords 'from your Council and Presence for ever'. David Ogg calls this 'one of the most important pronouncements of the reign, for it showed that the Tories were gradually adopting one of the fundamental positions of the Whigs, and in this way the principle of ministerial responsibility

with very little temper, but you will hardly conceive to what degree their uneasiness goes. In truth almost every one suffers by your act' (H.M.C. Portland MSS. iii. 624). One pamphleteer called the resumption 'a great Blow to the Protestant Interest in *Ireland*' (*Short Remarks upon the Late Act of Resumption of the Irish Forfeitures*, [May] 1701, p. 14), and another added that 'nothing could have been devised more Injurious and Detrimental to the *English* Protestant Interest in *Ireland*, than that fatal Bill' (*The Popish Pretenders to the Forfeited Estates*, 1702, p. 3). It is 'non-objective' statements like these that help explain Swift's *Discourse*.

came to be elevated above party strife'.[1] Bishop Burnet, however, objected that 'This was punishing before Trial, contrary to an indispensible Rule of Justice, of not judging before the Parties were heard', and Bonet added that 'Cette conduite irregulière et emportée est blamée de tous ceux qui ne sont pas prevenus pour les Tories'.[2] Ogg's comment, while obviously true, is no help in understanding the *Discourse*. The remarks of Burnet and Bonet, deprived of the gift of hindsight, provide some light on what Swift saw.

So in the following account of those passages in the Paper War which constitute the background of the *Discourse*, no attempt is made to be impartial. All that is attempted is to represent certain political and literary events of 1697–1701 as Swift saw them, with the further limitation that only those events which contributed to the making of the *Discourse* will be included. Another way of putting this is to say that the *Discourse* is not really concerned with the political history of 1697–1701 at all, but only with the political fables of the time. And it is with these fables, and the pamphlets which embodied and transmitted them, that the following account will be concerned. In the first paragraph of his *Parallel Lives* Plutarch expressed the hope that he might be able to purify the fables of the poets and make them take on at least the semblance of history. But he knew he could not succeed, for Fable 'obstinately disdains to make herself credible and refuses to admit any element of probability'.[3]

Collapse of the Whig Junto

With the signature of the Treaty of Ryswick in September 1697 the Whig junto, which had brought the country from military defeat and near-bankruptcy to an inconclusive conclusion to a nine-year war, began to disintegrate. The first to go was Sir William Temple's old

[1] Ogg, p. 508. [2] Burnet, ii. 267; B.M. Add. MS. 30000E, f. 146.
[3] Plutarch, *Theseus*, 1.

friend, the Lord Chamberlain, Robert Spencer, 2nd Earl of Sunderland. In December 1697, as Swift wrote to his successor at Kilroot, John Winder, 'Lord Sunderland fell and I with him'. December 1697 is also the date of The Epistle Dedicatory to *A Tale of a Tub* and it is difficult not to believe that this date represents some kind of turning-point in Swift's life. The year before, he had told Jane Waring that he would push his advancement 'with all the eagerness and courage imaginable' and did not doubt to succeed.[1] Now, he may have come to the conclusion, in Lady Gardiner's words, that 'A Court place is an unsartainty', and have decided to pursue 'other courses', as he hinted to John Winder. Swift was acutely aware that he was nearly thirty years old, virtually unemployed, and almost totally unknown. It is difficult to imagine that he had any alternative, 'as late in my life as it is', but party politics. For the moment, however, there was nothing to do but let his life 'drive on its old course' at Moor Park, finishing *The Battle of the Books*, reading and making long abstracts of the classical historians, and watching for an opportunity to make himself useful to the Whigs. For some reason he must have felt that it was not yet time to publish *A Tale of a Tub*, which was to be dedicated to Lord Somers. As Lord Chancellor, it was Somers's duty to bestow all ecclesiastical benefices in the King's gift. Perhaps Swift did not publish *A Tale of a Tub* in 1698 because Somers's influence was visibly waning.[2]

After the general election of August 1698 returned a strong majority of 'Wiggs mescontents et Tories', the only thing that held the junto together was, as Somers told Shrewsbury, the King's 'difficulty of . . . piecing with the other party; and the almost impossibility of finding

[1] *Corr.* i. 24. 18.

[2] Swift's latest editors accept his statement that 'The greatest Part' of *A Tale of a Tub* was finished in 1696 (*TT*, pp. xl–xliv; *Prose*, i. xv–xvi). The usual reason that is given for withholding publication of *A Tale of a Tub* is Temple's dislike of satire (*Miscellanea. The Second Part*, 1690, Essay I, p. 71), but Temple died in January 1699 and the *Tale* was not published until May 1704, when Somers's fortunes were again rising.

a set of Tories, who will unite'. By February 1699 James Vernon confessed: 'We are a dispersed routed party, [and] our opposers bear hard upon us.'[1]

The next to go was Edward Russell, Earl of Orford, First Lord of the Admiralty and hero of La Hougue, whose resignation was demanded in May 1699. In the same month Charles Montagu, hero of the financial reforms of 1694, resigned as Chancellor of the Exchequer, and Charles Talbot, Duke of Shrewsbury, gave up his post as Secretary of State. All of these places were filled with Tories, whether or not they were united. But, since William refused 'to declare for one party more than for another', he could not yet be prevailed upon to part with Somers. Robert Harley, still known as an 'Old' Whig, was just emerging as the Tory leader in the House of Commons, and opportunities for excluding the junto from ever coming into power again were being eagerly canvassed. This, of course, meant finding grounds for impeachment.

It was first assumed that grounds for impeachment could be found in the grants of forfeited estates in Ireland which the Whig ministers were alleged to have procured for themselves. In July 1699 Charles Davenant, *sergent-chef* of the Tory propaganda corps, wrote to Thomas Coke, the Tory M.P. for Derbyshire and a member of the Harley–Foley faction: 'I am very busy and putting myself in order to give the public an account of what our ancestors have done to such as being Ministers have presumed to pass grants to themselves of the Crown revenue. In short I shall endeavour to prepare the town to give the report of our Irish Commissioners a kind reception.'[2] The forfeited estates of Irish rebels had been a matter of contention between King and Commons for nine years. According to the basic law of the realm, property confiscated under an act of attainder reverted to 'the real and actual

1 *Miscellaneous State Papers*, [ed. Philip Yorke Hardwicke,] 2 vols., 1778, ii. 436; Vernon, ii. 262.

2 H.M.C. Cowper MSS. ii. 389.

possession and seizin of the crown'. Since 1690, however, the House of Commons had been trying to divert the income from these estates into the public treasury. But William, who told Halifax that 'hee did not come over to establish a Commonwealth', had not hesitated to make lavish grants of the forfeited estates to his favourites, most of whom were foreigners.

Finally, in April 1699, by the expedient of tacking it to a money bill, the Commons passed a Bill for an Account to be taken of the forfeited Estates in Ireland. To insure partisan control, four Tories and three Whigs were appointed to the commission. It was after 'this miserable session of Parliament', as William described it to Heinsius, that Orford, Montagu, and Shrewsbury were replaced by Tories. And it was 'to prepare the town to give the report of our Irish commissioners a kind reception' that Davenant wrote *A Discourse upon Grants and Resumptions, Showing How our Ancestors Have Proceeded with such Ministers As have Procured to Themselves Grants of the Crown-Revenue; And that the Forfeited Estates ought to be Applied towards the Payment of the Publick Debts.*

Davenant was the eldest son of Sir William D'Avenant, whom Swift had ridiculed in *The Battle of the Books*, and also a distant relation by marriage of Swift himself. His sister was married to Swift's uncle, the Reverend Thomas Swift. When he was elected to William's 4th Parliament in August 1698, Davenant had already published a number of controversial works in the field of public finance. Manuscript copies of four more of these, written in 1695–7 but apparently never published, were in Harley's possession at his death.[1] The Whigs claimed that Davenant wrote *A Discourse upon Grants and Resumptions* 'with the joint Assistance of some of his Party'. The bulk of this 445-page volume consists of parliamentary precedents for impeaching ministers who procured themselves grants of Crown lands. Harley, with his extensive knowledge of the 'records of parliament', is the one most likely to have

[1] They are preserved in B.M. Harleian MS. 1223.

provided the assistance which the Whigs suspected. But whether or not he assisted Davenant in writing *A Discourse upon Grants and Resumptions*, the book clearly serves Harley's purposes and on one occasion at least seems to repeat his very words.[1]

The Introduction to Davenant's work is full of dark threats against ministers 'who . . . had presum'd to procure to themselves Grants of the King's Lands', and of dark warnings to the King himself. William did not need to be reminded 'how fatal 'tis for the Soveraign to become the Head of any Party', for, as we have already seen, he steadfastly refused 'to declare for one party more than for another'. Davenant's sarcastic praise of the King for 'His so cheerfully disbanding the Army at the request of his Parliament' must have amused Harley, whose successful management of the Bill had driven William to write a speech of abdication.[2]

One paragraph in the Introduction must have attracted Swift's particular interest, for it seems to allude to Sir William Temple. Among the incidental disadvantages of fiscal corruption Davenant mentions that it frightens 'men of sublime Skill, Integrity and Virtue from meddling in Affairs':

> Indeed, the Ambition of Mankind consider'd, it was a wonder in former Reigns, to see Persons the most conspicuous for Understanding, deep Reach and Experience, employ their time with their Books, in making Gardens, or in Building, and that they should not rather seek those Dignities, to which their Birth and Superior Abilities did in a manner give 'em a just Right.

The story of Sir William Temple's many refusals of public office under Charles II was widely known. More par-

[1] *Animadversions on a late Factious Book, Entitled, Essays upon I. The Ballance of Power*, [May] 1701, p. 6. During violent debates in the Commons over the standing army, Harley told his father that there was no middle ground between 'disbanding the army or keeping it up, shutting up the Exchequer, governing by sword and edicts' (H.M.C. Portland MSS. iii. 601). Davenant similarly imagines 'bad Ministers . . . stopping the *Exchequer*, in order to set up an Army, and to subsist without a Parliament' (*A Discourse upon Grants and Resumptions*, [November 1699, but dated] 1700, p. 391).

[2] Coxe, 572–3.

ticularly, however, Davenant is replying to a paragraph in Temple's famous essay on gardening, which was published in 1690:

Some few in each Country make those higher Flights after Honour and Power . . . and nothing diverts nor busies Men more, than these pursuits, which are usually covered with the Pretences of serving a Mans Country, and of Publick Good. But the true Service of the Publick is a Business of so much Labour and so much Care, that though a good and wise Man may not refuse it, if He be called to it by His Prince or His Country, and thinks He can be of more than vulgar use, yet He will seldom or never seek it, but leaves it commonly to Men, who, under the disguise of Publick Good, pursue their own design of Wealth, Power, and such Bastard Honours as usually attend them.[1]

To this, Davenant replies that even retirement can be put to better use than books, gardening, and building:

The Writer of these Papers has continually endeavour'd to make his Studies tend to the Service of the Publick. . . . In order to which he has devoted his Hours of Leisure to Inquiries into Trade and Revenue of this Kingdom; And not serving his Country in an Active Life,[2] he hopes to make his Solitude and Contemplation of some use, so as to show himself not altogether an unprofitable Member of the Commonwealth.

Swift could not forget the false and pharisaical tone of these passages, and the implied criticism of that 'great and good Person', Sir William Temple. When he came to write the *Discourse* he reverted again and again to the point that what deters 'men of sublime Skill . . . from meddling in Affairs' is not fiscal mismanagement, but irresponsible impeachments.

Davenant's pose of labouring in the public interest, far above the dirty clash of party politics, is not borne out by the content of the book itself. It ransacks the past for

[1] *Miscellanea. The Second Part*, 1690, Essay II, pp. 4–5.

[2] Since, at the time of writing, Davenant was a Tory M.P. for Great Bedwin, Wilts., a virtually unpopulated borough controlled by the Bruce family, he may be said to have been 'not serving his Country' in a manner somewhat different from that implied in the text.

historical precedents for impeaching corrupt ministers and presents these in terms suggestive of the Whig junto.

Somers is identified, through his allegedly obscure origins, with Michael de la Pole, 'a Merchant's Son in *London*', who rose to be Richard II's Lord Chancellor, purchased royal 'Lands, Tenements, and Rents of a great Value', and was finally impeached for treason.[1]

The Dutchman Bentinck, William's favourite, who was raised to the peerage as Earl of Portland, is identified with the Gascon Piers Gaveston, Edward II's minion, who was elevated to the peerage as Earl of Cornwall and became 'presently a Minister of State' who 'plac'd only his own Creatures, or Foreigners about the King, and . . . caus'd the King to grant Lands, Tenements and Offices to himself. . . . For which he was Banish'd the Realm.'[2]

Edward Russell, Earl of Orford, who had resigned as First Lord of the Admiralty in May 1699, is glanced at in the person of William de la Pole, Duke of Suffolk, who was impeached during the minority of Henry VI for 'Grants out of the Crown Revenue procur'd for himself', and because 'the defence of [the] Rea[l]me, and the sauf kepyng of the Sea hadde not [been] kepte'. Sunderland is alluded to in the person of Simon de Burley, an earlier Lord Chamberlain who was impeached by the House of Commons in 1388 and beheaded on Tower Hill.[3]

The main attack, however, was reserved for Charles Montagu, who, as Vernon said, was 'the person they have the greatest mind to lower, as one that stands in their way'. Montagu is identified with no less than three villains of history: Ranulf Flambard, Lord Treasurer under an earlier William, William Rufus; Jean de Montaigu, a *surintendant des finances* under Charles VI of France, and Enguerrand de Marigny, the *grand chambellan* of Philip IV, who debased the currency, received large grants of Crown lands, and was finally 'condemn'd and hang'd'.[4]

[1] *A Discourse upon Grants and Resumptions*, [November 1699, but dated] 1700, pp. 317, 324, 334–5.

[2] Ibid., pp. 309, 312.

[3] Ibid., pp. 340, 343, 336.

[4] Ibid., pp. 307–8, 384, 383; Vernon, i. 461.

From this it is clear that the purpose of *A Discourse upon Grants and Resumptions* was to create popular support for impeachment of the Whig ministers. The 'Lesson' of the work is printed on page 357 in Gothic black letter: '**When the people of** ENGLAND **desire an Act of Resumption, the work must begin with impeaching corrupt ministers.**' Finally, after more protestations of impartiality, Davenant closed his book with another dark threat of further publication:

The Author thinks he cannot employ his Hours of Leisure more to his Country's Service than in Inquiries of this Nature. And next Year (if he finds a Continuation of these Foul Practices which have been so destructive to *England*, and so prejudicial to the King's Interest) he purposes to open a new Scene: That Zeal for the Publick which has now warm'd him shall not in the least cool, and though he should be left to stand alone, he will still combat on, and neither ask nor give Quarter in the Conflict he intends to maintain with the Corruptions of the Age.[1]

By the time Swift read *A Discourse upon Grants and Resumptions* he was back in Ireland. Sir William Temple had died in January 1699, and 'besides a Legacy [of £100] left [Swift] the care and trust and Advantage of publishing his posthumous Writings'. So Swift set off for London, where, according to his own account, he

applyed by Petition to King William, upon the Claym of a Promise his Majesty had mad[e] to Sr W T that he would give Mr Swift a Prebend of Canterbury or Westminster. The Earl of Rumney who professed much friendship for him, promised to second his Petition, but, as he was an old vitious illiterate Rake without any sense of Truth or Honor, said not a word to the King.[2]

So Swift made arrangements with Jacob Tonson, 'late Doorkeeper to the Honourable Society of Kit-Cats', to print Temple's letters.[3] Then he accepted a very

[1] *A Discourse upon Grants and Resumptions*, [November 1699, but dated] 1700, p. 448.

[2] *Prose*, v. 194, 195.

[3] *Letters Written by Sir W. Temple*, 2 vols., 1700, was actually published in November or December 1699. It was reviewed in *The History of the Works of the*

unpromising position as domestic chaplain to another of Temple's old friends, Charles Berkeley, 2nd Earl of Berkeley, who had been appointed one of the lords justices of Ireland in May 1699. Berkeley was 'an easy Man', with little influence or ambition, whom Swift found 'Intolerably lazy and indolent, and somewhat Covetous'.[1] On 18 July 1699 he left London in the Earl's entourage, bound for Bristol and the Irish Sea.

Publication of *A Discourse upon Grants and Resumptions* late in November 1699[2] was perfectly timed to produce the maximum propaganda effect. On 15 December the Report of the Commissioners to inquire into Forfeited Estates in Ireland was laid before the House of Commons. And, with the town so well 'prepared', it is surprising that there was no violence. For the size of some of William's grants to his foreign favourites was indeed regal: 135,820 acres to Willem Bentinck, Earl of Portland; 108,633 acres to Arnold Joost van Keppel, Earl of Albemarle; 36,148 acres to Henri de Massue de Ruvigny, Earl of Galway; 26,480 acres to Godard van Reede, Baron de Ginkel and 1st Earl of Athlone. The greatest surprise, however, was saved for the last paragraph: 'We shall now conclude our Report by laying before your Honours one other Grant of a considerable value, which we are apprehensive does not fall within the

Learned, i (December 1699), 748–52. Swift dedicated it 'To His Most Sacred Majesty William III', and wrote a brief Preface praising Temple for having 'advanced our English Tongue, to as great a Perfection as it can well bear'.

1 Ralph, ii. 815; *Prose*, v. 259. Swift said he also had expected to be appointed Berkeley's secretary (*Prose*, v. 195), a position which Matthew Prior had filled when Berkeley was William's envoy-extraordinary at The Hague in 1689–94. But the post finally went to one Arthur Bushe. Swift's disappointment illustrates his lack of patronage. Instead of 'an old vitious illiterate Rake' and an 'Intolerably lazy and indolent' lesser diplomat, Bushe's patrons were John Methuen, Lord Chancellor of Ireland, and Laurence Hyde, Earl of Rochester, who was soon to be appointed Lord Lieutenant of Ireland (B.M. Add. MSS. 28884, f. 323v, 28885, f. 101).

2 Vernon, ii. 373; *The Post Boy*, No. 727, 5–7 Dec. 1699. Its numerous misspellings, and errors in pagination and catchwords, confirm the fact announced on the fly-leaf that it was 'Printed off in haste'.

Letter of our Enquiry.'[1] This was a grant of 95,649 acres, 'all the Private Estate of the late King James', to Elizabeth Villiers, formerly William's mistress and now married off to James Hamilton, 1st Earl of Orkney. When he met her in 1712 Swift found her the wisest woman he ever saw, even if she did scrawl and spell 'like a Wapping wench'.

The Commissioners might very well have been apprehensive about including this grant in the Report, for these estates were Crown lands and they had not been forfeited. Three Commissioners refused to sign the Report because it included the grant to Elizabeth Villiers. When one of them objected that to include it would be flying in the face of the King, one of the Tory Commissioners revealed that it was his understanding that the report was intended to fly in the face of the King. And when Sir Richard Levinge carried his complaints against the Report on to the floor of the House of Commons, he was sent to the Tower, and the Report was ordered to be published.[2]

The Tories in the House of Commons remained 'strong and violent'. There were demands to impeach the Whig ministers who had advised William to pass such exorbitant grants. John Grubham Howe introduced a resolution that those who had advised William had 'highly failed in the Performance of their Trust and Duty'. Tempers were so high that when Harley merely 'advised looking forward for future amendments' Thomas Coke stalked out of the House and said 'he would never trust a Presbyterian rogue more'.[3]

[1] *The Report Made to the Honourable House of Commons, Decemb. 15, 1699. By the Commissioners appointed to Enquire into the Forfeited Estates of Ireland*, 1700, p. 27.

[2] *Corr.* v. 301. Levinge testified that when he objected to the inclusion of the grant to Elizabeth Villiers, John Trenchard 'did answer that it was a villanous Grant, and therefore fit to be exposed'. Trenchard, of course, denied the charge: 'that I called the Grant of the private Estate a villanous Grant, I directly deny it. 'Twas possible I might say 'twas an extravagant Grant, an unreasonable Grant, an unconscionable Grant . . . but that I used the word villanous I positively deny; 'tis a word I don't use in my ordinary Conversation, a word that never comes out of the mouth of a Gentleman, and is false'; in short, a villainous word (*The Report Made to the Honourable House of Commons, Decemb. 15, 1699*, 1700, pp. 37, 50).

[3] Vernon, ii. 411, 444; *C.J.* xiii. 130.

On the day that the Report of the Commissioners had been laid before them the House began another attempt to resume William's grants. Harley was one of the managers and by 11 January 1700, when the Bill had finally been drafted, he told his father that he had not had four hours of sleep during the past week. Once again the device of tacking was adopted, so that what finally emerged was ironically entitled 'An Act for granting an Aid to His Majesty by Sale of the forfeited Estates in Ireland, and by a Land-Tax in England'. It passed the Lower House on 2 April 1700 and was ordered to be carried to the House of Lords. There it produced 'a long, perplex'd, and passionate Debate'. On 4 April the French ambassador, Camille d'Hostun, duc de Tallard, reported to Louis XIV: 'c'est la plus grande scene qui se soit passé en Angleterre depuis la paix.' The Lords complained bitterly that unless the Bill were rejected no limits could be set to the power of the House of Commons, which was already acting as if it were absolute, dispensing favours here and withholding them there.[1] But the House voted 70–23 to read the Bill a second time. Eight lords, however, signed a protest against the second reading, on the grounds that 'tacking so many and different matters to a money bill is not only contrary to all the rules and methods of Parliament, but highly dangerous both to the undoubted prerogative of the Crown, and right of this House, putting it . . . in the power of the Commons to make any resolutions of their own as necessary, as any supply given for the support or emergencies of state'.[2]

After the third reading in the House of Lords the Bill was returned with certain minor amendments. But even these provoked a violent reaction in the House of Commons. Sir Edward Seymour blamed the influence of Somers, who was absent from the debates on account of

[1] Luttrell, iv. 594; P.R.O., Transcripts 3 (France) 185, f. 76; B.M. Add. MS. 17677UU, ff. 202v–3.

[2] J. E. Thorold Rogers, *The Protests of the Lords*, 3 vols., Oxford, 1875, i. 139–40.

illness, and 'reflected on . . . his religion, that he was a Hobbist'. Another member defended the right of the Commons to tack anything to bills of supply, even heads. A motion to refuse even to consider the Lords' amendments passed unanimously and a list of the Privy Council was ordered to be laid before the House. People in the street were saying that only 'bishops, beggars, and bastards' were against the Bill. At this moment the King seemed resolved 'to venture on all the ill consequences, that might follow the losing this Bill; tho' those', as Burnet said, 'would probably have been fatal'.[1]

The next day the House of Lords voted 47–34 to insist upon its amendments to the Bill and presented its reasons to the Commons at a conference on 10 April. Sir Edward Seymour, the chief manager of the Bill, restated the Commons' 'sole and entire Right' to grant subsidies and refused to discuss the matter any further. After hearing the Lords' reasons for their amendments the Commons again voted unanimously to reject them. Then, after ordering the lobby to be cleared of all strangers and the serjeant to be posted at the door, they began to consider the list of Privy Councillors one by one. The third name on the list was John, Lord Somers, Lord High Chancellor of England. It was on this occasion that Sir Christopher Musgrave moved an address to the King to remove Somers from his presence and Council forever, but the motion was defeated, 167–106. After candles had been brought in, however, the Marquis of Hartington's motion to exclude all foreigners from the Council passed without opposition. This attack—aimed primarily at the Duke of Schomberg and the Earl of Portland—must have fluttered the dove-cotes in Dublin Castle, for Henri de Massue de Ruvigny, Earl of Galway, was one of the lords justices of Ireland.[2]

[1] Vernon, iii. 13; B.M. Add. MS. 17677UU, ff. 207^{v}–8; *C.J.* xiii. 318; Vernon, iii. 17; Burnet, ii. 239.

[2] H.M.C. Lords MSS. 4 (new series), 142; B.M. Add. MS. 17677UU, f. 210; P.R.O., Transcripts 3 (France) 185, f. 81^{v}; *C.J.* xiii. 319–321; Vernon, iii. 23.

By this time the whole City of London was in an uproar and Westminster was so crowded with people that it was only with difficulty that anyone could get in or out of either House. Rumours were flying that the King had sent for the crown and was coming immediately to dissolve Parliament. In the Upper House, after Wharton, the sponsor of the amendments, had withdrawn, the Lords sat down to consider whether they should insist upon them. One speaker maintained, almost prophetically, 'que si une bonne fois pour toutes, ils ne s'oposoient pas aux communes, qu'à l'avenir elles pousseroient leurs pretentions jusques à l'infini, et qu'il ne faudroit plus regarder les privileges des pairs, que comme de vains titres qui ne signifiroient plus rien'. It was after a speech like this that the Lord Bishop of Salisbury so far forgot himself as to cry out 'Stuff, stuff', and 'had liked' to make reparation on his knees at the Bar of the House. When the question finally was put to stand by the amendments, the House divided 43–43, and, according to the rule, *semper praesumitur pro negante*, the motion was lost. After Burnet had tactfully hustled out the other bishops, the Lords voted 39–34 to accept the supply-*cum*-resumption Bill without amendments. As the news spread from the crowds surrounding Westminster throughout the rest of London, bonfires were lit and the celebration went on until morning. But Matthew Prior was less enthusiastic: '*God* knows how the Business will turn', he said, 'or where this Violence of the House of Commons will end.'[1]

The next morning William gave his assent to the supply-*cum*-resumption Bill and ended the second session of his 4th Parliament without even the customary speech of thanks. Tallard observed that 'l'autorité royalle et celle des seigneurs viennent de recevoir leur dernier coup et les communes deviennent absolument les maistresses de faire passer tout ce qu'il leur plaira dans la scéance prochaine en continuant à le joindre au bill d'argent'. That

[1] H.M.C. Lords MSS. 4 (new series), 142; B.M. Add. MSS. 30000D, f. 137, 17677UU, f. 210v; Vernon, iii. 24; Ralph, ii. 853.

'Presbyterian rogue', Harley, on the other hand, saw that the hand of God had intervened to save England from ruin.[1] Two weeks later, Somers was forced to resign and the rout of the Whig junto was now complete.

In retrospect, Bonet was impressed by the important part *A Discourse upon Grants and Resumptions* had played in this work: 'Ce livre qui étoit chargé de quantité de citations, fit une si grande impression sur les Parlementaires du second ordre, que sans autre examen, ils s'opignatrerent à revoquer entierement tous ces dons, comme il a paru.'[2] Davenant had been afraid that the book would 'seem tedious' and it does, but there can be no doubt about its effectiveness as propaganda. It was acknowledged even by the Whigs to have 'had a very publick influence'.[3]

The Partition of Spain

There was one respect, however, in which both Davenant's book and the Report of the Irish Commissioners were failures; they failed to provide grounds for impeaching the Whig ministers. The next hope was that these might be supplied by the Partition Treaties, news of which began to leak out in the summer of 1699. By July 1700 Davenant was already hard at work on the volume he had promised at the end of *A Discourse upon Grants and Resumptions*. Bonet reported that the party 'des Tories, et des mescontens a chargé le Docteur Davenant, qui a une plume assés heureuse, d'ecrire contre le Traité'.[4]

As soon as he heard the news of the attack on Galway, Swift must have concluded that his position as chaplain to the lords justices would soon be terminated. Fortunately, however, he had been instituted in March 1700 to the rectory of Agher and the vicarages of Laracor and Rathbeggan, which were in the gift of the lords justices. And

[1] Vernon, iii. 25; P.R.O., Transcripts 3 (France) 185, f. 82v; H.M.C. Portland MSS. iii. 618.

[2] B.M. Add. MS. 30000D, f. 226.

[3] *Jus Regium: Or, The King's Right to grant Forfeitures*, [April] 1701, p. 17. (Page references are to the quarto edition which collates *A*–F2G–K4L–M2N4).

[4] B.M. Add. MS. 30000D, f. 225.

in October 1700 he was to be installed prebend of Dunlavin in St. Patrick's Cathedral in Dublin.[1] So he was no longer 'unprovided both of friend and living'. It can be safely assumed, however, that he was no more content than Yorick to remain 'a lousy prebendary'. And in his first successful poem, written about this time, he makes Frances Harris recall that 'he hates to be call'd *Parson*, like the *Devil*'.[2] In May 1700 he was already anticipating his return to London. He observed to Jane Waring: 'our Government sits very loose, and I believe will change in a few months; whether our part will partake in the change, I know not, though I am very apt to believe it; and then I shall be at leisure for a short journey.'[3] Swift's guess was right, for in the same month the commissions of the three lords justices were revoked and in June the King offered the lord lieutenancy of Ireland to Laurence Hyde, Earl of Rochester.[4] On 1 May Rochester had written to Harley asking to be allowed to wait on him; on 5 September it was reported to Harley that Rochester and Godolphin had completely patched up their differences. Around these three men William proceeded to piece together a ministry during the summer of 1700. But he 'disoblig'd the *Whigs*, without gaining the *Tories*', for 'les Tories', as Bonet observed, 'ne seront satisfaits que quand ils auront tout le pouvoir en main'.[5]

Since it was in their imputed role as 'Lords Partitioners' that Somers, Montagu, Orford, and Portland were finally impeached, it will be necessary to say something about the vexed issue of the Partition Treaties of 1698–1700. These were 'the natural and almost inevitable consequence' of the failure of the Treaty of Ryswick to solve the problem

[1] Louis A. Landa, *Swift and the Church of Ireland*, Oxford, 1954, pp. 27, 34, 43 n. 4.

[2] *Poems*, p. 72.

[3] *Corr.* i. 33.

[4] B.M. Add. MS. 17677UU, f. 234^{v}; B.M. Add. MS. 30000D, ff. 212^{v}–213.

[5] Ralph, ii. 829; B.M. Add. MS 30000D, f. 211^{v}. It was Defoe who had urged William to take Tories into his government 'and thereby take off the edge and divide the party' (H.M.C. Portland MSS. iv. 148), but this time the strategy did not work.

of who was to succeed the childless Carlos II on the throne of Spain. In 1697, in fact, it had been possible to negotiate a treaty only by ignoring this *cauchemar perpétuel*, which had already overlain the peace of Europe for ten years, and was not finally dispelled until the Treaty of Utrecht brought another war to an end in 1713.[1]

William made two attempts to settle the issue short of war. In March 1698 negotiations were begun, in great secrecy, by Portland in Versailles and by Tallard and William in Kensington Palace. They were continued in Holland when William removed there in July. It was these negotiations, incidentally, which produced one of the most idyllic footnotes in the historical literature of the nineteenth century; it is a description of William's park at Loo:

> le parc, tout entier dans le style dit anglais, peut justement passer pour l'une des beautés de la Hollande et l'un des chefs d'œuvre de l'art du jardinier paysagiste. . . . Le plus rare peut-être de tous ces enchantements du regard, ce sont des hêtres et des chênes, plusieurs fois centenaires, où bondissent les écureuils, et sous la jeune ombre desquels se sont promenés sans doute Guillaume III, Heinsius, Tallard et Bonrepaus, devisant des plus grands intérêts du monde chrétien.[2]

In August William wrote to Somers, informing him of the secret negotiations and requesting him, if he approved of the terms, to send full powers under the Great Seal of England, with blanks for the names of the commissioners. After conferring hastily with Montagu, Orford, and Shrewsbury, Somers drafted a reply on 28 August. Not only did he *not* approve of the treaty, but he doubted England's ability to enforce it:

> entertaining a Proposal of this Nature seems to be attended with many ill Consequences, if the *French* did not act a sincere part. . . .

1 Coxe, p. 380; Arsène Legrelle, *La Diplomatie française et la Succession d'Espagne*, 4 vols., Paris, 1888–92, ii. 249.

2 Arsène Legrelle, *La Diplomatie française et la Succession d' Espagne*, 4 vols., Paris, 1888–92, ii. 442, n. 1.

But so far as relates to *England*, it would be Want of Duty not to give Your Majesty this clear Account: That there is a Deadness, and Want of Spirit in the Nation universally, so as not at all to be disposed to the Thought of entering into a new War; and that they seem to be tired out with Taxes, to a Degree beyond what was discerned, till it appeared upon Occasion of the late Elections.[1]

At the same time, however, he ordered Vernon to draw up a blank commission, affixed the Great Seal, and sent it off to Loo by special courier. William chose to ignore this ambiguous reply and the First Partition Treaty was concluded in September 1698. It was signed for England by Portland and Sir Joseph Williamson, the English ambassador to The Hague. Four months later the Tory majority in the new Parliament made it even less likely that England could enforce the secret Treaty by passing Harley's bill to reduce the strength of the standing army to 7,000. This, from the standpoint of the military historian, was 'an act of criminal imbecility, the most mischievous work of the most mischievous Parliament that has ever sat at Westminster', which left England virtually at the mercy of France.[2] William, of course, knew that it was 'ruinous', but, as David Ogg has said, 'as he could not explain, he could not hope to be understood'.[3]

The First Partition Treaty was nullified in January 1699 when Joseph Ferdinand, the 7-year-old Electoral Prince of Bavaria and the grand nephew of Carlos II, died in Brussels. This child had been named heir not only to Spain, but to Spanish America, the Lowlands, and Sardinia. When William learned of his death, he confessed to Heinsius that they were lost in a 'labyrinth'. Louis XIV promptly demanded a new treaty, threatening, if William hesitated, to support the claims of the Emperor, Leopold I, who was Carlos's brother-in-law, or the Dauphin, who was Carlos's cousin. Daniel Defoe, who was one of the

[1] *C.J.* xiii. 491.

[2] Sir John William Fortescue, *A History of the British Army*, 13 vols. in 14, 1910–35, i. 389.

[3] Vernon, ii. 237; Ogg, p. 450.

few people in England who knew of the existence of the Treaty, explains why neither of these terms was acceptable to William:

> I remember in that Famous Treaty, which I had the Honour to see, and something more in its Embrio—This Fundamental Maxim is laid down, as what all the Princes of *Europe* would acknowledge, *viz.* That it was Essential to the Safety and Peace of *Europe*, that the Kingdom of *Spain* should never Devolve on one Hand to any Prince that was Emperor of *Germany*, or on the other Hand, to any Prince that was King of *France*.[1]

So William set about doggedly to negotiate a second treaty.

These negotiations, which were not at all secret, were begun between William and Tallard in London and between Jean Baptiste Colbert, the Marquis de Torcy, Louis XIV's Foreign Minister, and Edward Villiers, Earl of Jersey, the English ambassador, in Versailles. Substantial agreement had been reached by May 1699, when Don Francisco Bernardo de Quirós, the Spanish ambassador to The Hague, dismissed it contemptuously as 'un alianza de papel' because it had not been ratified by Parliament. But for the rest, it was 'like an Alarum-Bell rung over all Europe'.[2] According to the terms of this Second Partition Treaty, the Archduke Charles, younger son of the Emperor, was named heir to the throne of Spain. France was to get the Spanish possessions in Italy, of which the duchy of Milan would be exchanged for the long-sought Duchy of Lorraine. Holland was to get the barrier fortresses in the Spanish Netherlands as protection against the power of France. The advantage to England was negative, but crucial: peace and the balance of power in Europe had been maintained.

In September 1699 Don Manuel de Coloma, Marqués de Canales, the Spanish ambassador to England, protested so violently against this dismemberment of Spanish power

[1] *Letters of William III. and Louis XIV*, ed. Paul Grimblot, 2 vols., 1848, ii. 255; *Review*, viii (28 Apr. 1711), 59.

[2] [Andrew Fletcher,] *A Speech upon the State of the Nation, in April 1701*, [1701], p. 10.

that he was declared *persona non grata* and given eighteen days to leave England. The Treaty was finally signed for England by Portland and Jersey on 21 February 1700. Despite de Quirós's protestations, it required no ratification by Parliament, for foreign affairs were still the exclusive prerogative of the Crown. As Nicholas Tindal explains, 'It is certain, that, by our Constitution, all foreign negotiations were trusted intirely to the Crown, that the King was under no obligation by law to communicate such secrets to his Council, or to hear, much less was he obliged to follow, their advice.'[1]

The Second Partition Treaty was to be no more successful than the First. In August 1700 the Emperor Leopold publicly renounced it and claimed the whole succession for himself. Carlos II reacted to this by drawing up another will. After directing that 100,000 masses be said for his soul, and that his body be buried in the Escorial, he left the entire Spanish empire to the 16-year-old second grandson of Louis XIV, Philippe, Duc d'Anjou. Only a month later, on 20 October 1700, Carlos II finally died, and the fate of the Second Partition Treaty was left hanging on the decision of Louis XIV.

As soon as the news of Carlos's death reached England, Defoe, who had 'had the Honour *from his Majesty's own Mouth* to hear many of his Reasons for making that Treaty', began to write in defence of it. In *The Two Great Questions Consider'd. I. What the French King will Do, with Respect to the Spanish Monarchy. II. What Measures the English ought to Take* Defoe answers the questions in his title by arguing very skilfully that all the advantages for Louis XIV lay in adhering to 'the *Postulata*' of the Second Partition Treaty, and by urging Englishmen 'to put themselves in such a posture as may prevent the French King seizing of Spain it self', in the event that

1 Tindal, iv. 223–4. Historians still acknowledge that 'William was within his rights in conducting his foreign policy without reference to parliament, or even to his ministers', but add that 'such conduct was no longer politic' (Ogg, p. 452). But without the benefit of hindsight, it could never occur to Tindal, or to Swift, that William should conduct his foreign affairs in any other fashion.

Louis 'shou'd so far forget himself' as to accept the throne of Spain for his grandson.[1]

But the Paper War could not keep up with the rush of events. Defoe had to add a Preface to *The Two Great Questions Consider'd* even before it was published: '*Since the Following Sheets were in the Press, some Letters from* France *advise, that the King of* France *has saluted his Grandson the Duke* D'Anjou, *as King of* Spain.' Louis had simply torn up the Second Partition Treaty, only ten months after it had been signed. Eleven years later Defoe could still recall William's words on receiving this shattering news: 'When his Majesty had the first News by an Express of the King of *France*'s having rejected the *Partition*, and set up his Grandson, he Paused some time, and said in French, *et bien don, le Roy de France est Ruin et L'Europe ausee*.'[2] The next day William wrote to Heinsius, 'We must confess we are dupes'. But if William was dejected, Harley was elated: 'This is . . . better than we could expect', he wrote to Thomas Thynne, Viscount Weymouth. William, however, was convinced by this second failure to settle the Spanish succession by treaty that war was inevitable. Despite the 'Deadness, and Want of Spirit in the Nation', which Somers had warned against in his letter of August 1698, and despite broad popular support for Louis's acceptance of the will, which seemed for the moment to avert war, William felt compelled to prepare England for the inevitable. 'I will engage people here, by a prudent conduct, by degrees', he wrote to Heinsius, 'not being able to play any other game with these people than engaging them imperceptibly.' And Defoe was almost his only pawn in this lonely game.[3]

Within five days of the publication of *The Two Great Questions Consider'd* an answer had appeared, called *Remarks Upon a Late Pamphlet Intitul'd, The Two Great*

[1] *The Two Great Questions Consider'd*, 1700, pp. 4–8, 22.

[2] [Daniel Defoe,] *The Felonious Treaty*, [December] 1711, p. 5.

[3] *Letters of William III. and Louis XIV*, ed. Paul Grimblot, 2 vols., 1848, ii. 477, 478–9; H.M.C. Portland MSS. iii. 634.

Questions Consider'd. While acknowledging that Defoe 'has gotten abundance of Reputation by writing this Book', the anonymous Tory author undermined all Defoe's arguments by appealing to the most primitive isolationist instincts: 'what have we to do to intermeddle with the Pretensions of Sovereign Princes, or to prevent the Natives of a Country from giving their Kingdom to whom they please?' On 2 December 1700 Defoe fired back *The Two Great Questions Further Considered, With some Reply to the Remarks*. The tone of this pamphlet is much more serious than the speculative tone of the first. Defoe complained of a Tory 'Pamphleteering Club' which was undermining 'the very Being of the English Monarchy' by asserting 'the People's Right to make Kings'. But the main object of this second pamphlet was to engage the people, imperceptibly, for war: 'Truly, If the French carry the Spanish Monarchy, that is, obtain the Possession of it to themselves, I appeal it to all the World if we are not in a dangerous Condition.'[1]

The swiftness with which events were moving in the late months of 1700 also forced a delay in the publication of the attack on the Second Partition Treaty which Davenant had begun in July. Even in July, Bonet had already acquired accurate information about the contents of the projected work:

> Pour cacher l'esprit de partis qui les [the Tories] guide, ils prenent pour pretexte le tort qu'un Traité de la nature de celui-la, et par lequel on cede à la France tous les Ports de mer que l'Espagne possede en Italie, peut porter à l'Angleterre, afin d'engager dans leurs partis, sous le voile de l'interet public, les Deputés des Provinces, qui sont pour la plus part si renfermés dans leurs Isle, qu'ils n'ont aucune connoissance des affaires étrangeres. Ce livre doit paraitre vers l'ouverture du Parlement prochain. . . . Il agitera meme la question, si les Rois d'Angleterre ont le droit de faire la guerre, et la Paix; et s'ils peuvent, sans la participation du Conseil, faire un Traité, ainsi qu'il est arrivé en dernier lieu.[2]

[1] *The Two Great Questions Further Considered. With some Reply to the Remarks*, [December] 1700, p. 15.

[2] B.M. Add. MS. 30000D, ff. 225v, 227v.

On 30 August, however, René L'Hermitage de Saulnières, the Dutch resident in London, reported a difference of opinion among the Tory propaganda managers: 'On continue à dire, que ce mesme docteur exerce son genie à écrire sur le partage de la succession d'Espagne, mais quelques uns de ses amis luÿ ont conseillé par avance de ne rendre pas son livre public'.[1] But Davenant, 'glorieux du Succés qu'eut son Livre dans le dernier Parlement', was still determined to publish his new book before the opening of the next session of Parliament. On 19 September he wrote to Harley at Brampton: 'Your man has delivered to me the records, of which about two months hence you will find I have made a plentiful use. The work goes on vigorously, but is infinitely of more labour than I expected.' On 5 November, after the news of the death of Carlos II had reached London, Bonet reported: 'Ce Davenant n'attend q'une occasion favorable pour mettre au jour le livre qu'il a fait pour examiner le *jus belli et pacis* des Roys d'Angleterre; Et s'ils peuvent faire indifferemment toute sorte de Traité et d'Alliance, sans les communiquer au Conseil Privé.'[2]

Now it began to be rumoured that the Tories had decided to suppress Davenant's book. But L'Hermitage reports only that Davenant himself decided to withhold publication: 'Le docteur Davenant, qui s'estoit preparé à mettre au jour un livre contre le traité du partage, trouvant la scene changée, et qu'il n'auroit plus l'applaudissement qu'il en attendoit, n'a pas jugé à propos de le faire: mais pour en quelque façon degager sa parole, en a publié un autre, sous un grand titre et qui est icÿ joint.'[3]

[1] B.M. Add. MS. 17677UU, ff. 302–302v.

[2] B.M. Add. MS. 30000D, ff. 272v, 312v; *Calendar of State Papers Domestic... 1700–1702*, ed. Edward Bateson, 1937, p. 119; H.M.C. Portland MSS. iv. 5.

[3] *Jus Regium: Or, The King's Right to grant Forfeitures*, [April] 1701, p. 80; B.M. Add. MS. 17677WW, f. 109v. This 'other' work of Davenant remains unidentified. It is tempting to suppose that it is the reply to Defoe, *The Two Great Questions Consider'd*, but *Remarks Upon a Late Pamphlet Intitul'd, The Two Great Questions Considered* is not a 'grand titre'. It is more likely that the 'other' work was a new edition of *The Emperour and the Empire Betray'd*, originally published in 1681. The Tories took up the cause of Leopold I when he refused to

In either case, publication of Davenant's *Essays Upon I. The Ballance of Power, II. The Right of making War, Peace, and Alliances. III. Universal Monarchy. To which is added, An Appendix Containing the Records Referr'd to in the Second Essay* was delayed for another three months. In the meantime Harley had found another writer and Davenant another patron, of almost limitless resources.

John Toland as 'Mr. Harley'*s Creature'*

The *fact* of Harley's patronage of John Toland is well established: Toland himself admitted in 1701 that he was 'Mr. *Harley*'s Creature'. But the details of this relationship are even more obscure than they are in the case of Davenant. They can only be inferred from what Toland wrote and published in 1700–1. It is not surprising, however, that this should be so. Harley would have every reason to conceal his patronage of a man who, it was believed, had trampled on the Book of Common Prayer while at Oxford, who had been 'driven out' of Ireland, and with whom 'it was even dangerous . . . to have been known once to converse', as William Molyneux warned John Locke.[1]

Harley learned immediately of Toland's difficulties from an informant in Ireland: 'we ordered his book [*Christianity not Mysterious*] to be burned and banishment to himselfe, which was accordingly done last markett day by the hands of the common hangman before the Parliament dore and the Tholsell in the citty. . . . Toland made his escape into England, where he had best stay.'[2] Toland arrived in England in 1697, the month the Treaty of Ryswick was signed. In the session of Parliament which

sign the Second Partition Treaty in August 1700. *The Emperour and the Empire Betray'd* is a 'grand titre' and it is cited in *England's Enemies Exposed*, [July] 1701, another product of the Tory propaganda mill.

[1] [Pierre Des Maizeaux,] *A Collection of Several Pieces of Mr. John Toland*, 2 vols., 1726, i. xxv, ii. 345, 348–9; *Notes and Queries*, 3rd series, i (4 Jan. 1862), 6–7.

[2] H.M.C. Portland MSS. iii. 586.

began in December 'The business of the standing Army', as he said later, 'became the very test . . . of Whig and Tory.' By writing against the standing army in *The Militia Reformed: Or an easy Scheme of furnishing England with a constant Land-force capable to prevent or to subdue any Foreign Power* Toland established an identity of purposes with Robert Harley, who was indifferent to party labels, but who was also the first politician to understand the overriding importance of propaganda in the constitutional monarchy which had been established by the Revolution.[1]

There were, indeed, even more compelling reasons for an understanding between Harley and Toland. Harley found Toland in exactly the same situation in which he found Defoe in 1703 and Swift in 1710. In Toland's own words, 'I thought my self neglected and ill-used by the Whig-Ministers'. Later he was to recall that his 'resentments against their persons' had implied 'no dislike of the Cause in which they pretend to be ingag'd'. But in 1698 his 'resentments against their persons' explains why a Whig 'Free-thinker' could be recruited alongside Jacobites like Davenant and non-jurors like Thomas Wagstaffe to attack the Whig junto. Toland admitted that he wholly approved of Harley's opposition to 'our corrupt Ministry' and of 'the strenuous efforts he made to dissolve it'.[2]

The first work which Toland is known for certain to have written for Harley was *The Oceana of James Harrington, Esq; And His Other Works . . . His Life Prefix'd by J. Toland*, published in August 1700, the same month in which Davenant's 'friends' were urging him not to publish his *Essays*. Harrington's account of the well-drilled and efficient militia of Oceana must have supplied the motive,

[1] [Pierre Des Maizeaux,] *A Collection of Several Pieces of Mr. John Toland*, 2 vols., 1726, ii. 341. *The Militia Reformed* was published in 1698. It is probably the 'new pamphlet . . . from the same club', which Vernon in November 1698 said was 'not writ with the same spirit as the last' (Vernon, ii. 216).

[2] [Pierre Des Maizeaux,] *A Collection of Several Pieces of Mr. John Toland*, 2 vols., 1726, ii. 346, 348–9.

for as Toland later reminded Harley, 'neither of us imagin'd the model it self to be practicable'.[1]

Thereafter Toland wrote at least three books under Harley's patronage. The first of these, *The Art of Governing by Parties*, the most coherent attack on the party-system to be written during the Paper War, was intended to have been published during the elections of December 1700–January 1701 as a straightforward Tory election pamphlet. Even while arguing that parties were 'the abominable fruits' of Charles II's 'policy', Toland makes it perfectly clear 'which of 'em has most Reason in my Opinion'. He holds up to infamy 'the apostat Whigs', deplores the 'past Mismanagements' of the junto in the same terms as Davenant, and even cites Davenant as his authority. All this, however, did not prevent Davenant from charging that Toland was really a tool of the Whigs and citing passages from *The Art of Governing by Parties* to prove it. The fact is that Toland attacks 'those quack Ministers' with enthusiasm, but betrays 'no dislike of the Cause in which they pretend to be ingag'd'. For this cause, the 'unalterable and indispensable' cause of 'civil Liberty, religious Toleration, and the Protestant Succession', Toland could not conceal his admiration. At bottom, he did not believe that the political merry-go-round had anything to do with principles: 'this party-business is . . . but a mere blind, for matters go on just as they did; where one left off, the other begins: in Tory out Whig, in Whig out Tory.' Toland assumed, just as Swift was to do in the *Discourse*, that party violence could only conclude in the loss of civil liberty and that 'the contending Parties . . .

[1] [Pierre Des Maizeaux,] *A Collection of Several Pieces of Mr. John Toland*, 2 vols., 1726, ii. 227; *A Transcript of the Registers of the Worshipful Company of Stationers, 1640–1708*, ed. G. E. B. Eyre and C. R. Rivington, 3 vols., 1913–14, iii. 492. It is an amusing sidelight on the bibliographical complexities of the Paper War that Toland was thought to be the author both of John Tutchin's violent Tory satire, *The Foreigners* (*Saul and Samuel; or, The Common Interest of our King and Country*, 1702, p. 16) and Defoe's famous rejoinder, *The True-Born Englishman* ([William Pittis,] *The True-born English Man: A Satyr, Answer'd Paragraph by Paragraph*, [February] 1701, p. 3). Furthermore, when Pittis published his savage attack on Toland, Toland was already at work for the Tories.

after they have mutually spent their Force against one another . . . easily become a common prey to Arbitrary Power'. In his conclusion, therefore, Toland advocates 'abolishing those fatal Distinctions of Whig and Tory, and making us at least bear with one another in Religion where we cannot agree'. It is easy to imagine why publication of this strange election pamphlet was deferred until the Tories were able to count a safe majority in the 5th Parliament of William III.[1]

The next work which Toland executed for Harley was a trial balloon for the Act of Settlement, entitled *Limitations for the Next Foreign Successor*, subscribed 3 March 1701 and published a few days later. The Act of Settlement had been made necessary by the tragic death in July 1700 of William, Duke of Gloucester, the last surviving child of Princess Anne. Although the Princess was pregnant again, she had already had fifteen miscarriages and was so fat that she could take no exercise. William was fifty years old, had no children and no inclination to remarry. So the death of this 11-year-old child was a serious blow to the Protestant Succession in England. 'God's ways', Harley wrote to his father, 'are unsearchable.'[2]

At its opening on 12 February 1701 William reminded his 5th Parliament that 'Our great misfortune in the loss of the Duke of *Gloucester*, hath made it absolutely necessary, that there should be a further provision for the succession to the crown in the protestant line'. And he urged that the matter should receive their 'early and effectual consideration'. But the House of Commons was too occupied with hearings on contested elections to give it either. Burnet observed that 'It was often put off from one day to another, and it gave place to the most trifling

[1] *The Art of Governing by Parties*, [February] 1701, pp. 9, 54, 110, 164, 177; [Pierre Des Maizeaux,] *A Collection of Several Pieces of Mr. John Toland*, 2 vols., 1726, ii. 227, 341, 349–50; [Charles Davenant,] *The Old and Modern Whig Truly Represented*, [December] 1701, p. 17. The passages from *The Art of Governing by Parties* which Davenant cites are pp. 53–54, 149–50.

[2] H.M.C. Portland MSS. iii. 624.

matters'. Finally, on 3 March, when 'a day was solemnly set for it, and all people expected, that it should pass without any difficulty, *Harley* moved, that some things previous to that might be first considered. . . . Nothing pressed them at present, so he moved they would settle some Conditions of Government, as Preliminaries, before they should proceed to the Nomination of the Person.' What these conditions were, was revealed to the world a few days later in Toland's pamphlet. They were, again in Burnet's words, 'such extravagant Limitations, as should quite change the Form of our Government, and render the Crown titular and precarious: The King was alarmed . . . for almost every particular, that was proposed, implied a reflection on him and his Administration.' In all, fifteen limitations were enumerated, including the following:

3. that no 'place-men' should sit in the House of Commons;
5. that the advice of Parliament be taken in the appointment of the Lord Chancellor, the Lord Treasurer, and the Lord Admiral;
8. that no leagues or treaties for peace or war be made without the consent of Parliament;
9. that the royal veto be limited;
15. that none but natives of the three kingdoms be capable of offices in the government.

Four of these conditions (3, 8, 9, and 15) were eventually embodied in the Bill, and Tory opposition to the House of Hanover was also reflected in Toland's preference for 'the Family of *Brandenburg*, who are of our own [reformed] Religion'.[1]

Bonet concluded, in a striking anticipation of what Swift was to say in the *Discourse*, that 'par ces limitations . . . le pouvoir sera presque tout dévolu au Peuple, ou plutot aux Chefs de la Chambre qui agissent par faction et par

[1] *C.J.* xiii. 375–6; Burnet, ii. 270; *Limitations for the Next Foreign Successor*, [March] 1701, pp. 11–13, 8; *C.J.* xiii. 400–1. There are at least two editions of *Limitations for the Next Foreign Successor* dated 1701, a folio and a quarto. These page references are to the quarto edition.

interet . . . et que les prerogatives du Roy, et celles des Seigneurs souffrent beaucoup par là. En un mot que la balance de ce Gouvernement sera otée, que c'est le chemin à une anarchie.'[1] The subsequent history of the Bill seemed to confirm that the Tories were reluctant to settle the Crown on the Electress Sophia of Hanover. After the limitations were agreed upon, and it became time to name the successor, Sir John Bolles, 'who was then disordered in his Senses, and soon after quite lost them, was set on by the Party, to be the first that should name the Electoress Dowager of *Brunswick*'. Burnet thought this was done 'to make it less serious, when moved by such a person', but Bonet had another explanation. He said the nomination was ordered to be made by 'un personnage peu estimé, afin de se moquer de ceux qui disoient que ce Bill etoit une pierre de touche pour connoitre les Jacobites'. Under Bolles's chairmanship, passage of the Bill was still postponed for many weeks. Burnet records that every time the motion was called for, 'all the members ran out of the house with so much indecency, that the contrivers seemed ashamed of this management'. Yet, as Bonet says, 'malgré les Tories', the Bill finally passed and was sent up to the House of Lords, where it encountered almost no opposition. Bonet attributed the passage of the Bill almost wholly to the force of public opinion which demanded it. And in the moulding of this opinion Toland's pamphlet must have played an important part.[2]

On 21 June 1701, nine days after William had given his reluctant assent to the Act of Settlement, Toland published a lengthy justification of the Act entitled *Anglia Libera, or the Limitation and Succession of the Crown of England explain'd and asserted; As grounded on his Majesty's Speech; The Proceedings in Parliament; The Desires of the People; The Safety of our Religion; The Nature of our*

[1] B.M. Add. MS. 30000E, f. 80.

[2] Burnet, ii. 271; B.M. Add. MS. 30000E, ff. 73ᵛ, 183. Bolles was one of four 'Patriots' who were urged in *A Tale of a Tub* to bring in a bill to recruit political, military, and religious leaders from Bedlam (*TT*, pp. 175–6).

Constitution; The Balance of Europe; and The Rights of all Mankind. Here for the first time Toland mentions Harley, a person of 'acknowledg'd Learning, and unparallel'd Ability in Parliamentary Affairs', and recalls hearing him 'declare his Opinion som Months ago', as he must indeed have done when he was writing *Limitations for the Next Foreign Successor.* The newsletters reported that *Anglia Libera* was written specifically to be presented to the Electress Sophia. George Stepney, in fact, called it 'the deceitfull message of the Speaker'. And it was Harley who secured Toland's appointment to the mission which William sent to Hanover to explain the provisions of the Act to the Electress. Upon his return to England in October 1701, however, Toland must have broken with Harley, for he published nothing more for the Tories, and in 1705 he protested 'by all that's awful' that he had not even communicated with Harley since the death of King William.[1]

Impeachment of the Whig Junto

The 5th Parliament of William III convened on 10 February 1701. Harley was elected Speaker, according to the plan which had been worked out when Rochester, Godolphin, and Harley had their first audience with William the previous November. With Davenant's attack on the Partition Treaty safely in reserve, the Speaker could allow the House of Commons to settle down to the pleasant, partisan business of deciding contested elections. The first irruption occurred on 15 February when John Howe, 'that Scandal of Parliaments', attacked the King in such violent terms that Bonet was afraid to report them. Howe said that 'the king's grants were squandered away upon buffoons and harlots, and called the treaty of partition a felonious treaty of three thieves'. But the momentum

[1] *Anglia Libera*, [June] 1701, pp. 50, 73; Luttrell, v. 67, 100; Bodleian MS. Montague d. 1, f. 69v; [Pierre Des Maizeaux,] *A Collection of Several Pieces of Mr. John Toland*, 2 vols., 1726, ii. 345.

gained from such a promising start was lost when the Commons allowed itself to be diverted into other affairs.[1]

At the end of February Bonet observed that while France was moving 60,000 soldiers into the Lowlands and building landing barges in all the ports facing England, the House of Commons was still amusing itself hearing evidence of election frauds. Defoe had 'some more than common reason to know' that the King was anxious about Parliament's delay in voting supplies for the 10,000 troops which had been promised to the Dutch.[2]

In the middle of March the attack on the junto was taken up in the House of Lords. John Sheffield, Marquis of Normanby, protested violently that a treaty committing the whole nation to war had been negotiated by two or three foreigners without even the advice of Council or Parliament. The great Whig, William Cavendish, Duke of Devonshire, offended because he had not been consulted by the King, demanded that those who had negotiated the Treaty ought to pay for it with their heads. When the Bishop of Salisbury interposed a remark in defence of the Treaty, Peterborough expressed surprise that an English bishop should utter sentiments appropriate to a Spanish cardinal. After this, not a word was spoken in defence of the Treaty during a debate of five hours. In conclusion, a committee was appointed to draft an address to the King.[3]

While the committee was framing an article begging the King not to conclude treaties without the advice of Council, the Earl of Portland upset the apple cart. 'Milord Portland débonda', as Tallard reported. He protested that the Partition Treaty had, in fact, been approved by the Privy Council. When challenged on this point, he named, among others, Somers and Montagu.

[1] B.M. Add. MS. 30000E, f. 44^{v}; Alexander Cunningham, *The History of Great Britain*, 2 vols., 1787, i. 208.

[2] B.M. Add. MS. 30000E, f. 61^{v}.

[3] P.R.O. Transcripts, 3 (France) 187, ff. 79–79^{v}; B.M. Add. MS. 30000E, ff. 91^{v}–92.

In his excitement, Portland had attributed to the Second Partition Treaty some of the circumstances of the First, secret Treaty, in the negotiation of which Somers's part was not even suspected.[1]

When Danby carried this astounding information on to the floor of the House, Somers defended himself by reminding the Lords that foreign negotiations were the exclusive prerogative of the Crown, that the King had commanded him to affix the seal to the Treaty, and that he could not have refused since the Treaty violated no known law of England. Three days later, while the address to the King was still in debate, Rochester made a motion to send to the House of Commons for their concurrence in the address. The motion was defeated, but by this time the Tory strategy had become apparent. 'It now plainly appeared', as Burnet records, 'that the design was, to set on the House of Commons, to impeach some of the Lords who had been concerned in the Partition Treaty.'[2]

On 14 March the Lords sent a message to the Commons to acquaint them of a Treaty 'extremely dangerous in itself, and transacted also in a most irregular manner'. The Commons finally took up the scent and voted 'to lay before his Majesty the ill consequences of the Treaty of Partition passed under the Great Seal of *England*, during the Sitting of Parliament, and without the Advice of the same'. Bonet recalled that the Treaty of Ryswick had been signed during the sitting of Parliament without any objections being made, but by this time the matter had passed beyond the stage of rational argument. An amendment to thank the King for his 'Care of these Nations, and the Peace of Europe' was defeated and Sir Edward Seymour was appointed chairman of the committee to draw up the address. The next day Davenant's *Essays Upon I. The Ballance of Power. II. The Right of making War, Peace, and Alliances. III. Universal Monarchy* was published, as 'conserté avec ceux de son partÿ', but with

[1] P.R.O. Transcripts, 3 (France) 187, f. 80; Burnet, ii. 264.

[2] P.R.O. Transcripts, 3 (France) 187, f. 82v; Burnet, ii. 262.

last-minute changes to fit the present situation. Publication was again perfectly timed to produce the maximum propaganda effect.[1]

The book begins with a virtual invitation to the London mob to demonstrate against the Lords Partitioners and even suggests a slogan:

> We have known the Times when the News of such a League as has lately been entred into without Advice of Parliament, would have created a general Consternation in the City. Thirty years ago[2] the Shops would have been shut up, if such a dangerous Union had been then made, between the strengths of *France* and *Spain*. . . . All the Town would have had nothing before 'em but a prospect of Universal Monarchy.

After repeating the charges made in *A Discourse upon Grants and Resumptions* that the junto had plundered the public treasury, Davenant opened up a new vein, following the lead that Sir Edward Seymour had afforded in his attack on Somers in 1700:

> As to Religion: 'Tis notorious that many of those lately in Play have us'd their utmost Endeavours to discountenance all Reveal'd Religion. . . . Good God! what a strange mixture of Men have we lately seen upon the Stage? Irreligious Phanaticks and Arbitrary Republicans! Are not a great many of us able to point out to several Persons, whom nothing has recommended to Places of the highest Trust, and often to rich Benefices and Dignities, but the open Enmity which they have almost from their Cradles professed to the Divinity of Christ.

But this charge was so manifestly absurd that the Archbishop of Canterbury immediately ordered a bill to be posted on the doors of Westminster Abbey demanding that the author should name those persons so that legal proceedings could be instituted against them, and the

[1] *Parl. Hist.* v. 1239; *C.J.* xiii. 419; B.M. Add. MS. 30000E, ff. 105–105^{v}; *The Post Boy*, No. 911, 20–22 March 1701; B.M. Add. MS. 17677WW, f. 203.

[2] This is an especially delightful irony, since 'thirty years ago' is almost exactly the date of Charles II's secret Treaty of Dover, which relegated England to the status of a Bourbon dependency.

Convocation declared the *Essays* to be 'a PUBLICK SCANDAL'.[1]

Davenant was not able to sustain this high level of invective throughout the 400-odd pages of his book. Most of it is devoted to dubious 'precedents' designed to prove that the House of Commons, from the time of William the Conqueror, had enjoyed 'a deliberative Voice' in the conduct of foreign affairs. The ingenuity which Davenant displays in reconciling the practice of Henry VIII, Elizabeth I, and Charles II with this theory is remarkable. When he refashions English history to suit Harley's purposes of the moment, he is indeed 'tedious', but he is not foolish. Even when he states blandly that 'We all know that [William III] had no part in this Treaty' he is not being naïve. He is deliberately contradicting a fact of common knowledge to assert the new and paradoxical principle that the *King*'s ministers must be 'accomptable to Parliament'. He foresaw that to destroy French dominance in Spain and to enforce a barrier in the Lowlands, which became the political objectives of the War of the Spanish Succession, would be 'a long, bloody, and expensive Enterprize'. And, finally, he never forgot that the purpose of his book was to create popular support for impeachment of the Lords Partitioners:

> To put us in a Condition to hold the Ballance [in Europe], our Distempers at Home must be first Cur'd: But in order to do this, the Sore must be Lanch'd, Prob'd, Search'd, and laid open; and if I do it with a rough Hand, let the Reader consider, I have stubborn and inveterate Diseases to deal with, which will baffle all gentle Remedies, and stand in need of the strongest Applications that can be thought on.[2]

The publication of Davenant's *Essays* must have taken the Whigs by complete surprise; it was six weeks before they could publish a reply, and even then they could not con-

[1] *Essays upon I. The Ballance of Power*, [March] 1701, pp. 38–40; Luttrell, v. 31; White Kennet, *The History of the Convocation*, 1702, pp. 75–76.

[2] *Essays upon I. The Ballance of Power*, [March] 1701, pp. 59, 186–7, 86, 33–34.

ceal their amazement that 'his Book [could] have such a run, and his Principles gain such footing'.[1]

Meanwhile the rough work of probing and searching for grounds for impeachment went ahead in the House of Commons. On 1 April the House of Commons again 'fell upon impeaching'. It was moved to impeach William, Earl of Portland, for high crimes and misdemeanors in negotiating the Second Treaty of Partition, 'which was destructive to the Trade of this Kingdom, and dangerous to the Peace of *Europe*'. Before putting the question, Harley observed that there was still time to turn back, but that, if the motion was voted in the negative, 'on pouvoit dire que dès ce moment, la cognée avoit esté mise à la racine de leurs libertés'. This so effectively stifled the opposition that Portland's impeachment was voted with only one dissenting voice. Davenant, Anthony Hammond, Sir Humphrey Mackworth, and other skirmishers in the Paper War, were appointed to the committee to draw up the articles of impeachment.[2]

But Portland was only a stalking horse for the junto. It was immediately pointed out that if Portland was guilty, Somers must be *more* guilty, for a foreigner could not be expected to know the laws of the realm as well as a lord chancellor. Somers had indeed affixed the Great Seal to 'that fatal treaty', as Vernon called it. Harley, 'contre sa prudence ordinaire, dit que si ce crime demeuroit impuni, qu'on pouvoit datter dès ce moment là la ruine de la liberté Anglicane'. But the same gambit failed to succeed twice and although the House sat until nine at night, a motion to impeach Somers was defeated 189–182.[3]

On 14 April the House of Commons returned to the attack, armed this time with the story of Somers's involvement in the secret negotiations of the First Partition

[1] *Animadversions on a late Factious Book, Entitled, Essays upon, I. The Ballance of Power*, [May] 1701, p. 40. This book is signed 'L. L. D. F.', apparently in an effort to associate it with the great popularity of Defoe, but it has not been admitted to the Defoe canon.

[2] *C.J.* xiii. 465; B.M. Add. MS. 17677WW, f. 212v.

[3] B.M. Add. MSS. 17677WW, f. 212v, 30000E, f. 121; Luttrell, v. 33.

Treaty. Portland's correspondence with Vernon, which was the source of this information, was read aloud letter by letter. Vernon was questioned so closely that he was brought to tears and even intimidated to speak against Somers himself. Harley very wisely neglected to ask Vernon whether Somers had in fact approved of the Treaty, for it would have surprised many of the members to learn that he had not. Instead, he gave 'un tour malin' to the debate by assuming that Somers *had* advised the Treaty, and then asking whether he were not guilty of high crimes and misdemeanors for having done so. When the Tory back-benchers learned that Somers had affixed the Great Seal to a blank commission they cried out that he might as well have sold England outright.[1]

At eight o'clock, Somers, who had received the King's permission to reveal the whole story of his involvement in the Treaty, appeared at the door of the House and asked permission to be heard in his own defence. After candles had been brought in, he was admitted and promptly challenged by Harley to reveal who had informed him that there was a debate in progress concerning himself. Somers offered to withdraw rather than do 'such a dishonourable Thing', but he was finally admitted and allowed to read the King's letter of August 1698 from Loo, and his own reply. Burnet believed that he spoke 'so fully and so clearly' that had the question of his impeachment been put immediately, it would again have been defeated. 'God knows', Matthew Prior exclaimed, 'what crime he is guilty of, but that of being a very great Man.'[2]

[1] *C.J.* xiii. 487, 489; P.R.O. Transcripts, 3 (France) 188, ff. 24v, 31; B.M. Add. MS. 30000E, ff. 143v–4. The actual letters which Vernon submitted to the House of Commons, including ten from Portland, are bound into the Brown University library copy of *Votes of the House of Commons* (Chester Kirby, 'The four lords and the partition treaty', *American Historical Review*, lii (1947), 477).

[2] Burnet, ii. 267; *C.J.* xiii. 489; *Miscellaneous Works of His late Excellency Matthew Prior*, 2 vols., 1740, i. 164. Such was 'the Madness and Fury of Parties' that Prior, who represented the rotten borough of East Grinstead, controlled by the great Tory magnate, the Earl of Dorset, felt compelled to vote for Somers's impeachment.

Harley, with his remarkable skill 'both of lengthening out and of perplexing debates', prevented the question from being put until the impression made by Somers's speech had 'much worn out', and then carried it upon a division, 198–188. Thereafter the impeachments of Montagu and Russell were carried by increasingly large majorities. A committee was appointed to go up to the Lords, and at their Bar, to impeach the leaders of the Whig junto 'in the name of the House of Commons, and of all the Commons of England'. It was after midnight when the House adjourned, and on the following day Jonathan Swift arrived in London in the entourage of Lord Berkeley.[1]

On Tuesday, 15 April, there were even more startling developments. First the House of Commons moved an address to the King to remove the four impeached lords from his presence and Council for ever. Not only was this 'punishing before Trial', as Burnet explained, but it cost the Commons popular support in all but the most high-flying Tory circles. Worst of all, this headstrong and unprecedented action cost the Commons the support of the Upper House, for the Lords saw immediately that it nullified their right of judicature in cases of impeachment.[2]

Two amusing incidents the next day served to emphasize the partisan nature of the address. It was discovered, first, that when a draft of the address was brought before the House, the name of William, Earl of Portland, had been omitted. Since Portland was not really a Whig and had been supplanted as William's favourite by the young Earl of Albemarle, the Tories had no real interest in impeaching him. Then, when Portland's name had hastily been added to the address, it was asked why the Earl of Jersey, who had signed the Second Partition

[1] Burnet, ii. 267; *Parl. Hist.* v. 1246; *C.J.* xiii. 489–90; B.M. Add. MSS. 30000E, f. 149v; 7078, f. 3.

[2] *C.J.* xiii. 492; Burnet, ii. 267; B.M. Add. MS. 30000E, f. 146; Vernon, iii. 144.

Treaty, was not also included. This was even more embarrassing, for Jersey had already bought his immunity. It was he who had suggested that Portland's letters to Vernon be looked into. Sir Edward Seymour saved the situation by turning it into a joke. He said that Jersey might be censured for some mismanagement of his cloak or wig, but that he could not be censured for mismanagements in affairs of state, for he was totally lacking in malice. After this *raillerie piquante* the address was ordered to be engrossed and presented to the King. Availing themselves of a fiction elaborated in Davenant's *Essays*, the drafting committee accused the impeached lords, among other things, of having endeavoured, under the King's sacred name, 'to seek Protection for what themselves had so advised'. The House of Lords rushed through an address on the same day, urging the King 'to pass no Censure or Punishment against the four Noble Lords . . . until the Impeachments depending against them in this House shall be tried'.[1]

The King did not reply to the Lords' address at all, but neither did he remove the names of the impeached lords from the Council book. To the House of Commons he replied pointedly that he would employ none in his service 'but such as shall be thought most likely to improve that mutual Trust and Confidence between us, which is so necessary, in this Conjuncture'. With fighting between France and the Empire already begun in Italy and with daily reports in the public prints of French preparations for a 'descent' on England, William did not have to explain what he meant by 'this Conjuncture'. In Kent the farmers were saying '*that they had sow'd their Corn, and the* French *were a coming to Reap it*'. And anyone who read the London newspapers must have had a pretty clear idea of what French dominance would mean to them. One item in *The Post Boy* reported that a young lawyer's wife in Paris had been fined fifty livres for wearing gold lace 'con-

[1] B.M. Add. MS. 30000E, ff. 156–156v; P.R.O. Transcripts 3 (France) 188, f. 31; *C.J.* xiii. 497; *L.J.* xvi. 654.

trary to the King's Ordinance'. An incident even more characteristic of the police state was the story of John Drummond, Earl of Melfort, who had gone into exile with James II. Having incurred Louis's displeasure, Melfort finally gained an audience with *le Grand Monarque* at Versailles. He was 'ordered to go home, where he might soon expect an Answer; accordingly he went to his Lodgings, where he found four Officers ready to carry him to the Bastile, in which place he is now a close Prisoner'.[1]

On 25 April Harley fell ill and proceedings in the House of Commons were suspended. Jean Baptiste Poussin, the French secretary of embassy in London, observed that the Commons' refusal to elect another Speaker was less a compliment to Harley than an indication of how anxious the House was to suspend its proceedings. It was also reported that 'The leading men in the House of Commons talke now of dispatching, when they meet again, and it is thereby understood that they will not prosecute their Impeachments this session, but only puff them in, and lett them by, 'till they meet again next year'.[2]

The Whig Counter-attack

If the Tories were abandoning the attack, 'thinking, that what they had already done had so marked those Lords, that the king could not employ them any more', the Whigs were quietly planning a counter-attack. The plan, which was rumoured to be the King's, was to appeal directly to the people. William had already come to regret his decision to admit Tories into his government. He was particularly 'uneasy with the Earl of *Rochester*, of whose imperious and intractable temper, he complained much'. It became increasingly clear to William that the Tories 'resolved to govern him in every thing, and not to be

[1] Burnet, ii. 268; *C.J.* xiii. 506. *The History of the Kentish Petition*, [September] 1701, p. 1; *The Post Boy*, No. 899, 20–22 Feb. 1701; No. 940, 27–29 May 1701.

[2] Luttrell, v. 42; P.R.O. Transcripts 3 (France) 188, f. 45; B.M. Add. MS. 7078, f. 5v.

governed by him in any one thing'. Furthermore, between January and April shares in the Bank of England had fallen from £122. 6*s*. to £104; Old East India Company had similarly declined from £117. 10*s*. to £75. 10*s*. As a consequence, bankers in the City were slow to finance the rearmament which William knew to be necessary. Of the £500,000 fund which had been voted to refit the navy, only £100,000 had been subscribed. So the Whigs decided to take their case to the country, to arouse the people to the danger of impending war, and, incidentally, as the Tories charged, 'to divert the *House* from their intended Prosecution' of the impeached lords.[1]

Almost all evidence for the behind-the-scenes management of this crisis in the Paper War is derived from hostile Tory sources, but the fact that the campaign was managed cannot be doubted. The Whigs themselves acknowledged the existence of 'Secret Committees' for propaganda and the meeting-place most frequently alleged for them was the Rummer, next door to Locket's, in Charing Cross. One meeting of the secret committee at the Red Lion inn, in Holborn, is also described. On this occasion 'Insolent *Calumnies*, begot at a *Club in Holbourn*, and brought forth by a Brace of *Abdicated Ministers* [Somers and Montagu], who gave the last Stroke to these Dull and Insipid *Paper Pot-Guns*', are 'Recommitted to the Faithful Hand of their Trusty Secretary *Jacob* [Tonson] (the Bird for the King) to Babble it abroad by the Hawkers'. The Vine tavern, in Longacre, was another centre from which pamphlets and broadsides were 'directed to gentlemen in the country under blank covers' or stuffed in portmanteaus and distributed in every town in England on market day, with 'Men posted to read the Libels' to the illiterate. So there is probably very little exaggeration in the Tory account of Whig activities in April 1701:

> Now they begin to put Pen to Paper; now they send about to all

[1] B.M. Add. MS. 30000E, f. 65^{v}; Burnet, ii. 280, 262; *Parl. Hist.* v. 1250; *The Source of Our Present Fears Discover'd*, 1703, p. 20.

their Agents and Dependants in every County, to solicite Petitions and Libels against the Parliament; now they send a thousand Lies about the Nation, that *the High Church-men are setting up for Persecution against all Dissenters*; that the Nation is undone by a *Jacobite* Parliament; that *French Lui-d'Ors* have been dispersed amongst the Members; that the Parliament is going to overturn the Government.[1]

However instigated, the petitions were indeed drawn up and presented, first in a trickle, but finally, by August 1701, in a flood which washed the 5th Parliament of William III completely out of existence. The most famous of these, of course, was the one from Kent. It is not unlikely that Daniel Defoe was the begetter, as well as the historian, of the Kentish petition. 'I had the Honour', he recalled later in one of his typical oblique allusions, 'to transact some things for his Majesty.' The Tories were certain that the Kentish petition originated, not in Kent, but in London, and was sent down to Kent five days before quarter-sessions was convened on 29 April. The Tory version of the Maidstone assizes differs sharply from Defoe's 'official' account in *The History of the Kentish Petition*; it goes as follows: 'the Justices of Peace, in Obedience to the Orders they had received from their Correspondents in *London* and *Westminster* . . ., put themselves upon the *Grand-Jury* . . .: the *Grand-Jury* . . . desire the *Chairman* [William Colepepper] to write them a Petition: He very gravely retires to Word *A Petition*

[1] *A Vindication of Dr. Charles Davenant*, [November 1701 but dated] 1702, p. 10; [Charles Davenant,] *The True Picture of a Modern Whig*, [August] 1701, p. 13; *A Letter to a Modern Dissenting Whig*, [September] 1701, p. 21; *The Legionites Plot*, [January ?] 1702, p. 6; *A Vindication of the Whigs*, [October] 1701, pp. 8–10; *The States-men of Abingdon*, [January] 1702, pp. 2–3; Luttrell, iv. 681; [Charles Davenant] *Tom Double Return'd out of the Country*, [January ?] 1702, p. 14; *A Justification of the Proceedings of the Honourable the House of Commons in the Last Sessions of Parliament*, [August] 1701, p. 22. This last work was 'said to be writ by the Speaker [Harley]' (Vernon, iii. 155–6). If this attribution is correct, it confers additional authority upon the account of Whig propaganda operations in April 1701, for 'It is certain', as Edward Harley said, that 'no person since the time of Secretary Walsingham ever had better intelligence or employed more money to procure it' (H.M.C. Portland MSS. v. 647).

that had been sent down from London, in his Verbis, *five Days before the Sessions.*'[1]

By 2 May Harley was fully recovered and the House resumed its sessions. Almost its first act was to lop £100,000 from the civil list allocation of £700,000 a year which had been voted to William for life in December 1697. This action clearly demonstrated that the Tory ministry had 'so little authority with their party as not to be able to restrain them from doing unreasonable and Extravagant things only to lessen the King, and it is not doubted but it will put the King upon employing the Whiggs again'. Bonet had remarked a few weeks earlier that the constant theme of the Tory literature was depreciation of the King in the eyes of the people.

At the same time the efforts of the Whig secret committee began to appear. A very circumstantial Tory account alleged that the Kentish petition was read 'in *Vicar's* Coffee-house, adjoyning to the Court of *Requests*, two Days before the Petitioners came to London'. On 6 May the members of parliament from Chester and Warwickshire received petitions from their constituents begging them to put England in a posture to defend itself against France. On the same day five gentlemen from Kent appeared at the door of St. Stephen's Chapel to present their petition in person. They were prevented from doing so for two days, but finally, on 8 May, the petition was read. It appealed to 'the Experience of all Ages' in pleading the necessity for national unity; it begged the Parliament to create no misunderstandings or distrust of the King, 'whose great Actions for this Nation are writ in the Hearts of his Subjects, and can never, without the blackest Ingratitude, be forgot'. Finally, it prayed that 'this Honourable House will have regard to the *Voice of the People* . . . that Your *Loyal Addresses* may

[1] P.R.O. Transcripts 3 (France) 189, f. 34v; B.M. Add. MS. 30000E, ff. 323–4; [Daniel Defoe,] *A Reply to a Pamphlet Entituled, the L[or]d H[aversham]'s Vindication of his Speech*, 1706, pp. 8–9; *The History of the Kentish Petition Answer'd*, [September] 1701, p. 11.

[2] B.M. Add. MSS. 7078, f. 9v; 7074, f. 15; 30000E, f. 151v.

be turned into *Bills of Supply*; and that His Most *Sacred Majesty* may be Enabled Powerfully to Assist His Allies before it is too late'. 'That which gave offence', as Somers observed, 'was, calling their *Addresses Loyal*: If they were *Loyal*, it cou'd be no Reflection to call them so; if they were not, they had Reason I confess to think it a Jeer.' Defoe recalled many years later that he had 'had more than common reason to know' that the King was uneasy over Parliament's failure to provide supplies.[1]

Never before in the annals of English history, Bonet observed, had the people demanded to be taxed. Poussin added that it was easy to guess the source of such a demand: 'Les whiggs en sont les instrumens et le Roy d'Angleterre l'ouvrier.' The Commons responded by declaring the petition to be 'scandalous, insolent, and seditious', and ordering the petitioners to be taken into the custody of the Serjeant-at-arms and imprisoned in the Gate House.[2]

Despite this show of bravado, the effect of the Kentish petition on the House of Commons was remarkable. Poussin remarked that 'Un changement de scène si extraordinaire en moins de deux jours, seroit . . . tres surprenant en tout autre pays qu'en Angleterre', thus confirming Danby's observation that nobody can know one day what the House of Commons will do the next. Poussin could not understand why the House should be intimidated by a petition signed by only 150 Whigs in Kent, but he reported to Louis XIV that on 9 May it voted 'de donner au Roy d'Angleterre les moyens de soutenir ses alliés et de maintenir la liberté de l'Europe, d'envoyer incessament le secours promis aux hollandois, et de presenter a La Majesté Britannique une adresse pour la prier de mettre devant la chambre un état de la dépense pour ce secours'. He went on to say that 'L'étourdissement' was so great that John Howe even proposed

[1] *The History of the Kentish Petition, Answer'd*, [September] 1701, p. 16; B.M. Add. MS. 30000E, f. 173v; [John Somers,] *Jura Populi Anglicani: Or The Subject's Right of Petitioning Set Forth*, [August] 1701, p. 48.

[2] *C.J.* xiii. 518; B.M. Add. MS. 30000E, f. 346v; P.R.O. Transcripts 3 (France) 188, f. 54v.

to restore to the civil list the £100,000 which had been subtracted only a week before. L'Hermitage reported to Heinsius that several members of the House 'ne vont pas plus dans les maisons à cafe, pour éviter les criailleries et de peur d'estre insultés; car presentement on ne laisse pas de reprocher le tems perdu'.[1]

The heaviest blow in the Paper War, however, was yet to be struck. On Wednesday, 14 May, Harley read to the House a letter which had been handed to him that morning by a stranger at the door of St. Stephen's Chapel. The stranger was Daniel Defoe. The letter was written in a disguised 'hand that stood the wrong way'. There was no salutation, but there was a postscript. It claimed to come from 200,000 Englishmen and it was signed LEGION. It ended as follows:

> *Englishmen* are no more to be slaves to *Parliament* than to a King.
> Our Name is LEGION, and we are many.
>
> Postscript. If you require to have this Memorial signed with our Names, it shall be done on your first Order, and Personally Presented.

Not only was the *Memorial* handed to Harley, it was simultaneously printed in so many editions that it is now impossible to determine which was the first, and 'upwards of thirty thousand' copies were distributed throughout England. To save on mailing costs, members' signatures were forged to frank the envelopes. This, as may be imagined, was highly resented and became the subject of still another resolution in the House of Commons. L'Hermitage remarked drily: 'cette lettre fait icÿ beaucoup de bruit.'[2] Nor is it surprising that it did, for nothing

[1] P.R.O. Transcripts, 3 (France) 188, ff. 57v–59v; *C.J.* xiii. 523; B.M. Add. MS. 17677WW, f. 255v.

[2] Despite much evidence that the Legion *Memorial* was simply sent by penny-post (B.M. Add. MSS. 7078, f. 25v; 17677WW, f. 260; 30000E, f. 193; P.R.O. Transcripts, 3 (France) 188, f. 62v; Luttrell, v. 50), Defoe's account (*The History of the Kentish Petition*, [September] 1701, p. 14), which he challenged the world to confute in 'the most trifling Circumstance', was accepted by the author of *The History of the Kentish Petition, Answer'd Paragraph by Paragraph*, [September] 1701, p. 27: 'let who will deliver it to Mr. *Speaker*, they vastly mistook the proper

like this had been seen in England since a wooden shoe had been found in the Speaker's chair in October 1673. Nor was the *wording* of the *Memorial* any less compromising; it was an unequivocal assertion of the right to resist arbitrary power 'by Extra-judicial Methods'. The Speaker was 'commanded' to present the *Memorial* to the Commons. The *Memorial* itself, after specifying fifteen abuses of power, did 'Require and Demand' that the Kentish petitioners be admitted to bail and receive the thanks of the House of Commons, and that John Howe be ordered 'to ask His Majesty Pardon for his Vile Reflections, or be immediately Expell'd the House'. More importantly, it demanded immediate payment of all public debts and immediate granting of '*Suitable Supplies*' to the King. Finally, it demanded 'That the *French* King be obliged to quit Flanders, or that His Majesty be address'd to declare War against him'.

The Impeachment Charges Dismissed

After this, if we can believe Defoe, several members quietly removed themselves to the country and John Howe stood in fear of his life. But Harley retained 'his usual haughty tone' and there was no panic. On 5 May, three weeks after the impeachments had been voted, the Commons was reminded, by a message from the House of Lords, that no articles had been exhibited against the accused lords. This occasioned some mutterings about impeachments for treason, instead of simple misdemeanors, but the House replied merely that the articles were 'preparing' and would be exhibited in due time. Four days later the articles against Russell were sent up

Person, for they should have deliver'd it to the *Hangman*. . . . The Manner in which it was deliver'd, shews its intended Mischief; for Truth needs no Force to support it, nor the whole County of *Kent* at the Heels of a single Gentleman to make it good'; *The History of the Kentish Petition*, [September] 1701, sig. A2r, 14; J. R. Moore, *A Checklist of the Writings of Daniel Defoe*, 1960, p. 15; [Charles Davenant,] *Tom Double Return'd out of the Country*, [January ?] 1702, p. 12; B.M. Add. MS. 17677WW, f. 302v; *C.J.* xiii. 637.

to the Lords—along with an unprecedented demand 'that he should give sufficient security to abide the Judgment of the House of Lords'. On 13 May the Commons again addressed the King to remove the four accused lords from his presence and Council for ever. Two days later a second message from the Lords urged that articles be presented against the remaining three lords.[1]

On 19 May the House of Commons sent up the articles against Somers. Two days later another message from the Lords urged that a time be set for the trial of Russell and that articles be presented against the two remaining lords. This message was repeated on 30 May. The next day the Commons replied that it would be 'most proper' to begin with the trial of Somers, at a time of which they 'as Prosecutors [were] the proper Judges'. At the same time another message from the Lords appointed 9 June for the trial of Russell and urged haste in presenting articles against the two remaining lords. At this point Bonet explained the reason for the Commons' delay: 'La verité est qu'il n'y a aucune accusation importante à alleguer contre ces deux Lords, et que les Communes voudroient bien, si elles pouvoient, assoupir cette affaire.'[2]

On Sunday, 1 June, however, carpenters began to build 'the Scaffolds in Westminster Hall for Trying the Lords Impeached, and Work'd all night'. Three days later another message from the Lords agreed that the Commons might 'proceed to the Tryal of any of the impeached Lords, whom the Commons should be first ready to begin with', but asserted that 'the Right of limiting a convenient Time' for the trial is lodged in the Lords, 'in whom the Judicature does intirely reside', not in the Commons 'as Prosecutors'. In reply the Commons found it necessary

[1] *Legion's New Paper*, [November ? 1701, but dated] 1702, p. 4; B.M. Add. MS. 30000E, f. 173v; *C.J.* xiii. 513, 539, 543; H.M.C. Lords MSS. 4 (new series), 296–7.

[2] *C.J.* xiii. 559, 587–8; H.M.C. Lords MSS. 4 (new series), 297; B.M. Add. MS. 30000E, f. 233. Burnet was also of the opinion that 'The Impeachments . . . would have been let sleep, if the Lords concerned had not moved for a Trial' (ii. 272).

to assert its 'undoubted Right' to determine which accused should be tried first, a concession which the Lords had just granted, and to deny the Lords' 'Right of limiting a convenient Time' without some previous signification that the Commons was ready to proceed. The Commons refused, in short, to try Russell on 9 June. Newsletters the next day reported: "Tis generally beleiv'd none of the impeach't lords will be tried this sessions; and that the parliament will rise in 10 dayes at farthest.'[1]

On 6 June the Commons requested that a committee of both Houses be appointed to consider the most proper ways and methods of proceeding on impeachments. Since the most proper ways and methods had been worked out in countless proceedings on impeachments over the past 300 years, the Whigs were naturally somewhat suspicious of the motives of such a request: 'if the Usage had settled it before, what need of settling it again?' The Lords, moreover, looked upon this unprecedented demand as a 'direct Invading of their Judicature' and flatly refused it. But the purpose of demanding such a committee is well explained by L'Hermitage:

> Qu'oÿ que les communes se soient proposées d'eluder le jugement des 4 seigneurs accusés, elles n'auroient pas voulu qu'il eut paru aux yeux du public, que toutes les dificultés qu'elles font naistre, procedent de cette cause, c'est pourquoÿ vendredÿ elles envoyerent un message aux seigneurs, qui donne une toute autre idee, paroissant disposées aux procedures du jugement, et demandant pour cet effet aux seigneurs de vouloir nommer un comité de leurs corps, pour conferer avec un comité qu'elles nommeroient de leur part, afin de tacher de convenir de la methode qu'on doit suivre, selon les usages du parlement, au sujet du jugement des pairs accusez.[2]

1 *The Post Boy*, No. 943, 31 May–3 June 1701; *C.J.* xiii. 594–5; Luttrell, v. 57.

2 *C.J.* xiii. 600, 637; *A Letter from Some Electors to One of their Representatives in Parliament*, [September?] 1701, p. 17; B.M. Add. MS. 17677WW, f. 285. Poussin agreed with L'Hermitage that the Commons' insistence upon a joint committee was a pretext to avoid prosecution: 'Les communes qui ne cherchent qu'à éluder . . . le jugement, se prevalent du refus fait par les Seigneurs d'un Comitté des deux Chambres qu'elles demandoient pour régler les préliminaires' (P.R.O. Transcripts, 3 (France) 188, ff. 93–93v).

On 9 June, the day originally appointed for the trial of Russell, the Commons heard the articles of impeachment against Montagu and ordered them to be engrossed. When Sir William St. Quintin proclaimed that the articles would tend to Montagu's 'eternall honour', he only escaped being called to the bar after a long debate. Poussin observed more soberly that the charges against Montagu 'se réduisent à six articles assez faibles', and that 'le party des thoris n'a d'autre vûe que de détourner pour cette session le jugement des quatre Lords, afin de les laisser dans le même embaras ou le Duc le Leeds se trouve depuis quelques années'. On the same day another message from the Lords appointed 13 June for the trial of Somers.[1]

On 10 June a message from the Lords appointed 17 June for the trial of Russell and the Commons made the further unprecedented demands that the accused lords, at their trials, should sit outside the Bar of the House 'as Criminals', and should be disqualified from voting in each other's cases. The next day the Commons complained of 'so short a Day' being appointed for the trial of Somers and again demanded the appointment of a committee of both Houses. A message from the Lords the next day replied that 'no Lord of Parliament . . . shall, upon his Tryal, be without the Bar' and that 'no Lord of Parliament . . . can be precluded from voting on any Occasion, except in his own Tryal', but also granted a postponement of the trial of Somers to 17 June.[2]

On Friday, 13 June, at a free conference in the Painted Chamber the Commons again urged the necessity of a committee of both Houses. Simon Harcourt said he wished the Lords had sent their reasons for insisting that none of the accused lords should sit outside the Bar, like criminals. When Sir Bartholomew Shower claimed that any other arrangement would be 'Abhorrent to Justice', John

[1] B.M. Add. MS. 7074, f. 29v; *C.J.* xiii. 606; P.R.O. Transcripts, 3 (France) 188, ff. 90, 94.

[2] H.M.C. Lords MSS. 4 (new series), 298; *C.J.* xiii. 614, 623, 627.

Thompson, Baron Haversham, seems to have lost his patience. 'The Lords', he said, 'hope Justice shall never be made use of as a Mask for any Design', and then went on to explain what this 'Design' might be:

> that the Commons think these Lords Innocent... is undeniable: For there are several Lords in the same Crimes. In the same Facts, there is no Distinction; and the Commons leave some of these Men at the Head of Affairs, near the King's Person, to do any Mischief, if their Persons are inclined to it; and Impeach others, when they are both alike Guilty, and concerned in the same Facts: This is a thing I was in hopes I should never have heard asserted, when the Beginning of it was from the House of Commons.

It was indeed remarkable that Sir Joseph Williamson, who had signed the First Partition Treaty, had not been prosecuted. But Williamson was a Tory, and had retired in 1699. But the Earl of Jersey, who had signed the Second Partition Treaty, had not retired. As Lord Chamberlain he was indeed near to the King's person. But it was Jersey, as stated before, who suggested that the Tories should examine the letters of 1698 between Portland and Vernon which provided grounds for impeaching Somers, Montagu, and Russell. And so he had not been prosecuted either. But as Burnet remarked: 'The House of Commons had now got a pretence to justify their not going further in these Trials; and they resolved to insist upon it.' The managers for the Commons promptly withdrew from the conference and reported Haversham's 'most scandalous Reproaches' to an indignant House. Harley, 'rusé & habille', must have been delighted. Now it was possible to accuse the Lords of 'delaying the Proceedings in the Impeachments' and to demand such punishment of Haversham 'as so high an Offense against the House of Commons does deserve'.[1]

On the following day the House refused to continue the free conference until they had received 'Reparation'

[1] *C.J.* xiii. 629–30; *A True Account of the Proceedings, Relating to the Charge of the House of Commons against John Lord Haversham*, [July?] 1701, pp. 1–3; Burnet, ii. 279.

for the indignity which they had suffered, and ordered the articles against Montagu to be sent up to the Lords. On Monday, 16 June, a message from the Lords described the ways and methods of proceeding to be followed in the trial of Somers. The Commons responded by ordering the committee on impeachments to consider reasons why they should not proceed to the trial. The next morning the Commons ordered that 'no Member of this House do presume to appear at the Place erected for the pretended Tryal of the Impeachment of the Lord Sommers, under the penalty of incurring the utmost Displeasure of this House', and then settled down to hear the reasons why they could not proceed to the trial. In spite of protests that they had acted 'with all imaginable Zeal' to expedite the trials, their reasons for refusing to proceed proved to be the old issues of a joint committee and whether the impeached lords were to sit as judges in each other's trials, together with their failure to receive satisfaction for the great indignity offered by Haversham.[1]

When this message was received in the Jerusalem Chamber on 17 June, the Lords voted 57–36 to try Somers 'upon the Scaffold in Westminster-Hall'. Accordingly, at 3.30 p.m., after Montagu and Russell had been granted permission to withdraw, the Lords proceeded 'in Form' to Westminster Hall, 'being all in their robes (except the Lord Sommers)', who 'sat in a chair within the Bar, uncovered'. A clerk read the articles of impeachment, Somers's answer to them (in which he pleaded not guilty), and the House of Commons' replication. Then the Lord Keeper, the Earl of Tankerville, declared that the Court would proceed to hear the evidence and desired the Lords to give their attention. He then turned to the empty benches reserved for the 513 members of the Lower House and instructed the Commons that they might now proceed with their evidence. Whereupon all this august company, which included the Earl of Carlisle, the Marshal of England, with the Earl of Lindsey, the Great Chamber-

[1] *C.J.* xiii. 631, 634, 636; *L.J.* xvi. 753–4.

lain of England, at his right, and the Earl of Jersey, the Great Chamberlain of the Court, on his left, all the peers of England, and the entire *corps diplomatique*, burst out laughing. After waiting 'un demy quart d'heure' Rochester arose and moved that the Lords adjourn to their House. At 8 o'clock the Lords filed back into Westminster Hall. When proclamation had been made for silence, the Lord Keeper put the question: 'That John Lord Sommers be acquitted of the Articles of Impeachment, against him exhibited by the House of Commons, and all Things therein contained: And that the said Impeachment be dismissed.' Then the Lord Keeper polled every lord whether Content or Not Content. When the tellers had counted the votes, the Lord Keeper declared that the majority was for acquitting. A great huzzah was made and the more than 600 ladies who were present 'rompirent leurs eventails'. When order was restored, the Lords again adjourned to the Jerusalem Chamber, where they ordered 'That the Proceedings in this House upon the Impeachments, be printed', thus confirming Bonet's observation that the Lords had been emboldened to this action because 'etant apuyés du Peuple . . . ils ne devoient pas user de lacheté'. The people responded satisfactorily by building 'Several bonefires'.[1]

Next morning the Lords appointed 23 June for the trial of Russell, but the Commons adjourned, to avoid receiving the message. On 20 June, when the Commons resumed its sessions, it complained bitterly that by 'the pretended Tryal' of Somers the House of Lords had invaded the liberties of the subject and overturned 'the Right of Impeachments, lodged in the House of Commons by the ancient Constitution of this Kingdom'. The Commons also reverted to its ancient demand for a committee of both Houses. The Lords replied that they could only infer from the Commons' persisting in this demand that 'they never designed to bring any of their Impeachments to a Trial'.[2]

[1] Luttrell, v. 62; B.M. Add. MSS. 30000E, ff. 278v–9; 7074, f. 33v.
[2] *C.J.* xiii. 639; *L.J.* xvi. 763.

'How this will end God onely knows', Evelyn wrote in his Diary, and Vernon foresaw that it might have no end: 'we are torn to pieces by parties and animosities; for my part, I see no end of them.' But if 'parties and animosities' could not be ended, they could at least be interrupted, and this the King did on 24 June when he intervened 'To interrupt these fatal Disputes between the two houses'. On the day before, the whole elaborate ceremonial which had been gone through on the occasion of Somers's trial, was punctiliously repeated with exactly the same result. The House of Lords voted unanimously to acquit Russell, and 'put another slur upon the Commons', as Vernon said, when they struck Sir Bartholomew Shower and Dr. Charles Davenant from the Commons' list of the commissioners to take the public accounts, 'one for being a lawyer and having other business to do, and the other for abusing the church in his last book'. The next day it dismissed the impeachment proceedings against Montagu and Portland, the charges against Haversham, and, with a fine flourish, the impeachment charges against Danby, which the Commons had failed to prosecute for more than six years. Then 'the King came to the House of Peers, between 3 and 4 a clock'. After being kept waiting for nearly two hours, he finally 'almost forced his way in'. 'Being seated on the Throne in his Royal Robes, according to the usual Solemnity', William gave the royal assent to four money bills, and made 'a most Gracious Speech'. He thanked the 'Gentlemen of the House of Commons, in particular, both for your dispatch of those necessary Supplies, which you have granted for the public occasions, and for the encouragements you have given me to enter into Alliances for the preservation of the Liberty of Europe'. Then he prorogued his 5th Parliament.[1]

The Whigs said that the King made his 'Gracious

[1] John Evelyn, *Diary*, ed. E. S. de Beer, 6 vols., 1955; v. 466; Vernon, iii. 148–50; *Parl. Hist.* v. 1321; A. S. Turberville, *The House of Lords in the Reign of William III* (Oxford Historical and Literary Studies, Volume 3), Oxford, 1913, p. 221; *The Post Boy*, No. 953, 24–26 June 1701; H.M.C. Cowper MSS. ii. 430.

II. The Five Kentish Petitioners

Speech' to enable the Tories to get home without being stoned, but Bonet observed that His Majesty 'a voulu adoucir par ce Discours les Mecontens et les autres esprits difficiles, lever cette malheureuse méfiance que plusieurs ont prise de S. M., et les amener aux justes fins qu'Elle se propose'. William had finally won his game of engaging 'these people' imperceptibly, and after allowing the four Lords Partitioners to kiss his hand, he sailed off to Holland to concert with his allies for the safety of Europe.[1]

With the rising of Parliament the Kentish petitioners were automatically freed. The people regarded them as martyrs, and even while in prison they had sat for their portraits by Robert White. These were now combined into a fine engraving (Fig. II), with a motto, *Non Auro Patriam*, reflecting on the recipients of French gold. While their pictures were hawked about the streets, the gentlemen themselves were splendidly entertained. The Fishmongers' Company treated them to a dinner at Fishmonger Hall and made them free of their Company. Then, on 1 July, they were 'nobly Treated' at the Mercers Chapel in Cheapside. 'The Entertainment was very splendid; there being present his Grace the Duke of Bolton, the Marquis of Hartington, and some other Noblemen' and members of parliament, and more than 200 persons of quality and citizens. On this occasion Daniel Defoe was seated next the guests of honour, or, as the Tory pamphleteer described it, 'Next the Worthies was placed their Secretary of State, the Author of the *Legion Letter*'.[2]

In all these celebrations the health of the four Lords Partitioners and the five Kentish Petitioners was drunk simultaneously in the favourite toast of the hour: 'To the health of the four five.' At the same time it was said that the favourite toast at Versailles and St. Germain was 'A la santé Monsieur Jaccou [Jack Howe]'. Defoe also

[1] B.M. Add. MS. 30000E, f. 297; P.R.O. Transcripts, 3 (France) 189, f. 13.

[2] B.M. Add. MS. 30000E, f. 195; Luttrell, v. 66–68; *The Post Boy*, No. 956, 1–3 July 1701; *The Legionites Plot*, 1702, p. 18.

accompanied the Kentish gentlemen on their triumphal homecoming: at Blackheath their coaches were met with 'Shouts and Joy' by 500 gentlemen on horseback; two miles from Maidstone they were met by the local gentry in their coaches, 'the Poor strowing the Ways with Greens and Flowers'.

John Howe, Knight of the Shire for Gloucester, was received in quite a different fashion. He was entertained at a local inn by four or five gentlemen. During dinner, as his hosts drew him out, he expanded on his accomplishments during the last session of Parliament. Perhaps he even boasted that he had called the Partition Treaty 'a felonious treaty of three thieves'. After dinner, when he offered to pay his share, the others protested, explaining that they had been ordered by the electors to entertain him, to thank him for his past services, and to say that they would no longer be needed in the future. At the next election, in December 1701, Howe's name stood at the bottom of the poll.[1]

Intensification of the Paper War

With the prorogation of Parliament and the King's departure for Holland, the tempo of the Paper War was greatly accelerated.

> The whole Kingdom [Ralph said] serv'd through the whole Summer, as a Stage for the two rival Factions to play the same detestable Parts, tho' under different Disguises. The two Houses had made their Appeal to the People, by a Publication of their respective Proceedings: These Appeals had been taken at the Rebound, by the Advocates Venal and Volunteer, conceal'd and avow'd, which had enroll'd themselves on both Sides. . . . Besides which, the Press produc'd several other general Accounts and Justifications, Apologies and Invectives; all equally enflam'd with the Violence of the Times, and visibly calculated to encrease it.

[1] B.M. Add. MS. 30000E, ff. 195, 302–3; [Daniel Defoe,] *The History of the Kentish Petition*, [September] 1701, pp. A3r, 15–16; B.M. Add. MS. 17677WW, ff. 322v–3.

Burnet confirms this:

> During the King's absence, the Nation was in a great ferment, which was increased by the many Books that were wrote, to expose the late Management in the House of Commons and the new Ministry, the Earl of *Rochester* in particular, [and then adds a curious comment:] The few Books that were published, on the other side, were so poorly writ, that it tempted one to think, they were writ by men who personated the being on their side, on design to expose them.

There were, in fact, several works written by Whigs 'personating' Tories. The first of these, published late in August, was a folio half-sheet entitled *The True Patriot Vindicated; or a Justification of his Excellency the Earl of Rochester, Lord Lieutenant of Ireland, from Several False and Scandalous Reports*. The 'vindication', of course, was undertaken 'only to rub up the memory' of Rochester's having served on the Court of Ecclesiastical Commission under James II, of his speech to the King of Poland in 1677, of the leaves he tore out of the treasury book to cover up his embezzlement of £8,000, and other old scandals. The irony, as Vernon observed, is 'carried on with a great deal of smartness', and the Tories' attribution of the work to Montagu may very well be correct.[1]

The mock-vindication of Rochester was immediately followed up by a mock-inscription: *An Inscription Intended to be set up for the E[ar]l of R[ocheste]r, When by the Happy Effects of his Ministry, the Chappel of St. Stephen's is become a Chappel of the Jesuites*. Poussin reported that this work was widely attributed to Somers. Rochester, who had finally taken up his post as Lord Lieutenant of Ireland, responded by ordering both works to be burnt by the common hangman in Dublin.[2]

Both the *Vindication* and the *Inscription* were 'industriously dispersed all over *England*, especially about the Country, where [they were] distributed *gratis* in great

[1] Ralph, ii. 997–8; Burnet, ii. 290; Vernon, iii. 156–7; [Charles Davenant ?] *The Old and Modern Whig Truly Represented*, [December] 1701, pp. 3, 21–22.

[2] P.R.O. Transcripts, 3 (France) 189, f. 59; B.M. Add. MS. 30000E, f. 370.

Numbers'. The Tories observed, somewhat ruefully, that the Whigs' 'Trade in scurrilous Lampoons, impudent Libels, scandalous Pamphlets, forg'd Accusations, and groundless Calumnies, has wonderfully improv'd since some of our late Ministry put themselves openly at the Head of 'em'. And although Vernon agrees that 'the chiefs seem to have a hand in it', Somers's role in the Paper War is even more difficult to document than Harley's.[1]

The only direct evidence that Somers was responsible for the Whig propaganda effort occurs in an exchange of letters with Sunderland in September–October 1701. Sunderland wrote on 15 September sketching the outline for a pamphlet:

> Among all the pamphlets which are come out, there ought to have been one, to have particularly explained the proceedings of the present ministry . . . the care which was taken by them and their friends upon the death of the King of Spain to persuade the world that all was well, and that a war would undo us; how, by this management, the French possessed themselves of Flanders, before the meeting of the Parliament; which was thought of so little importance to England, as not to be worth mentioning in the King's speech; all which disheartened so much our allies abroad, that the King of Portugal, despairing, made a treaty with France; &c., &c.

Somers agreed that such a pamphlet was 'wanting', but added that 'A thing of that nature has been promised'. Sunderland wrote back on 1 October insisting that 'nothing will be well done without such a paper as has been before wished for'. Somers again replied that the pamphlet 'was promised, and is believed to be ready printed. But for some reasons which the writer conceals, it has not yet appeared; and there is a doubt when it will.'[2]

The promised pamphlet, which was finally published in November 1701, was *Anguis in Herba; or the Fatal Consequences of a Treaty with France*. It was attributed to

[1] *The Source of our Present Fears Discover'd*, 1703, pp. 26–27; Vernon, iii. 155. Sixty quarto volumes of Somers's private papers were destroyed in a fire at Lincoln's Inn in 1752.

[2] *Miscellaneous State Papers*, [ed. Philip Yorke Hardwicke,] 2 vols., 1778, ii. 447, 450–2.

Somers himself but seems actually to have been written by Henry Maxwell. Since the pamphlet includes, besides the points suggested by Sunderland, an important statement of Whig war aims, the conclusion that it was written to Somers's specification seems inescapable.[1] In any case, it is clear that Sunderland addressed himself to Somers as the manager of Whig propaganda.

How long Somers had served in this capacity is difficult to determine. But during the controversy over the standing army in 1697–8 he was alleged to have written the most effective defence of William's position in *A Letter Ballancing the Necessity of Keeping a Land Force in Time of Peace, with the Dangers that may follow it.* The Tories, however, insisted that the balancing letter, as it was called, had been written by Bishop Burnet.[2] This episode anticipates by four years the pattern of Somers's involvement in *Anguis in Herba* and may supply a *terminus a quo* for his assumption of responsibility for Whig propaganda.

A similar pattern may be observed in the Whig reply to the *Discourse upon Grants and Resumptions*. There were, as a matter of fact, several immediate replies to Davenant's work, one of which, *The Case of the Forfeitures in Ireland fairly Stated*, was published early in 1700. But a full-scale refutation was delayed until April 1701, when its publication was timed to anticipate an appearance of three trustees of the forfeited estates before the House of Lords.[3] The

[1] New York Public Library MS. Hardwicke 33, p. 10: 'v. pamphlet entitled *Fatal consequences of a Treaty with France &c.* 1701. reprinted in 1711. 8°.—written by Ld. Somers.' Cf. Henry Maxwell, *Proposals To Render the Possession of Minorca, and Gibralter, More useful to the Commerce of Britain*, 1723, p. 3: 'Having written two former Discourses, (Tho' both without Name) one intituled *Anguis in Herba* or the fatal Consequences of a Treatie with *France*. . . .'

[2] 'Supposed to have been written by Bishop Burnet. Also attributed to Lord Somers' (*An Alphabetical Catalogue of an Extensive Collection of the Writings of Daniel Defoe*, 1830, p. 41). Cf. Tindal, iii. 396 n.: 'This piece has been generally ascribed to the Lord *Sommers*, but it is doubtful whether upon sufficient grounds.'

[3] Luttrell, v. 28. *The Post Boy* of 1–3 Apr. 1701 reported that 'Sir Henry Sheeres, Mr. Annesley, and Mr. Trenchard, three of the Trustees for the Forfeited Estates in Ireland', had reached Chester *en route* to London for the hearings. The next number of *The Post Boy* (No. 917, 3–5 Apr. 1701) announced publication of *Jus Regium.*

tenor of this work is evident from its title, *Jus Regium: Or, The King's Right to grant Forfeitures, and other Revenues of the Crown, fully set forth and trac'd from the beginning. His Majesty vindicated as to his Promise concerning his disposal of the Forfeited Estates. The Manifold Hardships of the Resumption, and the little Advantages we shall reap by it, Plainly demonstrated.* Some of the most effective passages in the work are those in which Davenant's own words are turned against him, a device which Swift was to use in the *Discourse.* But *Jus Regium* is only incidentally an attack on Davenant. It is essentially a defence of the King's foreign policy and a statement of the Whig position on the major issues of the day. As such, it was easily attributable to Somers, and this attribution has been widely accepted. A much more likely attribution, however, is one made on the title-page of the copy in the National Library at Dublin.

This manuscript note, in an old hand, ascribes the work to 'Dr. Ezechiel Burrige'. Burridge was a clergyman of the Church of Ireland who had already written several books on Ireland. The best guess, therefore, is that *Jus Regium* was written by Ezekiel Burridge, out of his own first-hand knowledge of the disruptive effects of the Act of Resumption on Irish land tenure, together with legal precedents, policy statements, and other information supplied by Somers. For it is quite unlikely that a clergyman would have access to the kind of secret intelligence implied by a quotation on page 15 of the work. Here it is stated that Davenant's 'Letter writ unto *Ireland* to one of our Commissioners for enquiring into Forfeitures . . . assures that Commissioner, that this Author's [i.e. Davenant's] Book should meet them here in the Winter'. Davenant apparently had written to one of the Tory Commissioners, exactly as he had done to Thomas Coke in July 1699, promising that he would 'prepare the town to give the report of our Irish Commissioners a kind reception'. This kind of information could only come to Somers from James Vernon, whose office controlled secret intelligence and regularly opened letters to Ireland.

The remaining evidence for Somers's intervention in the Paper War can be summarized very briefly. He is undoubtedly the 'great Man fallen from a greater Post in the Ministry' to whom *The Kentish Letter, for the Right Honourable the Lord Mayor, Aldermen, and Common Council of the City of London* was attributed. This work, published in May 1701, was a plea to the City government to petition the House of Commons in the same terms as did the Kentish petition.

The Tories also blamed Somers for 'a most elaborately dull Poem' celebrating the Kentish petitioners. This was *The Kentish Worthies*, which the poet laureate, Nahum Tate, published in August 1701. In the same month 'out came two Appeals to the People, one Intituled, the *History of the* Kentish *Petition*, and the other, *Jura Populi Anglicani*, or the *Subject's Right of Petitioning set forth*, &c. In these', the Tory critic continues, 'the very essence and being of a *House of Commons* was assaulted.' The latter work, which Keith Feiling has called 'The fiercest of all Whig pamphlets in this generation', was Somers's attack, not, of course, on the 'essence and being of a *House of Commons*', but on 'Ro—rt Har—y' and the 'very fatal consequence in breaking the Ballance of Civil Power, and shewing the Grand Enemy where he is to make his Attack to subdue a People whom his Arms cannot hurt'. Warrants were immediately issued for the arrest of the author and printer, but not even after a 'great search' was the well-known author of this 'seditious libell' discovered.[1]

Among the books published on the Tory side during the summer of 1701 were two, *not* so poorly written that Burnet could suspect them to be the work of Whigs, which Swift notices in the *Discourse*. The first of these, *The Claims of the People of England, Essayed. In a Letter from the Country*, appeared in July. The third edition of

[1] *The History of the Kentish Petition, Answered*, [September] 1701, p. 12; *A Letter to a Modern Dissenting Whig*, [September] 1701, p. 21; *Jura Populi Anglicani: . . . Answer'd*, [September] 1701, p. iii; *The Source of Our Present Fears Discover'd*, 1703, p. 33; Keith Feiling, *A History of the Tory Party 1640–1714*, Oxford, 1924, p. 311; Luttrell, v. 86.

1782 states the author to be G. Sharp, about whom, however, nothing else is known. This work, like the *Discourse*, undertakes to discover the 'Causes of popular Tumults'. It finds them, of course, 'in Oppression and Male-Administration', Tory cant phrases for the government of the Whig junto. Individual members of the junto are attacked in the persons of Piers Gaveston and Michael de la Pole, just as Davenant had done in his *Discourse upon Grants and Resumptions*.

The second of these books, *A Vindication of the Rights of the Commons of England*, was published on 22 August. No name appears on the title-page, but the dedicatory epistles are signed by Sir Humphrey Mackworth and the work was advertised as his in *The Post Boy*. It was almost certainly concerted with Harley, however, for Henry St. John recalled that his 'political bantering friend . . . had a paper ready for the press, and I suppose it is that which I find in the newspapers styled a *Vindication of the Rights of the Commons of England*'. The style of the work, as St. John observed, is 'barren and dry', deliberately adapted 'to the meanest Capacity'. But its tone and content are highly sophistical.[1]

Mackworth explicitly adopts an equable, almost deferential tone: 'The Writer . . . doth not pretend *to Assert*, *but Argue*; *not to Determine*, *but to Submit to better Judgment*.' Actually, however, what he asserts is the infallibility of the House of Commons, and he determines every point at issue between the two Houses in favour of the Commons. He pretends to deplore those late 'Unhappy Divisions' and to be seeking 'to reconcile the Difference'. Actually, however, the book is a point-by-point vindication of the Tory committee on impeachments by a writer

[1] H.M.C. Downshire MSS. I. ii. 806. Vernon wrote to the King on 22 Aug.: 'Sir Humphry Mackworth has publisht a book Entitled a Vindication of the rights of the Commons. . . . I thought by his preface recommending Union, that hee would have proposed some methods for accommodation but I find his Drift is to condemn the Lords proceedings in the late Impeachments and in the Conclusion hee finds fault with petitions and addresses for medling in matters they have nothing to do with' (B.M. Add. MS. 40775, vol. v, f. 85v).

who was a member of that committee. And although Mackworth, who was a lawyer, insists that 'we must not argue like *Lawyers* in *Westminster-Hall*, from the *Narrow Foundation* of Private Causes of *meum* and *tuum*', he does exactly this when he argues, for example, that the Lords could not be entrusted with the right to set the time and place for trials of impeachment because they might 'appoint the following day for the Tryal to be had at *Truro* in *Cornwall*'.[1]

Mackworth similarly acknowledges that a private suit in law may be brought 'out of Malice and private Revenge', but denies that a public assembly is subject to the same motives: 'it is not to be imagin'd', he wrote, 'that a Majority of so numerous a Body of Gentlemen, can be Influenc'd against Reason and Justice.' But this is precisely the 'Supposition' on which Swift bases his *Discourse* and which evokes some of his most eloquent rhetoric. Mackworth also has a great deal to say about 'reserving a just Ballance of Power' between King, Lords, and Commons, but he gives himself away when he remarks that 'Power in this Government is chiefly Lodged in the Commons'. Swift saw in this imbalance of power 'an Appearance of Fatality' which could lead only to 'a *Dominatio Plebis*, or *Tyranny of the Commons*'.[2]

Charles Davenant brought to 'Philippize'

In all this ferment of writing Davenant's pen was curiously quiet. Since November 1700, when he finished his *Essays*, Davenant apparently had written only 'a remarkable Half-sheet in Folio' called *Parliamentary Authorities, Justifying the Proceedings of the Commons against the Four Impeached Lords*, which he published on 1 May 1701. There were, however, reasons for his silence.[3]

His *Discourse upon Grants and Resumptions* was acknowledged even by the Whigs to have had 'a very publick

[1] *A Vindication of the Rights of the Commons of England*, [August] 1701, pp. 40, 4, 20. [2] Ibid., pp. 23–24, 30. [3] Ralph, ii. 997.

influence'. 'Glorieux de succés qu'eut son Livre', he can easily be imagined to have resented the efforts, made late in 1700, to delay publication of, or even to suppress, his *Essays*. If he did, he must also have been aware that Harley was by no means the only source of patronage.[1]

In any case on 23 December 1700, with a copy of *A Discourse upon Grants and Resumptions* in hand, 'the adroit Dr. *Davenant*' paid a private visit to the house of the French ambassador. Tallard reported this visit immediately, and in cipher, to Torcy at Versailles: 'Le plus célèbre député de la chambre basse du party opposé a la cour, m'est venu me voir ce matin et m'a aporté un livre qu'il a presenté au Parlement sur les affaires d'Irlande.' Thereafter, 'a great *foreign Minister*'s Coach' at Davenant's door and other marks of Tallard's 'bienveillance' were repeatedly noted.[2]

Unfortunately Davenant had little time to exploit this promising new connexion, for Tallard was unexpectedly recalled early in April 1701. Tallard left England in such a hurry that he was unable to introduce Davenant to Jean Baptiste Poussin, 'une espece de Secretaire' who succeeded him but who never was formally accredited as *chargé d'affaires*. Poussin complained to Torcy 'que dans le tems que je vins icy et qu'il [Tallard] partit, ses amis étoient si réservés alors qu'il ne put m'en laisser aucun'. So Poussin had to set to work to build up a new *réseau* from scratch. Thus it was not until 30 July, when he spent the whole day with Poussin in the house of a common friend, that Davenant was able to re-establish contact with the French. On this occasion Davenant described the entire contents of his new book, *The True Picture of a Modern Whig*, which was ready for publication. When Poussin observed that several passages were not in the interest of France, Davenant readily agreed to cut them out.[3]

[1] *Jus Regium: Or, The King's Right to grant Forfeitures*, [April] 1701, p. 21; B.M. Add. MS. 30000D, f. 272^{v}.

[2] P.R.O. Transcripts 3 (France) 185, f. 3; *Jus Regium: Or, The King's Right to grant Forfeitures*, [April] 1701, p. 18; B.M. Add. MS. 17677WW, f. 271^{v}.

[3] Luttrell, v. 35; B.M. Add. MS. 30000E, ff. 133, 162^{v}; P.R.O. Transcripts 3

Two weeks later Poussin received permission to continue his cultivation of Davenant. The difficulty, as Poussin explained to Torcy, was that Davenant was already so compromised that it was impossible to meet him frequently: 'apres tout ce que ses ennemis ont publié de ses prétendus engagemens avec la France, et dans une conjuncture aussy délicate que celle-cy, je ne pourrais pas le voir souvent sans le compromettre. Mais il n'y a gueres de jour que je n'aye de ses nouvelles par un de nos amis communs.' At another meeting in a private house, near the end of August, Poussin concluded that Davenant was ready for recruitment into the French service. During this conversation, Davenant repeatedly expressed regret that his advances to Tallard had met with so little success. Poussin pretended not to understand this, but in fact he understood very well: what Davenant regretted was that he had put too high a price on his services and was now ready to be more reasonable. Poussin's report of this meeting concludes with a cold-blooded assessment of Davenant's motives, resources, and price. And because it affords such a surprising example of how '*the most Christian King . . . dealing large Money among some popular Orators . . .* brought many of them . . . to *Philippize*', it is worth quoting at length:

Le Sr. Davenant est plus lié que jamais aux chefs des thoris. Les Lords Rochester, Godolphin et Normanby prennent en luy une entiére confiance, et ont une grande déference pour ses sentimens.

(France) 189, ff. 28v, 45–45v. Davenant's *The True Picture of a Modern Whig, Set Forth in a Dialogue between Mr. Whiglove & Mr. Double, Two Under-Spur-Leathers to the late Ministry* was published in 29 August 1701 (P.R.O. Transcripts 3 (France) 189, f. 47v). It is a very different kind of work from Davenant's earlier compilations of precedents and statistics. What it possesses of wit and humour may derive from Charles Mordaunt, 3rd Earl of Peterborough, who was later to become Swift's great friend. The pamphlet was immediately assumed to be his (*Remarks By Way of Answer, Paragraph by Paragraph, to The Character of a Modern Whig*, 1701, p. 1). Peterborough and Davenant are also alleged to have collaborated in *Memoirs of Secret Service*, 1699, which appeared under the name of Matthew Smith, a notorious intelligence 'Novelist' (J. R. Moore, *A Checklist of the Writings of Daniel Defoe*, Bloomington, 1960, p. 158; Ralph, ii. 828). A copy of *The True Picture of a Modern Whig* was in Swift's library at his death.

Le Sr. Musgrave et le Sr. How sont ses plus intimes amis. D'ailleurs non seulement par luy, mais par plusieurs autres personnes, je scay les bonnes intentions qu'il a pour le Prince de Galles.

Toutes ces considerations, Monseigneur, me persuadent qu'il seroit tres avantageux pour le présent et l'avenir de pouvoir compter sur luy, pouvant par ses ecrits et par ses amis faire autant de bien que de mal. Il a une grosse famille avec peu de bien; d'une autre cote on peut luy faire envisager une grande fortune par l'establissement du Prince de Galles en Angleterre; et aujourd'huy, Monseigneur, a la veille des nouvelles seances [parliament had been prorogued to 18 September], je croirois qu'on pourroit commencer a l'engager par un diament de trois ou quatre cens pistolles.

Si c'etoit l'intention de Sa Majeste, il seroit tres utile de luy faire recevoir le plutot qu'il seroit possible. Par luy on seroit bien informé de toutes les affaires et des intrigues secrets du Parlement, et par luy on pourroit insinuer tout ce qu'on jugeroit convenir aux interets de Sa Majeste.

The intentions of Louis XIV in this matter were made evident on 11 September when Poussin received a diamond, together with authorization to bestow upon Davenant this mark of His Most Christian Majesty's esteem. A week later Davenant seems finally to have settled down to work under French patronage, and Poussin could report satisfactory progress: 'Le docteur Davenant travaille à donner au public un nouvel ouvrage sur les affaires presentes de l'Europe, et la necessité de la guerre si la France et l'Espagne ne veuillent pas concourir aux moyens qui peuvent assurer la paix. Je tacheray qu'il n'oublie pas les inconveniens qu'il y auroit a craindre pour la nation anglaise dans le renouvellement d'une guerre.' But again, Davenant had little time to exploit this promising new connexion.[1]

[1] P.R.O. Transcripts 3 (France) 189, ff. 36, 47–47^{v}, 57, 62. The 'nouvel ouvrage' in the last reference is probably *Tempus Adest: Or, A War Inevitable*, published in November 1701 (*The History of the Works of the Learned*, iii.704), as a reply to Defoe's ironic *Reasons against a War with France*. Henry St. John describes this book on 30 Sept.: 'Dr. D——t is writing a book . . . to shew the justice that lies on the side of the H. of Austria in this quarrel, and the game England ought to play, with respect to it' (H.M.C. Downshire MSS. 1. ii. 808).

This time, ironically, it was the death of James II that broke off Davenant's treasonable conversations. James died on 5 September at St. Germain. Louis had promised the dying King to recognize his 13-year-old son as King of England, but he had also undertaken in the fourth article of the Treaty of Ryswick not to disturb William III 'en quelque Facon que ce soit' in the possession of the throne of England. As Louis pondered this dilemma, he discovered that his honour was more deeply involved in his 'parole' to a dead king than in a published treaty with a living usurper. So he allowed James Francis Edward, Prince of Wales, to be proclaimed James III, King of England, Scotland, and Ireland.[1]

On 7 September Torcy ordered Poussin to explain to the lords justices, who were governing England in William's absence, that Louis fully intended to honour the Treaty of Ryswick and that his recognition of James III was 'juste, digne de générosité, conforme aux Traictez et a ce qu'il a faict pour le feu Roy d'Angleterre depuis qu'il a cherché son asile en France'. William responded to this nonsense by ordering his ambassador to quit Versailles without even a final audience with Louis. On 20 September the lords justices received William's order to declare Poussin *persona non grata*.[2]

Poussin was prevented from presenting Louis's memorandum to the lords justices on the grounds that he was not properly accredited. Accordingly, he caused it to be translated and published, also on 20 September, as *The French King's Reasons for Owning the Pretended Prince of Wales*. This pamphlet achieved such wide distribution that the Government issued warrants for the arrest of both translator and printer on suspicion of treason. Still unaware of William's order, but strongly convinced that diplomatic relations between France and England would

[1] *An Exact Account of the Sickness and Death of the Late King James II. As Also Of the Proceedings at St. Germains thereupon*, [September] 1701, p. 3; M. A. Thomson, 'Louis XIV and the origins of the War of the Spanish Succession', *Transactions of the Royal Historical Society*, 5th Series, iv (1954), 125–30.

[2] P.R.O., Transcripts 3 (France) 189, ff. 52–53^{v}; Burnet, ii. 294.

soon be broken, Poussin arranged a private dinner for his most valuable informants at the Blue Posts in the Haymarket on 23 September. The choice of the Blue Posts was unfortunate, for it had long been known to the Government as a Jacobite centre.

On the same day, 23 September, the lords justices issued the order for Poussin's expulsion. When the master of ceremonies, who was serving the order, finally caught up with Poussin at nine o'clock that night, he found him in a very distinguished company. It included John Sheffield, the Marquis of Normanby, Don Francisco Antonio de Navarro, the Spanish *chargé d'affaires*, and three of the leading Tory publicists, all members of parliament: John Tredenham, Anthony Hammond, and Charles Davenant. When the party was interrupted, Poussin hastily withdrew to the hall, where he was served with an order to depart the kingdom within eight days. When he returned to the party and disclosed what had happened, his guests, as he reported somewhat ruefully to Torcy, 'me parurent fort touchés de cette nouvelle, moins par amitie pour moy que par raport aux suites qu'ils voyent bien ne pouvoir être que tristes pour eux. Ils sont plus persuadés que jamais qu'un succes en Italie n'embarasseroit pas peu le Roy de la Grand Bretagne.'[1]

The consequences were indeed remarkable. All 'the Triobolary Writers of Pye-Corner and White-Fryers' joined in the hue and cry after the Poussineers, as Tredenham, Hammond, and Davenant soon came to be called. The 'Secret Committee' for Whig propaganda gleefully turned out another round of mock-vindications. The first of these, written in the person of a simple-minded Jacobite, was a folio half-sheet entitled *A full and true Relation of a horrid and detestable Conspiracy against the Lives, Estates and Reputations of Three Worthy Members of this Present Parliament, which God long preserve*. This was fol-

[1] Luttrell, v. 91, 95; P.R.O. Transcripts 3 (France) 189, ff. 65, 68; B.M. Add. MS. 40775, vol. v. f. 109; *Calendar of State Papers Domestic . . . 1700–1702*, ed. Edward Bateson, 1937, pp. 424–7.

lowed by *A Vindication of Dr. Charles Davenant, Anthony Hammond, Esq., and John Tredenham, Esq., From The Scurrilous Reflections Cast upon them in a Late Paper, called A Full and True Relation of a Horrid and Detestable Conspiracy against the Lives, Estates, and Reputations of Three Worthy Members of this present Parliament.* This more sophisticated product of the Kit-Cat Club introduces, with almost uncanny accuracy, Poussin telling Davenant what to write, inducing him to delete passages 'likely to prove so fatal to France', and urging him to append a 'Qualifying Postscript' in favour of Louis XIV. But while all this merriment was taking place in London, Swift was back in Ireland, waiting, anxiously it may be supposed, for the publication of his first book.

2. TEXT AND NOTES

A DISCOURSE

OF THE

Contests and *Dissensions*

BETWEEN THE

NOBLES and the COMMONS

IN

ATHENS and *ROME*,[1]

WITH THE

Consequences they had upon both those

STATES.

——*Si tibi vera videtur*
Dede manus; *& si falsa est accingere contra.* Lucret.[2]

LONDON:

Printed for *John Nutt* near *Stationers-Hall*. 1701.

CHAP. I

'TIS agreed that in all Government there is an absolute unlimited Power, which naturally and originally seems to be placed in the whole Body, wherever the Executive Part of it lies. This holds in the Body natural; For wherever we place the beginning of Motion, whether from the Head, or the Heart, or the animal Spirits in general, the Body moves and acts by a Consent of all its Parts. This unlimited Power placed fundamentally in the Body of a People, is what the Legislators of all Ages have endeavour'd in their several Schemes or Institutions of Government, to deposite in such Hands as would preserve the People from Rapine and Oppression within, as well as Violence from without. Most of them seem to agree in this, that it was a Trust too great to be committed to any one Man or Assembly, and therefore they left the Right still in the whole Body, but the Administration or Executive part, in the hands of *One*, the *Few*, or the *Many*, into which three powers all independent Bodies of Men seem naturally to divide; for by all I have read of those innumerable and petty Commonwealths in *Italy*, *Greece*, and *Sicily*, as well as the great ones of *Carthage* and *Rome*; it seems to me, that a free People met together, whether by *Compact* or *Family Government*, as soon as they fall into any Acts of Civil Society, do of themselves divide into three Powers. The first is that of some one eminent Spirit, who having signalized his Valour and Fortune in Defence of his Country, or by the Practice of popular Arts at home, becomes to have great Influence on the People, to grow their Leader in Warlike Expeditions, and to preside, after a sort, in their Civil Assemblies: And this is grounded upon the Principles of Nature and common Reason, which in all Difficulties or Dangers, where Prudence or Courage is required, do rather incite us to fly for Counsel or Assistance to a single Person than a Multitude. The second natural Division of Power, is of such Men who have acquired large Possessions, and consequently Dependances, or descend from Ancestors who have left them great Inheritances, together with an Hereditary Authority. These easily uniting in Thoughts and Opinions, and acting in Concert, begin to enter upon Measures for securing their Properties, which are best upheld by preparing against Invasions from abroad, and maintaining Peace at home: This commences a great Council or Senate of Nobles for the weighty Affairs of the Nation. The last Division is of the Mass or Body of the People, whose Part of Power is great and undisputable, whenever they can unite either collectively or by Deputation to exert it. Now the three Forms of Government so generally known in the Schools, differ only by the Civil Administration being placed in the Hands of One, or sometimes Two (as in *Sparta*) who were call'd *Kings*, or in a Senate, who were call'd the *Nobles*, or in the People Collective or Representative, who may be called the *Commons*: each of these had frequently the Executive Power in *Greece*, and sometimes in *Rome*: but the Power in the last Resort was always meant by Legislators to be held in Balance among all three. And it will be an eternal Rule in Politicks among every free People, that there is a Balance of Power to be carefully held by every State within itself, as well as among several States with each other.

The true Meaning of a Balance of Power, either without or within a State, is best conceived by considering what the nature of a Balance is. It supposes three Things. First, the Part which is held, together with the Hand that holds it; and then the two Scales, with whatever is weighed therein. Now consider several States in a Neighbourhood: In order to preserve Peace between these States, it is necessary they should be form'd into a Balance, whereof one or more are to be Directors, who are to divide the rest into equal Scales, and upon Occasions remove from one into the other, or else fall with their own Weight into the Lightest. So in a State within itself, the Balance must be held by a third Hand; who is to deal the remaining Power with utmost Exactness into the several Scales. Now, it is not necessary that the Power should be equally divided between these three; For the Balance may be held by the Weakest, who, by his Address and Conduct, removing from either Scale, and adding of his own, may keep the Scales duly pois'd. Such was that of the two Kings of *Sparta*, the Consular Power in *Rome*: that of the Kings of *Media* before the Reign of *Cyrus*, as represented by *Xenophon*, and that of the several limited States in the *Gothick* Institution.

When the Balance is broke, whether by the Negligence, Folly, or Weakness of the Hand that held it, or by mighty Weights fallen into either Scale, the Power will never continue long in equal Division between the two remaining Parties, but (till the Balance is fixed anew) will run entirely into one. This gives the truest account of what is understood in the most ancient and approved *Greek* Authors by the Word *Tyranny*, which is not meant for the seizing of the uncontrouled or absolute Power into the Hands of a single Person (as many superficial Men have grosly mistaken) but for the breaking of the Balance by whatever Hand, and leaving the Power wholly in one Scale. For *Tyranny* and *Usurpation* in a State, are by no means confined to any Number, as might easily appear from Examples enough, and because the Point is material, I shall cite a few to prove it.

The *Romans* having sent to *Athens*, and the *Greek* Cities of *Italy*, for the Copies of the best Laws, chose Ten Legislators to put them into form, and during the Exercise of their Office, suspended the Consular Power, leaving the Administration of Affairs in their Hands. These very Men, though chosen for such a Work, as the digesting a Body of Laws for the Government of a free

State, did immediately usurp Arbitrary Power, ran into all the Forms of it, had their Guards and Spies, after the Practice of the Tyrants of those Ages, affected Kingly State, destroy'd the Nobles, and opprest the People; One of them proceeding so far as to endeavour to force a Lady of great Virtue: the very Crime which gave Occasion to the Expulsion of the Regal Power but sixty Years before, as this Attempt did to that of the *Decemviri*.

The *Ephori* in *Sparta* were at first only certain Persons deputed by the Kings to judge in Civil Matters, while *They* were employ'd in the Wars. These Men, at several times, usurp'd the absolute Authority, and were as cruel Tyrants as any in their Age.

Soon after the unfortunate Expedition into *Sicily*, the *Athenians* chose four hundred Men for Administration of Affairs, who became a Body of Tyrants, and were called in the Language of those Ages, an *Oligarchy*, or Tyranny of the *Few*; under which hateful Denomination, they were soon after deposed in great Rage by the People.

When *Athens* was subdued by *Lysander*, he appointed thirty Men for the Administration of that City, who immediately fell into the rankest Tyranny: But this was not all; For conceiving their Power not founded on a *Basis* large enough, they admitted three thousand into a Share of the Government; and thus fortified, became the cruellest Tyranny upon Record. They murder'd, in cold Blood, great numbers of the best Men, without any Provocation, from the meer Lust of Cruelty, like *Nero* or *Caligula*. This was such a Number of Tyrants together, as amounted to near a third part of the whole City. For *Xenophon* tells us, that the City contain'd about ten thousand Houses, and allowing one Man to every House, who could have any Share in the Government (the rest consisting of Women, Children, and Servants) and making other obvious Abatements, these Tyrants, if they had been careful to adhere together, might have been a Majority even of the People Collective.

In the time of the second *Punick* War, the Balance of

Power in *Carthage* was got on the side of the People, and that to a Degree, that some Authors reckon the Government to have been then among them a *Dominatio Plebis*, or *Tyranny of the Commons*, which it seems they were at all times apt to fall into, and was at last among the Causes that ruined their State: And the frequent Murders of their Generals, which *Diodorus* tells us was grown to an establish'd Custom among them, may be another Instance that Tyranny is not confined to Numbers.

I shall mention but one Example more among a great Number that might be produced; It is related by the Author last cited. The Orators of the People at *Argos* (whether you will stile them in modern Phrase, *Great Speakers in the House*, or only in general, Representatives of the People Collective) stirred up the Commons against the Nobles; of whom 1600 were Murdered at once, and at last, the Orators themselves, because they left off their Accusations, or to speak Intelligibly, because they *withdrew their Impeachments*; having, it seems, raised a Spirit they were not able to lay. And this last Circumstance, as Cases have lately stood, may perhaps be worth noting.

From what hath been already advanced, several Conclusions may be drawn.

First, That a mixt Government partaking of the known Forms received in the Schools, is by no means of *Gothick* Invention, but has place in Nature and Reason, seems very well to agree with the Sentiments of most Legislators, and to have been follow'd in most States, whether they have appear'd under the name of Monarchies, Aristocracies, or Democracies. For, not to mention the several Republicks of this Composition in *Gaul* and *Germany*, described by *Caesar* and *Tacitus*; *Polybius* tells us, the best Government is that which consists of three Forms, *Regno*, *Optimatium*, & *Populi imperio*: Which may be fairly Translated, the *King*, *Lords* and *Commons*. Such was that of *Sparta* in its Primitive Institution by *Lycurgus*; who observing the Corruptions and Depravations to which every of these was subject, compounded his Scheme out of all; so that it was made up of *Reges*, *Seniores*, & *Populus*: Such also was the State of *Rome*, under its Consuls; And the Author tells us, that the *Romans* fell upon this Model purely by chance, (which I take to have been Nature and common Reason) but the *Spartans* by Thought and Design. And such at *Carthage* was the *summa Reipublicae*, or Power in the last Resort; For they had their Kings call'd *Suffetes*, and a Senate which had the Power of *Nobles*, and the *People* had a share establish'd too.

Secondly, It will follow, That those Reasoners who employ so much of their Zeal, their Wit and their Leisure for upholding the Balance of Power in Christendom, at the same time that by their Practices they are endeavouring to destroy it at home, are not such mighty Patriots, or so much in the true Interest of their Country, as they would affect to be thought, but seem to be employed like a Man who pulls down with his right Hand what he has been Building with his left.

Thirdly, This makes appear the Error of those who conceive, that Power is safer lodged in many Hands than in one. For if those many Hands be made up only of one of the three Divisions before mentioned, 'tis plain from those Examples already produced, and easie to be parallel'd in other Ages and Countries, that they are as capable of Enslaving the Nation, and of acting all manner of Tyranny and Oppression as it is possible for a single Person to be; tho' we should suppose their number to be not only of Four or Five Hundred, but above Three Thousand.

Again, it is manifest from what has been said, that in order to preserve the Balance in a mix'd State, the Limits of Power deposited with each Party ought to be ascertained, and generally known. The defect of this is the cause that introduces those strugglings in a State about *Prerogative* and *Liberty*, about Encroachments of the *Few*, upon the Rights of the *Many*, and of the *Many* upon the Privileges of the *Few*, which ever did and ever will conclude in a Tyranny; First, either of the *Few*, or the *Many*, but at last infallibly of a single Person. For, which ever of the three Divisions in a State is upon the Scramble for more Power than its own (as one or other of them generally is) unless due care be taken by the other two; upon every new Question that arises, they will be sure to decide in favour of themselves, talk much of Inherent Right; they will nourish up a dormant Power, and reserve Privileges in *petto*, to exert upon Occasions, to serve Expedients, and to urge upon Necessities. They will make large Demands, and scanty Concessions, ever coming off considerable Gainers: Thus at length the Balance is broke, and Tyranny let in, from which Door of the three it matters not.

To pretend to a declarative Right upon any occasion whatsoever, is little less than to make use of the whole Power: That is, to declare an opinion to be Law, which has always been contested, or perhaps never started at all before such an incident brought it on the Stage. Not to consent to the Enacting of such a Law, which has no view beside the general Good, unless another Law shall at the same time pass, with no other view but that of advancing the Power of one Party alone; What is this but to claim a positive Voice as well as a negative? To pretend that great Changes and Alienations of Property have created new and great dependances, and consequently new additions of Power, as some Reasoners have done, is a most dangerous Tenet: If Dominion must follow Property, let it follow in the same pace: For Changes in Property thro' the Bulk of a Nation make slow Marches, and its due Power always attends it. To conclude, that whatever attempt is begun by an Assembly, ought to be pursued to the end, without regard to the greatest incidents that may happen to alter the Case; To count it mean, and below the *Dignity of a House* to quit a Prosecution; To resolve upon a Conclusion before it is possible to be apprised of the Premises; To act thus, I say, is to affect not only absolute Power, but infallibility too. Yet such unaccountable Proceedings as these have Popular Assemblies engaged in, for want of fixing the due Limits of *Power* and *Privilege*.

Great Changes may indeed be made in a Government, yet the Form continue, and the Balance be held; but large Intervals of Time must pass between every such Innovation, enough to melt down and make it of a Piece with the Constitution. Such we are told were the Proceedings of *Solon*, when he Modelled anew the *Athenian* Commonwealth: And what Convulsions in our own as well as other States have been bred by a neglect of this Rule, is fresh and notorious enough: 'Tis too soon in all conscience to repeat this Error again.

Having shewn that there is a natural Balance of Power in all free States, and how it has been divided sometimes by the People themselves, as in *Rome*, at others by the Institutions of Legislators, as in the several States of *Greece* and *Sicily*: The next thing is to examine what Methods have been taken to break or overthrow this Balance; which every one of the three Parties have continually endeavour'd, as opportunities have served; which might appear from the Stories of most Ages and Countries. For, Absolute Power in a particular State, is of the same nature with universal Monarchy in several States adjoyning to each other. So endless and exorbitant are the desires of Men, whether consider'd in their Persons or their States, that they will grasp at all, and can form no Scheme of perfect Happiness with less. Ever since Men have been united into Governments, the Hopes and Endeavours after universal Monarchy have been bandied among them, from the Reign of *Ninus* to this of the *Most Christian King*; in which pursuits Commonwealths have had their share as well as Monarchs: So the *Athenians*, the *Spartans*, the *Thebans* and the *Achaians*, did at several times aim at the universal Monarchy of *Greece*; So the Commonwealths of *Carthage* and *Rome* affected the universal Monarchy of the then known World. In like manner has absolute Power been pursued by the several Parties of each particular State, wherein single Persons have met with most Success, tho' the endeavours of the *Few* and the *Many* have been frequent enough; But, being neither so uniform in their Designs, nor so direct in their Views, they neither could manage nor maintain the Power they had got; but were ever deceived by the Popularity and Ambition of some single Person. So that it will be always a wrong step in Policy, for the *Nobles* or *Commons* to carry their Endeavours after Power so far, as to overthrow the Balance: And it would be enough to damp their warmth in such Pursuits, if they could once reflect, that in such a Course they will be sure to run upon the very Rock they meant to avoid, which I suppose they would have us think is the Tyranny of a single Person.

Many Examples might be produced of the Endeavours from each of these three Rivals after absolute Power; But I shall suit my Discourse to the Time I am Writing in, and Relate only such Dissentions between the *Nobles* and *Commons*, with the Consequences of them, in *Greece* and *Rome*, wherein the latter were the Aggressors.

I shall begin with *Greece*, where my Observations shall be confin'd to *Athens*, tho' several Instances might be brought from other States thereof.

CHAP. II.

Of the Dissensions in Athens, *between the* Few *and the* Many.

Theseus is the first who is Recorded with any appearance of Truth to have brought the *Grecians* from a barbarous manner of Life among scattered Villages, into Cities, and to have establish'd the *Popular State* in *Athens*, assigning to himself the Guardianship of the Laws, and chief Command in War. He was forced after some time to leave the *Athenians* to their own measures, upon account of their seditious Temper, which ever continu'd with them till the final Dissolution of their Government by the *Romans*. It seems, the Country about *Attica* was the most Barren of any in *Greece*; thro' which means it happened that the Natives were never expelled by the Fury of Invaders, (who thought it not worth a Conquest) but continued always *Aborigines*; and therefore retained thro' all Revolutions a tincture of that turbulent Spirit wherewith their Government began. This Institution of *Theseus* appears to have been rather a sort of mixt Monarchy than a popular State, and for ought we know, might continue so during the Series of Kings till the Death of *Codrus*. From this last Prince, *Solon* was said to be descended; who finding the People engaged in two violent Factions, of the Poor and the Rich, and in great confusions thereupon; refusing the Monarchy which was offered him, chose rather to cast the Government after another Model, wherein he made due provision for settling the Balance of Power, chusing a Senate of 400, and disposing the Magistracies and Offices according to Mens Estates; leaving to the Multitude their Votes in Electing, and the Power of judging certain Processes by Appeal. This Council of 400 was Chosen, 100 out of each Tribe, and seems to have been a Body Representative of the People; tho' the People collective reserved a share of Power to themselves. It is a Point of History perplexed enough; but thus much is certain, that the Balance of Power was provided for; else *Pysistratus*, (called by Authors the Tyrant of *Athens*) could never have govern'd so peaceably as he did, without changing any of *Solon*'s Laws. These several Powers, together with that of the *Archon*, or Chief Magistrate, made up the Form of Government in *Athens*, at what time it began to appear upon the Scene of Action and Story.

The first great Man bred up under this Institution was *Miltiades*, who lived about Ninety Years after *Solon*, and is reckon'd to have been the first great Captain not only of *Athens*, but of all *Greece*. From the time of *Miltiades* to that of *Phocion*, who is look'd upon as the last famous General of *Athens*, are about 130 years: After which they were subdued and insulted by *Alexander*'s Captains, and continued under several Revolutions a small truckling State of no Name or Reputation, till they fell with the rest of *Greece* under the Power of the *Romans*.

During this Period from *Miltiades* to *Phocion*, I shall trace the Conduct of the *Athenians*, with relation to their Dissensions between the People and some of their Generals; who at that time by their Power and Credit in the Army, in a Warlike Commonwealth, and often supported by each other, were, with the Magistrates and other Civil Officers, a sort of Counterpoise to the Power of the People, who since the Death of *Solon* had already made great Encroachments. What these Dissensions were, how founded, and what the Consequences of them, I shall briefly and impartially Relate.

I must here premise, that the *Nobles* in *Athens* being not at this time a Corporate Assembly that I can gather; therefore the Resentments of the Commons were usually turned against particular Persons, and by way of Articles of Impeachment. Whereas, the Commons in *Rome*, and some other States, (as will appear in proper Place) tho' they followed this Method upon occasion, yet generally pursued the Enlargement of their Power, by more set Quarrels of one entire Assembly against another. However, the Custom of particular Impeachments being not limited to former Ages, any more than that of general Struggles and Dissensions betwixt fix'd Assemblies of Nobles and Commons; And the Ruin of *Greece* having been owing to the former, as that of *Rome* was to the latter; I shall treat on both expresly; that those States who are concerned in either (if at least, there be any such now in the World) may by observing the Means and the Issues of former Dissensions, learn whether the Causes are alike in theirs, and if they find them to be so, may consider whether they ought not justly to apprehend the same Effects.

To speak of every particular Person impeach'd by the Commons of *Athens*, within the compass designed, would introduce the History of almost every great Man they had among them. I shall therefore take notice only of Six, who living in that Period of Time when *Athens* was at the height of its Glory (as indeed it could not be otherwise while such Hands were at the Helm) tho' *impeach'd for high Crimes and Misdemeanors*, such as *Bribery*, *Arbitrary Proceedings*, *misapplying or imbesling publick Funds*, *ill Conduct at Sea*, and the like, were honored and lamented by their Country, as the Preservers of it, and have had the Veneration of all Ages since paid justly to their Memories.

Miltiades was one of the *Athenian* Generals against the *Persian* Power, and the famous Victory at *Marathon* was chiefly owing to his Valour and Conduct. Being sent some time after to reduce the Island *Paros*, he mistook a great Fire at distance, for the *Persian* Fleet, and being no ways a Match for them, set Sail for *Athens*; at his Arrival he was *impeach'd* by the Commons for Treachery, tho' not able to appear by reason of his Wounds, fined 30000 Crowns, and died in Prison. Tho' the Consequences of this Proceeding upon the Affairs of *Athens*, were no other than the untimely Loss of so great and good a Man, yet I could not forbear relating it.

Their next great Man was *Aristides*: Beside the mighty Service he had done his Country in the Wars; he was a Person of the strictest Justice, and best acquainted with the Laws as well as Forms of their Government, so that he was in a manner the Chancellor of *Athens*. This Man upon a slight and false Accusation of *favouring Arbitrary Power*, was banish'd by *Ostracism*, which rendered into modern *English*, would signify that they voted *he should be removed from their Presence and Councils for ever*. But, however, they had the Wit to recal him, and to that Action owed the Preservation of their State by his future Services. For it must be still confessed in behalf of the *Athenian* People, that they never conceived themselves perfectly infallible, nor arrived to the Heights of *modern Assemblies*, to make *Obstinacy* confirm what *sudden Heat* and *Temerity* began. They thought it not below the Dignity of an

Assembly to endeavour at correcting an ill Step; at least to repent, tho' it often fell out too late.

Themistocles was at first a *Commoner* himself. It was he that raised the *Athenians* to their Greatness at Sea, which he thought to be the true and constant Interest of that Commonwealth; and the famous Naval Victory over the *Persians* at *Salamis* was owing to his Conduct. It seems the People observed somewhat of Haughtiness in his Temper and Behavior, and therefore banisht him for five Years; but finding some slight matter of Accusation against him, they sent to seize his Person, and he hardly escaped to the *Persian* Court; from whence if the love of his Country had not surmounted its base Ingratitude to him, he had many Invitations to return at the Head of the *Persian* Fleet, and take a terrible Revenge; But he rather chose a voluntary Death.

The People of *Athens* Impeached *Pericles* for *Misapplying the Publick Revenues to his own Private Use*. He had been a Person of great Deservings from the Republick, was an *admirable Speaker*, and very Popular; *His Accounts were confused*, *and he could not then give them up*; therefore meerly to divert that Difficulty, and the Consequences of it, he was forced to engage his Country in the *Peloponnesian* War, the longest that ever was known in *Greece*, and which ended in the utter Ruin of *Athens*.

The same People having resolved to subdue *Sicily*, sent a mighty Fleet under the command of *Nicias*, *Lamachus*, and *Alcibiades*: the two former, Persons of Age and Experience; the last a young Man of noble Birth, excellent Education, and a plentiful Fortune. A little before the Fleet set Sail, it seems, one Night, the Stone Images of *Mercury* placed in several parts of the City were all pared in the Face: This Action the *Athenians* interpreted for a Design of destroying the Popular State; and *Alcibiades* having been formerly noted for the like Frolicks and Excursions, was immediately accused of this. He, whether Conscious of his Innocence or assured of the Secrecy, offered to come to his Tryal before he went to his Command; this the *Athenians* refused; but as soon as he was got to *Sicily*, they sent for him back, designing to take the Advantage, and Prosecute him in the Absence of his Friends, and of the Army, where he was very Powerful. It seems, he understood the Resentments of a Popular Assembly too well to trust them; and therefore instead of returning, escaped to *Sparta*; where his desires of Revenge prevailing over his Love to his Country, he became its greatest Enemy. Mean while, the *Athenians* before *Sicily*, by the Death of one Commander, and the Superstition, Weakness, and perfect ill Conduct of the other, were utterly destroyed, the whole Fleet taken, a miserable Slaughter made of the Army, whereof hardly one ever returned. Some time after this, *Alcibiades* was recalled upon his Conditions, by the Necessities of the People, and made chief Commander at Sea and Land; but his Lieutenant engaging against his positive Orders, and being beaten by *Lysander*, *Alcibiades* was again disgraced and banished. However, the *Athenians* having lost all Strength and Heart since their Misfortune at *Sicily*, and now deprived of the only Person that was able to recover their Losses, repent of their Rashness, and endeavour in vain for his Restoration; the *Persian* Lieutenant, to whose Protection he fled, making him a Sacrifice to the Resentments of *Lysander* the General of the *Lacedemonians*, who now reduces all the Dominions of the *Athenians*, takes the City, razes their Walls, ruins their Works, and changes the Form of their Government; which though again restored for some time by *Thrasybulus* (as their Walls were rebuilt by *Conon*) yet here we must date the Fall of the *Athenian* Greatness; the Dominion and chief Power in *Greece*, from that Period, to the time of *Alexander* the Great, which was about fifty Years, being divided between the *Spartans* and *Thebans*. Though *Philip*, *Alexander*'s Father (*the Most Christian King* of that Age) had indeed some time before begun to break in upon the Republicks of *Greece*, by Conquest or *Bribery*; particularly *dealing large Money among some Popular Orators*, by which he brought many of them, (as the term of Art was then) to *Philippize*.

In the time of *Alexander* and his Captains, the *Athenians* were offered an Opportunity of preserving their Liberty, and being restored to their former State; but the wise Turn they thought to give the Matter, was by an Impeachment and Sacrifice of the Author, to hinder the Success. For, after the Destruction of *Thebes* by *Alexander*, this Prince designing the Conquest of *Athens*, was prevented by *Phocion* the *Athenian* General, then Ambassador from that State; who by his great Wisdom and Skill at Negotiation, diverted *Alexander* from his Design, and restored the *Athenians* to his Favour. The very same Success he had with *Antipater* after *Alexander*'s Death, at which time the Government was new regulated by *Solon*'s Laws: But *Polyperchon*, in hatred to *Phocion*, having by Order of the young King (whose Governor he was) restored those whom *Phocion* had banished; the Plot succeeded, *Phocion* was accused by Popular Orators, and put to Death.

Thus was the most powerful Commonwealth of all *Greece*, after great degeneracies from the Institution of *Solon*, utterly destroyed by that rash, jealous, and inconstant humour of the People, which was never satisfied to see a General either *Victorious* or *Unfortunate*; such ill Judges, as well as Rewarders, are *Popular Assemblies*, of those who best deserve from them.

Now the Circumstance which makes these Examples of more Importance, is, that this very Power of the People in *Athens*, claimed so confidently for an *inherent Right*, and insisted on as the *undoubted Privilege of an* Athenian *born*, was the rankest Encroachment imaginable, and the grossest Degeneracy from the Form that *Solon* left them. In short, their Government was grown into a *Dominatio plebis*, or *Tyranny of the People*, who by degrees had broke and overthrown the Balance which that Legislator had very well fixed and provided for. This appears not only from what has been already said of that Lawgiver; but more manifestly from a Passage in *Diodorus*; who tells us, That Antipater *one of* Alexander'*s Captains, abrogated the Popular Government* (*in* Athens) *and restored the Power of Suffrages and Magistracy, to such only as were worth two thousand Drachmas; by which means,* (*says he*) *that Republick came to be* [*again*] *administred by the Laws of* Solon. By this Quotation, 'tis manifest, that great Author look'd upon *Solon*'s Institution, and a Popular Government to be two different Things. And as for this Restoration by *Antipater*, it had neither Consequence nor Continuance worth observing.

I might easily produce many more Examples, but these are sufficient, and it may be worth the Readers time to reflect a little upon the Merits of the Cause, as well as of the Men who had been thus dealt with by their Country. I shall direct him no further than by repeating, that *Aristides* was the most renowned by the People themselves for his exact *Justice and Knowledge in the Law*; That *Themistocles* was a most fortunate Admiral, and had got *a mighty Victory over the great King of* Persia'*s Fleet*; That *Pericles* was an *able Minister of State, an excellent Orator, and a Man of Letters*; And lastly, that *Phocion*, besides the Success of his Arms, was also renowned for his *Negotiations abroad, having in an Embassy brought the greatest Monarch of the World at that time, to the Terms of an honourable Peace, by which his Country was preserved.*

I shall conclude my Remarks upon *Athens*, with the Character given us of that People by *Polybius*. About this time (says he) the *Athenians* were Governed by two Men, quite sunk in their Affairs; had little or no Commerce with the rest of *Greece*, and were become great Reverencers of Crown'd Heads.

For from the time of *Alexander*'s Captains, till *Greece* was subdued by the *Romans* (to the latter part of which this Description of *Polybius* falls in) *Athens* never produced one famous Man either for Councils or Arms, or hardly for Learning. And indeed it was a dark insipid Period through all *Greece*: for except the *Achaian* League under

Aratus and *Philopœmen*, and the endeavours of *Agis* and *Cleomenes* to restore the State of *Sparta*, so frequently harassed by Tyrannies occasioned by the Popular Practices of the *Ephori*, there was very little worth Recording. All which Consequences may perhaps be justly imputed to this Degeneracy of *Athens*.

CHAP. III.

Of the Dissensions between the Patricians and Plebeians in Rome, *with the Consequences they had upon that State.*

HAVING in the foregoing Chapter confined my self to the Proceedings of the Commons, only by the Method of *Impeachments* against particular Persons, with the fatal Effects they had upon the State of *Athens*; I shall now treat of the Dissensions at *Rome* between the People and the Collective Body of the *Patricians* or *Nobles*. It is a large Subject, but I shall draw it into as narrow a Compass as I can.

As *Greece*, from the most antient Accounts we have of it, was divided into several Kingdoms, so was most part of *Italy* into several petty Commonwealths. And as those Kings in *Greece* are said to have been deposed by their People upon the Score of their Arbitrary Proceedings; so on the contrary, the Commonwealths of *Italy* were all swallowed up, and concluded in the Tyranny of the *Roman* Emperors. However, the Differences between those *Grecian* Monarchies, and *Italian* Republicks, were not very great: For, by the Accounts *Homer* gives us of those *Grecian* Princes who came to the Siege of *Troy*, as well as by several Passages in the *Odysses*; it is manifest, that the Power of these Princes in their several States, was much of a size with that of the Kings in *Sparta*, the

Archon at *Athens*, the Suffetes at *Carthage*, and the Consuls in *Rome*: So that a limited and divided Power seems to have been the most antient and inherent Principle of both those People in Matters of Government. And such did that of *Rome* continue from the time of *Romulus*, tho' with some interruptions, to *Julius Cæsar*, when it ended in the Tyranny of a single Person. During which Period, (not many Years longer than from the *Norman* Conquest to our Age) the Commons were growing by degrees into Power and Property, gaining Ground upon the Patricians as it were Inch by Inch, till at last they quite overturned the Balance, leaving all Doors open to the Practices of popular and ambitious Men, who destroyed the Wisest Republick, and enslaved the Noblest People that ever entred upon the Stage of the World. By what Steps and Degrees this was brought to pass, shall be the Subject of my present Enquiry.

While *Rome* was governed by Kings, the Monarchy was altogether Elective. *Romulus* himself, when he had built the City, was declared King by the universal Consent of the People, and by Augury, which was then understood for *Divine Appointment*. Among other Divisions he made of the People, one was into *Patricians* and *Plebeians*: The former were like the Barons of *England* some time after the Conquest; and the latter are also described to be almost exactly what our Commons were then. For they were Dependants upon the Patricians, whom they chose for their Patrons and Protectors, to answer for their Appearance, and defend them in any Process: They also supplied their Patrons with Money in exchange for their Protection. This Custom of *Patronage*, it seems, was very antient, and long practised among the *Greeks*.

Out of these Patricians, *Romulus* chose an hundred to be a *Senate* or *Grand Council*, for Advice and Assistance to him in the Administration. The Senate therefore, originally consisted all of *Nobles*, and were of themselves a *Standing Council*, the *People* being only convoked upon such Occasions as by this Institution of *Romulus* fell into their Cognizance: Those were, to constitute Magistrates, to give their Votes for making Laws, and to advise upon entring on a War. But the two former of these popular Privileges were to be confirmed by Authority of the Senate; and the last was only permitted at the King's Pleasure. This was the utmost Extent of Power pretended by the *Commons* in the time of *Romulus*; all the rest being divided between the King and the Senate, the whole agreeing very nearly with the Constitution of *England* for some Centuries after the Conquest.

After a Year's *interregnum* from the Death of *Romulus*, the Senate of their own Authority chose a Successor, and a Stranger, meerly upon the Fame of his Virtue, without asking the Consent of the Commons; which Custom they likewise observed in the two following Kings. But in the Election of *Tarquinius Priscus*, the fifth King, we first hear mentioned that it was done, *Populi impetratâ veniâ*, which indeed was but very reasonable for a free People to expect; tho' I cannot remember in my little reading, by what Incidents they were brought to advance so great a Step. However it were, this Prince, in Gratitude to the People by whose Consent he was chosen, elected a hundred Senators out of the Commons, whose Number with former Additions was now amounted to three hundred.

The People having once discovered their own Strength, did soon take occasion to exert it, and that by very great Degrees. For, at this King's Death (who was murdered by the Sons of a former) being at a loss for a Successor, *Servius Tullius*, a Stranger, and of mean Extraction, was chosen Protector of the Kingdom, by the *People*, without the Consent of the Senate; at which the Nobles being displeased, he wholly applied himself to gratify the Commons, and was by them declared and confirmed no longer Protector but King.

This Prince first introduced the Custom of giving freedom to Servants, so as to become Citizens of equal Privileges with the rest, which very much contributed to encrease the Power of the *People*.

Thus in a very few Years the Commons proceeded so far as to wrest even the Power of chusing a King, entirely out of the Hands of the Nobles; which was so great a Leap, and caused such a Convulsion and Struggle in the State, that the Constitution could not bear it; but Civil Dissensions arose, which immediately were followed by the Tyranny of a single Person, as this was by the utter Subversion of the Regal Government, and by a Settlement upon a new Foundation. For the Nobles spighted at this Indignity done them by the Commons, firmly united in a Body, deposed this Prince by plain force, and chose *Tarquin the Proud*, who running into all the Forms and Methods of Tyranny, after a cruel Reign was expelled by an universal Concurrence of Nobles and People, whom the Miseries of his Reign had reconciled.

When the Consular Government began, the Balance of power between the Nobles and Plebeians was fixed anew. The two first Consuls were nominated by the Nobles, and confirmed by the Commons; and a Law was enacted that no Person should bear any Magistracy in *Rome*, *injussu Populi*; that is, without *Consent of the Commons*.

In such turbulent Times as these, many of the poorer Citizens had contracted numerous Debts, either to the richer sort among themselves, or to Senators and other Nobles: and the Case of Debtors in *Rome* for the first four Centuries, was, after the set time for Payment, no Choice but either to pay or be the Creditor's Slave. In this Juncture the Commons quit the City in Mutiny and Discontent, and will not return but upon condition to be acquitted of all their Debts; and moreover, that certain Magistrates be chosen yearly; whose Business it shall be to defend the Commons from Injuries. These are called *Tribunes of the People*, their Persons are held Sacred and Inviolable, and the People bind themselves by Oath never to abrogate the Office. By these Tribunes, in process of time, the People were grosly imposed on to serve the Turns and Occasions of revengeful or ambitious Men, and to commit such Exorbitances as could not end, but in the Dissolution of the Government.

These Tribunes a year or two after their Institution kindled great Dissensions between the Nobles and the Commons, on the account of *Coriolanus*, a Nobleman, whom the latter had *Impeached*, and the Consequences of whose Impeachment (if I had not confined my self to *Grecian* Examples for that part of my Subject) had like to have been so fatal to their State. And from this time the Tribunes began a Custom of accusing to the People whatever Noble they pleas'd, several of whom were Banish'd or put to Death in every Age.

At this time the *Romans* were very much engaged in Wars with their Neighbouring States; but upon the least Intervals of Peace, the Quarrels between the Nobles and the Plebeians would revive; and one of the most frequent Subjects of their Differences was the *Conquered Lands*, which the Commons would fain have divided among the Publick; but the Senate could not be brought to give their Consent. For several of the wisest among the Nobles began to apprehend the growing Power of the People; and therefore knowing what an Accession thereof would accrue to them by such an Addition of Property, used all means to prevent it: For this the *Appian* Family was most noted, and thereupon most hated by the Commons. One of them having made a Speech against this Division of Lands, was Impeach'd by the People of High Treason, and a Day appointed for his Tryal; but disdaining to make his Defence, chose rather the usual *Roman* Remedy of killing himself: After whose Death the Commons prevailed, and the Lands were divided among them.

This point was no sooner gained, but new Dissensions began: For the Plebeians would fain have a Law Enacted, to lay all Mens Rights and Privileges upon the same level; and to enlarge the Power of every Magistrate within his own Jurisdiction, as much as that of the Consuls. The Tribunes also obtain'd to have their Number doubled, which before was Five, and the Author tells us, that their

Insolence and Power encreased with their Number, and the Seditions were also doubled with it.

By the beginning of the Fourth Century from the Building of *Rome*, the Tribunes proceeded so far in the name of the Commons, as to accuse and fine the Consuls themselves, who represented the Kingly Power. And the Senate observing, how in all Contentions they were forc'd to yield to the Tribunes and People, thought it their wisest course to give way also to Time: Therefore a Decree was made to send Ambassadors to *Athens*, and to the other *Grecian* Commonwealths planted in that part of *Italy*, call'd *Græcia Major*, to make a Collection of the best Laws; out of which and some of their own, a new complete Body of Law was formed, afterwards known by the name of the *Laws of the Twelve Tables.*

To digest these Laws into Order, Ten Men were Chosen, and the Administration of all Affairs left in their Hands; what use they made of it has been already shewn. It was certainly a great Revolution, produc'd entirely by the many unjust Encroachments of the People; and might have wholly changed the Fate of *Rome*, if the Folly and Vice of those who were chiefly concern'd, could have suffered it to take Root.

A few Years after, the Commons made further Advances on the Power of the Nobles; demanding among the rest, that the Consulship, which hitherto had only been disposed to the former, should now lie in common to the Pretensions of any *Roman* whatsoever. This, tho' it fail'd at present, yet afterward obtain'd, and was a mighty Step to the Ruin of the Commonwealth.

What I have hitherto said of *Rome* has been chiefly Collected out of that exact and diligent Writer *Dionysius Halicarnasseus*; whose History (thro' the injury of Time) reaches no farther than to the beginning of the fourth Century after the Building of *Rome*. The rest I shall supply from other Authors; tho' I do not think it necessary to deduce this Matter any further, so very particularly as I have hitherto done.

To point at what Time the Balance of Power was most equally held between the *Lords* and *Commons* in *Rome*, would perhaps admit a Controversie. *Polybius* tells us, that in the second *Punick* War, the *Carthaginians* were declining, because the Balance was got too much on the side of the People; whereas the *Romans* were in their greatest Vigour, by the Power remaining in the Senate; yet this was between Two and Three Hundred Years after the Period *Dionysius* ends with; in which time the Commons had made several further Acquisitions. This however must be granted, that (till about the middle of the fourth Century) when the Senate appeared resolute at any time upon exerting their Authority, and adhered closely together, they did often carry their point. Besides, it is observed by the best Authors, that in all the Quarrels and Tumults at *Rome*, from the expulsion of the Kings; tho' the People frequently proceeded to rude contumelious Language, and sometimes so far as to pull and hale one another about the *Forum*; yet no Blood was ever drawn in any popular Commotions till the time of the *Gracchi*. However, I am of Opinion, that the Balance had begun many years before to lean to the popular side; But this default was corrected, partly by the Principle just mentioned, of never drawing Blood in a Tumult; partly by the Warlike Genius of the People, which in those Ages was almost perpetually employed; and partly by their great Commanders, who by the Credit they had in their Armies, fell into the Scales as a further counterpoise to the growing Power of the People. Besides, *Polybius*, who liv'd in the time of *Scipio Africanus* the younger, had the same apprehensions of the continual Encroachments made by the Commons; and being a Person of as great Abilities, and as much Sagacity as any of his Age; from observing the Corruptions which he says had already entred into the *Roman* Constitution, did very nearly foretel what would be the Issue of them. His Words are very remarkable, and with little addition may be rendred to this purpose. *That those Abuses and Corruptions which in time destroy a Government, are sown along with the very Seeds of it, and both grow up together. And that as Rust eats away Iron, and Worms devour Wood, and both are a sort of Plagues born and bred along with the substance they destroy; so with every Form and Scheme of Government that Man can invent, some Vice or Corruption creeps in with the very Institution, which grows up along with, and at last destroys it.* The same Author in another place, ventures so far as to guess at the particular Fate which would attend the *Roman* Government. He says, its Ruin would arise from popular Tumults, which would introduce a *Dominatio Plebis*, or Tyranny of the People; wherein 'tis certain he had reason; and therefore might have adventured to pursue his conjectures so far, as to the Consequences of a popular Tyranny, which as perpetual Experience teaches, never fails to be followed by the Arbitrary Government of a single Person.

About the middle of the Fourth Century from the Building of *Rome*, it was declared lawful for *Nobles* and *Plebeians* to intermarry; which Custom among many other States, has proved the most effectual means to ruin the former, and raise the latter.

And now the greatest Employments in the State were one after another, by Laws forceably Enacted by the *Commons*, made free to the People; the *Consulship* it self, the Office of *Censor*, that of the *Questors*, or *Commissioners of the Treasury*, the Office of *Prætor*, or Chief Justice, the *Priesthood*, and even that of *Dictator*. The Senate after long Opposition, yielding meerly for present quiet to the continual urging Clamors of the *Commons*, and of the *Tribunes* their Advocates. A Law was likewise Enacted, that the *Plebiscita*, or *A Vote of the House of Commons*, should be of universal Obligation; nay in time the method of Enacting Laws was wholly inverted: For whereas the Senate used of old to confirm the *Plebiscita*; the People did at last as they pleased, confirm or disanul the *Senatusconsulta*.

Appius Claudius brought in a Custom of admitting to the Senate the Sons of Freed Men, or of such who had once been Slaves; by which, and succeeding alterations of the like nature, that great Council degenerated into a most corrupt and factious Body of Men, divided against it self; and its Authority became despis'd.

The Century and half following, to the end of the third *Punick* War, by the entire destruction of *Carthage*, was a very busie Period at *Rome*: The Intervals between every War being so short, that the *Tribunes* and *People* had hardly Leisure or Breath to engage in Domestick Dissensions; However, the little time they could spare, was generally employed the same way. So *Terentius Leo*, a *Tribune*, is recorded to have basely prostituted the Privileges of a *Roman* Citizen, in perfect spight to the *Nobles*. So the great *African Scipio* and his Brother, after all their mighty Services were Impeached by an ungrateful *Commons*.

However, the Warlike Genius of the People, and continual Employment they had for it, served to divert this Humor from running into a Head, till the Age of the *Gracchi*.

These Persons entring the Scene in the time of a full Peace, fell violently upon advancing the Power of the People, by reducing into practice all those Encroachments which they had been so many years a gaining. There were at that time certain *Conquered Lands*, to be divided, beside a *great private Estate left by a King*. These the Tribunes, by procurement of the elder *Gracchus*, declar'd by their Legislative Authority, were not to be disposed of by the *Nobles*, but by the *Commons* only. The younger Brother pursued the same design; and besides, obtained a Law, that all *Italians* should vote at Elections, as well as the Citizens of *Rome*: in short, the whole Endeavours of them both perpetually turned upon retrenching the *Nobles* Authority in all things, but especially in the matter of *Judicature*. And tho' they both lost their Lives in those pursuits, yet they traced out such ways as were afterwards followed by *Marius*, *Sylla*, *Pompey*, and *Cæsar*, to the Ruin of the *Roman* freedom and greatness.

For, in the time of *Marius*, *Saturninus*, a Tribune, procur'd a Law that the Senate should be bound by Oath to agree to whatever the People would Enact: And *Marius* himself, while he was in that Office of Tribune is recorded to have with great Industry used all Endeavours for depressing the *Nobles*, and raising the People; particularly for cramping the former in their *Power of Judicature*, which was *their most ancient and inherent Right.*

Sylla, by the same measures became perfect Tyrant of *Rome*; He added Three Hundred Commons to the Senate, which perplexed the Power of the whole Order, and rendred it ineffectual; then flinging off the Mask, he abolished the Office of Tribune, as being only a Scaffold to Tyranny, whereof he had no further use.

As to *Pompey* and *Cæsar*, *Plutarch* tells us, that their union for pulling down the *Nobles*, (by their credit with the People) was the cause of the Civil War, which ended in the Tyranny of the latter; both of them in their Consulships having used all endeavours and occasions for sinking the Authority of the *Patricians*, and giving way to all Encroachments of the People, wherein they expected best to find their own Accounts.

From this deduction of popular Encroachments in *Rome*, the Reader will easily judge how much the Balance was fallen upon that side. Indeed by this time the very Foundation was removed, and it was a moral impossibility that the Republick could subsist any longer. For the Commons having usurped the Offices of the State, and trampled on the Senate, there was no Government left but a *dominatio Plebis*: Let us therefore examine how they proceeded in this conjuncture.

I think it is an universal Truth, that the People are much more dexterous at pulling down and setting up, than at preserving what is fixt; And they are not fonder of seizing more than their own, than they are of delivering it up again to the *worst Bidder*, with their own into the bargain. For altho' in their corrupt Notions of Divine Worship, they are apt to multiply their Gods; yet their Earthly Devotion is seldom paid to above one Idol at a time, of their own Creation; whose *Oar* they pull with less murmuring and much more Skill than when they *share the Lading*, or even *hold the Helm.*

The several Provinces of the *Roman* Empire were now Govern'd by the great Men of their State; those upon the Frontiers with powerful Armies, either for Conquest or Defence. These Governors upon any designs of Revenge or Ambition, were sure to meet with a divided Power at home, and therefore bent all their Thoughts and Applications to close in with the People, who were now by many degrees the stronger Party. Two of the greatest Spirits that *Rome* ever produced, happen'd to live at the same time, and to be engaged in the same Pursuit; and this at a juncture the most dangerous for such a Contest. These were *Pompey* and *Cæsar*, two Stars of such a Magnitude, that their *Conjunction* was as likely to be Fatal as their *Opposition.*

The *Tribunes* and People having now Subdued all Competitors, began the last game of a prevalent Populace, which is that of chusing themselves a *Master*; while the Nobles foresaw, and used all endeavours left them, to prevent it. The People at first made *Pompey* their Admiral with full power over all the *Mediterranean*; soon after Captain General of all the *Roman* Forces, and Governor of *Asia. Pompey* on the other side restored the Office of *Tribune*, which *Sylla* had put down; and in his Consulship procur'd a Law for *examining into the Miscarriages of Men in Office or Command for Twenty Years past.* Many other Examples of *Pompey*'s Popularity are left us on Record, who was a perfect Favorite of the People, and design'd to be more; but his pretensions grew stale, for want of a timely opportunity of introducing them upon the Stage. For *Cæsar*, with his Legions in *Gaul*, was a perpetual Check upon his Designs; and in the Arts of pleasing the People, did soon after get many Lengths beyond him. For he tells us himself that the Senate by a bold effort having made some severe Decrees against his Proceedings, and against the Tribunes; these all left the City and went over to his Party, and consequently along with them, the

Affections and Interests of the People; which is further manifest from the Accounts he gives us of the Citizens in several Towns, mutinying against their Commanders, and delivering both to his Devotion. Besides, *Cæsar*'s publick and avowed Pretensions for beginning the Civil-War, were to restore the Tribunes and the People opprest (as he pretended) by the *Nobles*.

This forced *Pompey* against his Inclinations, upon the Necessity of changing sides, for fear of being forsaken by both; and of closing in with the Senate and chief Magistrates, by whom he was chosen General against *Cæsar*.

Thus at length, the *Senate* (at least the Primitive part of them, the Nobles) under *Pompey*, and the *Commons* under *Cæsar*, came to a final Decision of the long Quarrels between them. For, I think, the Ambition of private Men, did by no means begin or occasion this War; though Civil Dissensions never fail of introducing and spiriting the Ambition of private Men; who thus become indeed the great Instruments for deciding of such Quarrels, and at last are sure to seize on the Prize. But no Man that sees a Flock of Vultures hovering over two Armies just ready to engage, can justly charge the Blood drawn in the Battle to them; though the Carcases fall to their share. For while the Balance of Power is equally held, the Ambition of private Men, whether Orators or great Commanders, gives neither Danger nor Fear, nor can possibly enslave their Country; but That once broken, the divided Parties are forced to unite each to its Head, under whose Conduct or Fortune one side is at first Victorious, and at last both are Slaves. And to put it past dispute, that this entire Subversion of the *Roman* Liberty and Constitution, was altogether owing to those Measures which had broke the Balance between the *Patricians* and *Plebeians*, whereof the Ambition of particular Men was but an Effect and Consequence; we need only consider, that when the uncorrupted Part of the Senate, had by the Death of *Cæsar* made one great Effort to restore their former State and Liberty; the Success did not answer their hopes, but that whole Assembly was so sunk in its Authority, that those Patriots were forced to fly, and give way to the Madness of the People; who by their own Dispositions stirred up with the Harangues of their Orators, were now wholly bent upon Single and Despotick Slavery. Else, how could such a Profligate as *Antony*, or a Boy of eighteen, like *Octavius*, ever dare to dream of giving the Law to such an Empire and People? wherein the latter succeeded, and entailed the vilest Tyranny that Heaven in its Anger ever inflicted on a Corrupt and Poison'd People. And this, with so little Appearance at *Cæsar*'s Death, that when *Cicero* wrote to *Brutus*, how he had prevailed by his Credit with *Octavius*, to promise him (*Brutus*) Pardon and Security for his Person; that Great *Roman* received the Notice with the utmost Indignity, and returned *Cicero* an Answer (yet upon Record) full of the highest Resentment and Contempt for such an Offer, and from such a Hand.

Here ended all Shew or Shadow of Liberty in *Rome*. Here was the Repository of all the wise Contentions and Struggles for Power, between the Nobles and Commons, lapt up safely in the Bosom of a *Nero* and a *Caligula*, a *Tiberius* and a *Domitian*.

Let us now see from this Deduction of particular Impeachments, and general Dissensions in *Greece* and *Rome*, what Conclusions may naturally be formed for Instruction of any other State, that may haply upon many Points labour under the like Circumstances.

CHAP. IV.

UPON the Subject of *Impeachments* we may observe that the Custom of accusing the *Nobles* to the *People*, either by themselves or their Orators (now stiled *An Impeachment in the Name of the Commons*) has been very antient both in *Greece* and *Rome*, as well as *Carthage*; and therefore may seem to be the inherent Right of a free People; nay perhaps it is really so; But then, it is to be considered, First, that this Custom was peculiar to Republicks, or such States where the Administration was principally in the Hands of the Commons, and ever raged more or less according to their Encroachments upon absolute Power; having been always lookt upon by the wisest Men, and best Authors of those times, as an Effect of Licentiousness, and not of Liberty; a Distinction which no Multitude either *Represented* or *Collective*, has been at any time very Nice in observing. However, perhaps this Custom in a Popular State, of Impeaching particular Men, may seem to be nothing else but the Peoples chusing, upon Occasion, to exercise their own Jurisdiction in Person, as if a King of *England* should sit as Chief Justice in his Court of *King*'s *Bench*, which they say, in former times, he sometimes did. But in *Sparta*, which was called a kingly Government, though the People were perfectly free, yet because the Administration was in the two Kings, and the *Ephori* (with the Assistance of the Senate) we read of no Impeachments by the People, nor was the Process against great Men, either upon account of Ambition or ill Conduct, though it reacht sometimes to Kings themselves, ever formed that way, as I can recollect: but only past through those Hands where the Administration lay. So likewise during the Regal Government in *Rome*, though it was instituted a mixt Monarchy, and the People made great Advances in Power; yet I do not remember to have read of one Impeachment from the Commons against a Patrician, till the Consular State began, and the People had made great Encroachments upon the Administration.

Another thing to be considered is, That, allowing this Right of Impeaching to be as inherent as they please: Yet, if the Commons have been perpetually mistaken in the Merits of the Causes and the Persons, as well as in the Consequences of such Impeachments upon the Peace of the State; one cannot conclude less, than that the Commons in *Greece* and *Rome*, (whatever they may be in other States) were by no means qualified either as Prosecutors or Judges in such matters; and therefore, that it would have been prudent, to have reserved these Privileges dormant, never to be produced but upon very great and urging Occasions, where the State is in apparent danger, the universal Body of the People in Clamours against the Administration, and no other Remedy in view. But for a few Popular Orators or Tribunes upon the Score of *Personal Picques*; or *to employ the Pride they conceive in seeing themselves at the Head of a Party*; Or *as a Method for Advancement*; Or *moved by certain powerful Arguments that could make* Demosthenes *Philippize*; For such Men, I say, when the State would of it self gladly be quiet, and has besides Affairs of the last Importance upon the Anvil, to *Impeach* Miltiades *after a great Naval Victory for not pursuing the* Persian *Fleet*; *To Impeach* Aristides, *the Person most versed among them in the Knowledge and Practice of their Laws, for a blind suspicion of his acting in an Arbitrary way*; (*that is, as they expounded it, not in Concert with the People*); *To Impeach* Pericles, *after all his Services, for a few Paultry Accounts*; *Or to Impeach* Phocion, *who had been guilty of no other Crime but negotiating a Treaty for the Peace and Security of his Country*: what could the Continuance of such Proceedings end in, but the utter Discouragement of all virtuous Actions and Persons, and consequently in the Ruin of a State? Therefore the Historians of those Ages seldom fail to set this Matter in all its Lights; leaving us the highest and most honorable *Ideas* of those Persons, who suffered by the Persecution of the People, together with the fatal Consequences they had, and how the Persecutors seldom failed to repent when it was too late.

These Impeachments perpetually falling upon many of the best Men both in *Greece* and *Rome*, are a Cloud of Witnesses, and Examples enough to discourage Men of Virtue and Abilities from engaging in the Service of the Publick; and help on t'other side, to introduce the Ambitious, the Covetous, the Superficial, and the ill-designing; who are as apt to be Bold, and Forward, and Meddling, as the former are to be Cautious, and Modest, and Reserved. This was so well known in *Greece*, that an Eagerness after Employments in the State, was lookt upon by wise Men, as the worst Title one could set up; and made *Plato* say, *That if all Men were as good as they ought, the Quarrel in a Commonwealth would be, not as it is now, who* should *be Ministers of State, but who should not be so.* And *Socrates* is introduced by *Xenophon* severely chiding a Friend of his for not entring into the Publick Service, when he was every way qualified for it. Such a Backwardness there was at that time among good Men to engage with an usurping People, and a Set of *pragmatical ambitious Orators.* And *Diodorus* tells us, that when the *Petalism* was erected at *Syracuse*, in imitation of the *Ostracism* at *Athens*, it was so notoriously levelled against all who had either Birth or Merit to recommend them, that whoever had either, withdrew for Fear, and would have no Concern in Publick Affairs. So that the People themselves were forced to abrogate it for fear of bringing all things into Confusion.

There is one thing more to be observed, wherein all the Popular Impeachments in *Greece* and *Rome*, seem to have agreed; and that was, a Notion they had of being concerned in *Point of Honour* to condemn whatever Person they Impeached, however frivolous the Articles were upon which they began, or however weak the Surmises whereon they were to proceed in their Proofs. For, to conceive, that the Body of the People could be mistaken, was an Indignity not to be imagined, till the Consequences had convinced them when it was past Remedy. And I look upon this as a Fate to which all Popular Accusations are Subject; though I should think that the saying, *Vox Populi, Vox Dei*, ought to be understood of the Universal Bent and Current of a People, not of the *bare Majority* of a few Representatives; which is often procured by *little Arts*, and great Industry and Application, wherein those who engage in the Pursuits of Malice and Revenge, are much more Sedulous than such as would prevent them.

From what has been deduced of the *Dissensions* in *Rome*, between the two Bodies of Patricians and Plebeians, several Reflections may be made.

First, That when the Balance of Power is duly fixed in a State, nothing is more dangerous or unwise than to give way to the *first Steps* of Popular Encroachments; which is usually done either in hopes of procuring Ease and Quiet from some vexatious Clamor, or else *made Merchandise, and meerly Bought and Sold*. This is breaking into a Constitution to serve a present Expedient, or supply a present Exigency: The Remedy of an Empirick, to stifle the present Pain, but with certain Prospect of sudden and terrible Returns. When a Child grows easie and content by being humoured; and when a Lover becomes satisfied by small Compliances, without further Pursuits; then expect to find Popular Assemblies content with small Concessions. If there could one single Example be brought from the whole Compass of History, of any one Popular Assembly, who after beginning to contend for Power, ever sate down quietly with a certain Share: Or, if one Instance could be produced of a Popular Assembly, that ever knew, or proposed, or declared what share of Power was their due; then might there be some hopes, that it were a Matter to be adjusted, by Reasonings, by Conferences, or Debates: But since all that is manifestly otherwise, I see no Course to be taken in a settled State, but a steddy constant Resolution in those to whom the rest of the Balance is entrusted, never to give way so far to Popular Clamours, as to make the least Breach in the Constitution, through which a Million of Abuses and Encroachments will certainly in time force their way.

Again, from this Deduction, it will not be difficult to gather and assign certain Marks of Popular Encroachments; by observing of which, those who hold the Balance in a State, may judge of the Degrees, and by early Remedies and Application, put a Stop to the fatal Consequences that would otherwise ensue. What those Marks are, has been at large deduced, and need not be here repeated.

Another Consequence is this: That (with all Respect for popular Assemblies be it spoke) it is hard to recollect one Folly, Infirmity or Vice, to which a single Man is subjected, and from which a Body of Commons either collective or represented can be wholly exempt. For, besides that they are composed of Men with all their Infirmities about them; they have also the ill Fortune to be generally led and influenced by the very worst among themselves; I mean, *Popular Orators*, *Tribunes*, or as they are now stiled, *Great Speakers*, *Leading Men*, and the like. From whence it comes to pass, that in their Results we have sometimes found the same Spirit of Cruelty and Revenge, of Malice and Pride; the same Blindness and Obstinacy, and Unsteadiness; the same ungovernable Rage and Anger; the same Injustice, Sophistry, and Fraud, that ever lodged in the Breast of any Individual.

Again, In all Free States the Evil to be avoided is Tyranny: That is to say, the *Summa Imperii*, or unlimited Power solely in the Hands of the *One*, the *Few*, or the *Many*. Now, we have shewn, that although most Revolutions of Government in *Greece* and *Rome* began with the Tyranny of the People, yet they generally concluded in that of a Single Person; so that an usurping Populace is its own *Dupe*; a meer Underworker, and a Purchaser in Trust for some Single Tyrant, whose State and Power they advance to their own Ruin, with as blind an Instinct, as those Worms that die with weaving magnificent Habits for Beings of a Superior Nature to their own.

CHAP. V.

Some Reflections upon the late publick Proceedings among us, and that variety of Factions into which we are still so intricately engaged, gave Occasion to this Discourse. I am not conscious that I have forced one Example, or put it into any other Light than it appeared to me, long before I had Thoughts of producing it.

I cannot conclude without adding some particular Remarks upon the present Posture of Affairs and Dispositions in this Kingdom.

The Fate of Empire is grown a common place: That all Forms of Government having been instituted by Men, must be mortal like their Authors, and have their Periods of Duration limited as well as those of private Persons, this is a Truth of vulgar Knowledge and Observation: But there are few who turn their Thoughts to examine how those Diseases in a State are bred, that hasten its End; which would however be a very useful Enquiry. For tho' we cannot prolong the Period of a Commonwealth beyond the Decree of Heaven, or the Date of its Nature, any more than Human Life beyond the Strength of the Seminal Virtue; yet, we may manage a sickly Constitution, and preserve a strong one; we may watch and prevent Accidents; we may turn off a great Blow from without, and purge away an ill Humour that is lurking within: And by these, and other such Methods, render a State long-lived, tho' not immortal. Yet some Physicians have thought, that if it were practicable to keep the several Humours of the Body, in an exact equal Balance of each with its opposite, it might be immortal; and so perhaps would a political Body, if the Balance of Power could be always held exactly even. But I doubt, this is as impossible in the Practice as the other.

It has an Appearance of Fatality, and that the Period of a State approaches, when a Concurrence of many Circumstances both within and without, unite toward its Ruin; while the whole Body of the People are either stupidly negligent, or else giving in with all their Might, to those very Practices that are working their Destruction. To see whole Bodies of Men breaking a Constitution by the very same Errors that so many have been broke before; To observe opposite Parties, who can agree in nothing else, yet firmly united in such Measures as must certainly ruin their Country; In short, to be encompass'd with the greatest Dangers from without, to be torn by many virulent Factions within; then to be secure and sensless under all this, and to make it the very least of our Concern; These and some others that might be named, appear to me to be the most likely Symptoms in a State, of a *Sickness unto Death.*

Quod procul à nobis flectat Fortuna gubernans:
Et ratio potius, quam res persuadeat ipsa. Lucr.

There are some Conjunctures wherein the Death or Dissolution of Government is more lamentable in its Consequences than it would be in others. And, I think, a State can never arrive to its Period in a more deplorable *Crisis,* than at a time when some *Prince in the Neighbourhood,* of vast Power and Ambition lies hovering like a Vulture to devour, or at least, dismember its dying Carcass; by which means it becomes only a Province or Acquisition to some mighty Monarchy, without hopes of a Resurrection.

I know very well, there is a Set of sanguine Tempers, who deride and ridicule in the Number of Fopperies all such apprehensions as these. They have it ready in their Mouths, that the People of *England* are of a Genius and Temper, never to admit Slavery among them; and they are furnish'd with a great many common places upon that Subject. But, it seems to me, that such Discoursers do reason upon short Views, and a very moderate compass of Thought. For, I think it a great Error to count upon the Genius of a Nation as a standing Argument in all Ages; since there is hardly a Spot of Ground in *Europe,* where the Inhabitants have not frequently and entirely changed their Temper and Genius. Neither can I see any Reason why the Genius of a Nation should be more fixed in the Point of Government, than in their Morals, their Learning, their Religion, their common Humour and Conversation, their Diet, and their Complexion; which do all notoriously vary almost in every Age, and may every one of them have great Effects upon Mens Notions of Government.

Since the *Norman* Conquest, the Balance of Power in *England* has often varied and sometimes been wholly overturned; the Part which the Commons had in it, *that most disputed Point in its Original, Progress and Extent*, was, by their own Confessions, but a very inconsiderable share. Generally speaking, they have been gaining ever since, tho' with frequent Interruptions, and slow Progress. The abolishing of *Villanage*, together with the Custom introduced (or permitted) among the Nobles of selling their Lands in the Reign of *Henry* the Seventh, was a mighty Addition to the Power of the Commons; yet I think a much greater happened in the time of his Successor, at the Dissolution of the Abbies. For this turned the *Clergy* wholly out of the Scale, who had so long filled it; and placed the *Commons* in their stead; who in a few Years became possessed of vast Quantities of those and other Lands, by Grant or Purchase. About the middle of Queen *Elizabeth*'s Reign, I take the Power between the Nobles and the Commons to have been in more equal Balance, than it was ever before or since. But then, or soon after, arose a Faction in *England*, which under the Name of Puritan, began to grow Popular, by molding up their new Schemes of Religion with Republican Principles in Government; and gaining upon the *Prerogative*, as well as the *Nobles*, under several Denominations for the space of about sixty Years, did at last overthrow the Constitution, and according to the usual course of such Revolutions, did introduce a Tyranny, first of the People, and then of a single Person.

In a short time after, the old Government was revived. But the Progress and Affairs for almost Thirty Years under the Reigns of two weak Princes, is a Subject of a very different Nature; when the Balance was in danger to be overturned by the Hands that held it, which was at last very seasonably prevented by the late Revolution. However, as it is the Talent of human Nature to run from one Extream to another; so, in a very few Years we have made mighty Leaps from Prerogative Heights into the

Depths of Popularity; and I doubt, to the very last degree that our Constitution will bear. It were to be wish'd, that the most August Assembly of the Commons would please to form a *Pandect* of their own Power and Privileges, to be confirmed by the entire Legislative Authority, and that in as solemn a manner (if they please) as the *Magna Charta*. But to fix one Foot of their Compass wherever they think fit, and extend the other to such terrible Lengths, without describing any Circumference at all, is to leave us and themselves in a very uncertain State, and in a sort of *Rotation*, that the Author of the *Oceana* never dreamt on. I believe the most hardy Tribune will not venture to affirm at present, that any just Fears of Encroachment are given us from the Regal Power or the *Few*: And, is it then impossible to err on the other side? How far must we proceed, or where shall we stop? *The Raging of the Sea*, and *the Madness of the People* are put together in Holy Writ; and 'tis God alone who can say to either, *Hitherto shalt thou pass, and no further*.

The Balance of Power in a limited State is of such absolute Necessity, that *Cromwell* himself, before he had perfectly confirmed his Tyranny, having some Occasions for the Appearance of a Parliament, was forced to create and erect an entire new House of Lords (such as it was) for a Counterpoise to the Commons. And indeed, considering the vileness of the Clay, I have sometimes wonder'd, that no Tribune of that Age durst ever venture to ask the *Potter*, *What dost thou make*? But it was then about the last Act of a Popular Usurpation, and *Fate* or *Cromwell* had already prepared them for that of a single Person.

I have been often amazed at the rude, passionate and mistaken Results, which have at certain Times fallen from great Assemblies both Antient and Modern, and of other Countries as well as our own. This gave me the Opinion I mentioned a while ago, That publick Conventions are liable to all the Infirmities, Follies and Vices of private Men. To which, if there be any Exception, it must be of such Assemblies who act by *universal Concert, upon Publick Principles, and for Publick Ends*; such as proceed upon Debates without *unbecoming Warmths*, or *Influence from particular Leaders and Inflamers*; such, whose Members instead of *canvassing to procure Majorities for their private Opinions, are ready to comply with general sober Results, tho' contrary to their own Sentiments.* Whatever Assemblies act by these and other Methods of the like Nature, must be allowed to be exempt from several Imperfections to which particular Men are subjected. But I think the Source of most Mistakes and Miscarriages in Matters debated by Publick Assemblies, arises from the Influence of private Persons upon great Numbers; stiled in common Phrase, *Leading Men and Parties.* And therefore, when we sometimes meet a *few Words* put together, which is called the *Vote* or *Resolution* of an Assembly, and which we cannot possibly reconcile to *Prudence* or *Publick Good*, it is most charitable to conjecture that such a Vote has been conceived, and born and bred in a private Brain, afterwards raised and supported by an obsequious Party, and then with usual Method confirmed by an *artificial* Majority. For, let us suppose five hundred Men, mixt in point of Sense and Honesty, as usually Assemblies are: And let us suppose these Men, proposing, debating, resolving, voting, according to the meer natural Motions of their own little or much Reason and Understanding; I do allow, that abundance of indigested and abortive, many pernicious and foolish Overtures would arise and float a few Minutes; but then they would die and disappear. Because, this must be said in behalf of Human kind, that common Sense and plain Reason, while Men are disengaged from acquired Opinions, will ever have some general Influence upon their Minds; whereas the species of Folly and Vice are infinite, and so different in every Individual, that they could never procure a Majority, if other Corruptions did not enter to pervert Mens Understandings, and misguide their Wills.

To describe how Parties are bred in an Assembly,

would be a Work too difficult at present, and perhaps not altogether safe. *Periculosæ plenum opus aleæ*. Whether those who are Leaders, usually arrive at that Station more by a sort of Instinct, or secret Composition of their Nature, or Influence of the Stars, than by the Possession of any great Abilities, may be a Point of much Dispute. But when the Leader is once fixed, there will never fail to be Followers. And Man is so apt to *imitate*, so much of the Nature of *Sheep*, (*Imitatores, servum Pecus*) that whoever is so bold to give the first *great Leap over the Heads of those about him*, (tho' he be the worst of the Flock) shall be quickly followed by the rest. Besides, when Parties are once formed, the Stragglers look so ridiculous, and become so insignificant, that they have no other way, but to run into the Herd, which at least will hide and protect them; and where to be much considered, requires only to be very violent.

But there is one Circumstance with Relation to Parties, which I take to be of all others most pernicious in a State; and I would be glad any Partisan would help me to a tolerable Reason, that because *Clodius* and *Curio* happen to agree with me in a few singular Notions, I must therefore blindly follow them in all: Or, to state it at best, that because *Bibulus* the *Party-man* is persuaded that *Clodius* and *Curio* do really propose the Good of their Country as their chief End; therefore *Bibulus* shall be wholly guided and governed by them, in the Means and Measures towards it. Is it enough for *Bibulus* and the rest of the Herd to say without further examining, *I am of the side with* Clodius, *or I vote with* Curio? Are these proper Methods to form and make up what they think fit to call the *united Wisdom of the Nation*? Is it not possible, that upon some Occasions *Clodius* may be bold and insolent, born away by his Passion, malicious and revengeful; that *Curio* may be corrupt and expose to sale his Tongue or his Pen. I conceive it far below the Dignity both of Human Nature, and Human Reason, to be engaged in any Party, the most plausible soever, upon such servile Conditions.

This Influence of *One* upon *Many*, which seems to be as great in a People *Represented*, as it was of old in the Commons *Collective*, together with the Consequences it has had upon the Legislature; has given me frequent Occasion to reflect upon what *Diodorus* tells us of one *Charondas*, a Lawgiver to the *Sybarites*, an antient People of *Italy*; who was so averse to all Innovation, especially when it was to proceed from particular Persons: And I suppose, that he might put it out of the Power of Men fond of their own Notions, to disturb the Constitution at their Pleasures by advancing private Schemes; that he provided a Statute, that whoever proposed any Alteration to be made, should step out, and do it with a Rope about his Neck: If the Matter proposed, were generally approved, then it should pass into a Law; if it went in the Negative, the Proposer to be immediately *hang'd*. Great Ministers may talk of what Projects they please; but I am deceived, if a more effectual one could ever be found for *taking off* (as the present Phrase is) those hot, unquiet Spirits, who disturb Assemblies, and obstruct Publick Affairs, by gratifying their Pride, their Malice, their Ambition, or their Avarice.

Those who in a late Reign began the Distinction between the *Personal* and *Politick* Capacity, seem to have had Reason, if they judged of Princes by themselves; for, I think, there is hardly to be found thro' all Nature, a greater Difference between two Things, than there is between a Representing Commoner in the Function of his Publick Calling, and the same Person, when he acts in the common Offices of Life. Here, he allows himself to be upon a Level with the rest of Mortals: Here, he follows his own Reason, and his own Way; and rather affects a Singularity in his Actions and Thoughts, than servilely to copy either from the wisest of his Neighbours. In short, here his Folly, and his Wisdom, his Reason, and his Passions, are all of his own Growth, not the Eccho or Infusion of other Men. But when he is got near the Walls of his Assembly, he assumes and affects an entire Set of very different Airs; he conceives himself a Being of a Superiour Nature to those *without*, and acting in a Sphere where the vulgar Methods for the Conduct of Human Life can be of no Use. He is listed in a Party where he neither knows the Temper, nor Designs, nor perhaps the Person of his Leader; but whose Opinions he follows and maintains with a Zeal and Faith as violent, as a young Scholar does those of a Philosopher, whose Sect he is taught to profess. He has neither Opinions, nor Thoughts, nor Actions, nor Talk, that he can call his own, but all conveyed to him by his Leader, as Wind is thro' an Organ. The Nourishment he receives has been not only *chewed*, but *digested* before it comes into his Mouth. Thus instructed, he follows the *Party* right or wrong thro' all its Sentiments, and acquires a Courage and Stiffness of Opinion not at all congenial with him.

This encourages me to hope, that during this lucid Interval, the Members retired to their Homes, may suspend a while their *acquired Complexions*, and taught by the Calmness of the Scene and the Season, reassume the native sedateness of their Temper. If this should be so, it would be wise in them, as individual and private Mortals, to look back a little upon the Storms they have *raised*, as well as those they have *escaped*: To reflect, that they have been Authors of a new and wonderful Thing in *England*, which is, for a House of Commons to lose the universal Favour of the Numbers they represent; To observe, how those whom they thought fit to persecute for Righteousness sake, have been openly caress'd by the People; and to remember how themselves sat in fear of their Persons from popular Rage. Now, if they would know the Secret of all this unpresidented Proceeding in their Masters; they must not impute it to their Freedom in Debate, or declaring their Opinions; but to that unparliamentary Abuse of setting Individuals upon their Shoulders, who were hated by God and Man. For, it seems, the Mass of the People, in such Conjunctures as this, have opened their Eyes, and will not endure to be governed by *Clodius* and *Curio* at the

Head of their *Myrmidons*, tho' these be ever so numerous, and composed of their own Representatives.

This Aversion of the People to the late Proceedings of the Commons, is an Accident, that if it last a while, might be improved to good Uses for setting the Balance of Power a little more upon an Equality, than their late Measures seem to promise or admit. This Accident may be imputed to two Causes. The first, is an universal Fear and Apprehension of the Greatness and Power of *France*, whereof the People in general seem to be very much and justly possess'd, and therefore cannot but resent to see it in so critical a Juncture, wholly laid aside by their Ministers, the Commons. The other Cause, is a great Love and Sense of Gratitude in the People towards their present King, grounded upon a long Opinion and Sense of his Merit, as well as Concessions to all their reasonable Desires; so that it is for some time they have begun to say, and to fetch Instances where he has in many things been hardly used. How long these Humours may last, (for Passions are momentary, and especially those of a Multitude) or what Consequences they may produce, a little time may discover. But whenever it comes to pass, that a popular Assembly, free from such obstructions, and already possess'd of more Power, than an equal Balance will allow, shall continue to think they have not enough, but by cramping the Hand that holds the Balance, and by Impeachments or Dissensions with the Nobles, endeavour still for more; I cannot possibly see in the common course of things, how the same Causes can produce different Effects and Consequences among us, than they did in *Greece* and *Rome*.

There is one thing I must needs add, tho' I reckon it will appear to many as a very unreasonable Paradox. When the Act Passed some years ago against Bribing of Elections; I remember to have said upon occasion, to some Persons of both Houses, that we should be very much deceived in the Consequences of that Act: And upon some Discourse of the Conveniences of it, and the contrary (which will admit Reasoning enough) they seem'd to be of the same Opinion. It has appear'd since, that our Conjectures were right: For I think the late Parliament was the first-fruits of that Act; the Proceedings whereof, as well as of the present, have been such, as to make many Persons wish that things were upon the old Foot in that matter. Whether it be that so great a Reformation was too many Degrees beyond so corrupt an Age as this; or that according to the present turn and disposition of Men in our Nation, it were a less abuse to Bribe Elections, than leave them to the discretion of the Chusers. This at least was *Cato*'s Opinion, when things in *Rome* were at a Crisis, much resembling ours; who is recorded to have gone about with great Industry, dealing Mony among the People to favour *Pompey* (as I remember) upon a certain Election in opposition to *Cæsar*; And he excused himself in it upon the necessities of the occasion, and the corruptions of the People; an Action that might well have excus'd *Cicero*'s censure of him, that he reasoned and acted, *tanquam in Republica Platonis, non in fæce Romuli.* However it be, 'tis certain that the Talents which qualifie a Man for the Service of his Country in Parliament, are very different from those which give him a dexterity at making his court to the People; and do not often meet in the same subject. Then for the moral part, the difference is inconsiderable; and whoever practices upon the Weakness and Vanity of the People, is guilty of an immoral action as much as if he did it upon their Avarice. Besides, the two Trees may be judged by their Fruits. The former produces a set of popular Men, fond of their own Merits and Abilities, their Opinions, and their Eloquence; whereas the bribing of Elections seems to be at worst, but an ill means of keeping things upon the old foot, by leaving the defence of our Properties, chiefly in the hands of those who will be the greatest sufferers, whenever they are endangered. It is easie to observe in the late and present Parliament, that several Boroughs and some Counties have been represented by Persons, who little thought to have ever had such hopes before: And how far this may proceed, when such a Way is lay'd open for the Exercise and Encouragement of popular Arts, one may best judge from the Consequences that the same Causes produced both in *Athens* and *Rome*. For, let Speculative Men Reason, or rather Refine as they please; it ever will be true among us, that as long as men engage in the Publick service upon private Ends, and whilst all Pretences to a Sincere *Roman* Love of our Country, are lookt upon as an Affectation, a Foppery, or a Disguise; (which has been a good while our Case, and is likely to continue so;) it will be safer to trust our Property and Constitution in the hands of such, who have pay'd for their Elections, than of those who have obtained them by servile Flatteries of the People.

FINIS.

NOTES

[1] Allen cites Sir William Temple, *Miscellanea*, 1680, p. 90: 'the frequent tumults, seditions, and alterations in the Commonwealths of *Athens* and *Rome*.' Cf. 'Dissentions between the *Nobles* and *Commons*, with the Consequences of them, in *Greece* and *Rome*' (I. 312–13).

[2] Lucretius, *De rerum natura*, ii. 1042–3.

CHAPTER I

l. 4. Cf. Temple, *Miscellanea*, 1680, p. 54: '*Power . . . is always in those that are governed*.' This was one of the few issues in 1701 on which Whig and Tory could agree.

l. 16. The Tories denied that the power, once it was delegated, remained with the people; *England's Enemies Exposed*, 2d ed., 1701, p. 30: 'the Power of Electing Members to serve in Parliament, is the sole Right of the Electors; but as soon as they have made their Choice . . . the Power and Rights of the Electors devolves intirely upon their Representatives. . . . [The electors] have no Power to compel their Members to Vote or Act . . . tho' the whole Country . . . were of a contrary Opinion to that of their Representatives.'

l. 17. Cf. Aristotle, *Politica*, 1279a: 'the government, which is the supreme authority in states, must be in the hands of one, or of a few, or of the many'; Polybius, vi. 4; Locke, *Two Treatises of Government*, 1690, p. 351.

l. 23. On the issue of the *origins* of political power, on which Temple and Locke were in total disagreement, Swift pointedly refuses to commit himself.

l. 25. The issue of the *division* of powers was one other on which Whig and Tory were agreed. Although Hobbes had insisted that the *summum imperium* was indivisible, the Tories now agreed with Swift that in a 'Mixt Government . . . the States (or *Tres Ordinis Regni*) are so mixt, as the Soveraignty is joyntly in them all . . . as in [a] Corporation' (J. H., *Letters to Parliament-Men in Reference to Some Proceedings in The House of Commons During the Last Session*, [December]1701, p. 21).

l. 30. This sentence introduces the 'way of Allegory'. 'One eminent Spirit' is William III; the two other 'Powers' are, of course, the two Houses of Parliament. 'After a sort' is probably ironical. William's 'minding Affairs so little' is a constant complaint of Bishop Burnet. In 1689 when Halifax urged the new King to attend debates in the House of Lords, he noted that William 'was extreamely averse from coming to the house, Saying with some anger, that hee had no time for it' (*The Life and Letters of Sir George Savile, Bart., First Marquis of Halifax*, ed. H. C. Foxcroft, 2 vols., 1898, ii. 244).

l. 80. Cf. *The History of the Four Last Years of the Queen*: 'where the Prince holds the Balance between Two great Powers, the Nobility and People; It is of the very nature of his Office to remove from One Scale into Another; or sometimes put his own Weight into the lightest, so to bring both to an Equilibrium' (*Prose*, vii. 20–21).

l. 95. The Tories in general used the word 'tyranny' in the limited sense in which James Harrington had defined it in *The Rota*: 'The Government of one against the Balance, is Tyranny' (*The Rota: Or, A Model of a Free-state, or Equall Commonwealth: Once Proposed and Debated in Brief, and to be Again More at Large Proposed*, 1660, p. 3), but Swift is about to elaborate a new concept, namely that there is no safety in numbers. More particularly it was Charles Davenant who had 'grosly' misrepresented William's ambition and insinuated that tyranny could be imposed only by '*One*', not by 'the *Few*, or the *Many*': 'Princes . . . are never satisfied till they can grasp the whole' (*Essays Upon I. The Ballance of Power*, [March] 1701, sig. R2[v]–R3[r]).

l. 100. Cf. Locke, *Two Treatises of Government*, 1690, pp. 422–3: ''Tis a Mistake, to think this Fault [tyranny] is proper only to Monarchies, other Forms of Government are liable to it, as well as that: for where-ever the Power, that is put in any hands, for the Government of the People, and the Preservation of their Properties, is applied to other ends . . . it presently becomes Tyranny, whether those, that thus use it, are one or many. Thus we read of the Thirty Tyrants at *Athens*, as well as one at *Syracuse*; and the intolerable Dominion of the *Decemviri* at *Rome*, was nothing better.' The Thirty Tyrants and the Decemviri are among the examples which Swift cites below.

l. 115. *Dionys, Halicarn. lib.* 10 [Swift's marginal note]. Actually the paragraph abridges Dionysius, x. 54–xi. 46. The 'Lady of great Virtue' is Verginia and her would-be abductor is the decemvir Appius Claudius. The earlier rape of Lucretia by Sextus Tarquinius, which 'gave Occasion to the Expulsion of the Regal Power', is recounted in Dionysius, iv. 64–67.

l. 120. Plutarch, *Cleomenes*, x. 2–3. Cf. Sir Thomas North's translation: 'the kings being alwaies employed in that warre, whereby they could not attend the affairs of the common wealth at home, did choose certaine of their frendes to sit in iudgement in their steades, to determine controversies of lawe: which were called Ephores, and did governe long time as the kinges ministers, howbeit that afterwards, by litle and litle, they tooke apon them absolute government by them selves . . . licentiously abusing their authoritie' (*The Lives of the Noble Grecians and Romanes, Compared . . .: Translated . . . by Thomas North*, 1579, p. 860).

l. 126. *Thucid. lib.* 8 [67–68, 82, 92–95] [Swift's marginal note].

l. 135. *Xenoph. de Rebus Graec.* l[ib]. *2.* [iii. 1–22] [Swift's marginal note].

l. 144. [Xenophon,] *Memorab. lib. 3.* [vi. 14] [Swift's marginal note].

l. 151. *Polyb. Frag. lib. 6.* [51] [Swift's marginal note]. Swift translates Polybius's 'oligarchia' (vi. 4)—'dominatum . . . paucorum' in the Latin version of Casaubon—as '*Oligarchy*, or Tyranny of the *Few*'. But he renders Polybius's 'ochlocracia'—'dominatum . . . turbae vulgaris' in the Latin—more consistently than the Latin, and very pointedly, as '*Dominatio Plebis*, or *Tyranny of the Commons*' (Polybius, *Historiae*, ed. Isaac Casaubon, Paris, 1609, p. 452).

l. 152. [Diodorus Siculus,] *lib. 20.* [10] [Swift's marginal note]. Diodorus nowhere states that the murder of generals was an established custom among the Carthaginians. What he does say is that 'they bring false charges against them through envy and load them with fines', but George Booth translated the latter clause 'put them to death', and Swift, whether wittingly or not, repeats Booth's error (Diodorus, *The Historical Library . . . Made English, By G. Booth*, 2 vols., 1700, ii. 661).

l. 166. [Diodorus Siculus,] *lib. 15.* [58] [Swift's marginal note]. The phraseology may have been influenced by George Booth's translation: '*Argos* was Govern'd by a Democracy; the Orators, and those that affected Popularity, stirr'd up the Mob . . . so that there were Executed above Sixteen hundred of the greatest and most powerful Men of the City: Neither were the Orators themselves spar'd; for when they slack'd in the Prosecution of Calumnies . . . the People concluded that they had deserted their Cause, which put them into such a ferment of Rage and Fury, that they kill'd all the Orators that were then in the City; which seem'd to be Executed upon them by . . . some revenging Deity, as a reward of their Villanies' (Diodorus, *The Historical Library . . . Made English, By G. Booth*, 2 vols., 1700, ii. 433). These lines state the major cautionary theme of the *Discourse*. Cf. III. 266 *n*.

l. 171. Swift is contradicting Davenant: 'these Swarms from the North . . . chang'd every thing, introducing . . . new Customs, other Manners, Languages, different ways of making War, new Laws, and new Forms of Government. . . . And whoever looks into the Antient Constitutions of *England*, *France*, *Spain*, *Denmark* and *Sweeden*, will find, that all these Nations, had one and the same Form of Government; and tho' they might very in some Circumstances, yet they all agreed in certain Fundamentals, which were, That the People should have their Rights and Priviledges; That the Nobles, or Men of Chief Rank, should have some Participation of Power, and That the Regal Authority should be limited by Laws' (*A Discourse upon Grants and Resumptions*, [November 1699, but dated] 1700, pp. 91–92). Cf. *Essays Upon I. The Ballance of Power*, [March] 1701, p. 236.

l. 179. [Polybius,] *Frag. lib. 6.* [3] [Swift's marginal note]. The Latin phrases derive from Casaubon's translation: 'tres Rerumpublicarum formas enumerent; quarum unam vocant regnum, alteram optimatium principatum, tertiam populi imperium . . . quum eam Rempublicam censeri debere optimam liquidò constet, quae ex omnibus illis quas diximus formis sit composita' (Polybius, *Historiae*, ed. Isaac Casaubon, Paris, 1609, pp. 451–2).

l. 189. [Polybius, vi. 10] [Swift's marginal note, Id. ib.]: 'As for the *Romans*, tho they have arriv'd at the same End, in the establishing of their Commonwealth, they have not done it by the Force of *Reason* and *Discourse*' (*The History . . . Translated by Sir H*[*enry*] *S*[*heeres*], 2nd ed., 3 vols. in 2, 1698, iii. 15–16).

l. 192. Polybius, vi. 51.

l. 201. The irony is directed at Davenant's insistence that his writings, which were extremely inflammatory and divisive in their tendency, were undertaken solely as a public service: 'This Diabolical Practice' had already been noticed (*Animadversions on a Late Factious Book, Entitled, Essays upon I. The Ballance of Power*, [May] 1701, p. 13).

l. 204. Swift probably alludes to the Commons' arrest and imprisonment of the five Kentish Petitioners in May 1701. A Whig broadside, *Some Queries, which may deserve Consideration*, [August] 1701, referring to the same event, asks very pointedly 'Whether, as the Case stands, the *Habeas Corpus* Act be a sufficient Security for the Liberty of the Subject? And whether Arbitrary Power be not less terrible in the Hands of One, than of Many; since in the first Case Shame or Pity may sometimes prevail, but never in the other?' Cf. Temple, *Miscellanea*, 1680, pp. 49–50: 'popular tumults have worse effects upon common safety than the rankest Tyranny.'

l. 215. The clearest illustration of the bitter partisan conflict over the issue of 'the Limits of Power' occurred in June 1701. The Lords concluded a routine message to the Commons by observing that the best way to preserve good correspondence between the Houses was 'for neither of the two Houses to exceed those limits which the law and custom of Parliaments had already established'. Twenty-two lords, including all the Tory ministers, promptly protested, 'Because we know not that the law and custom of Parliaments have established any certain limits' (J. E. Thorold Rogers, *The Protests of the Lords*, 3 vols., Oxford, 1875, i. 153); cf. V. 124.

l. 221. Swift's conclusion, that contentions between the legislative branches of a government invariably terminate, by a kind of historical law, in dictatorship, had already been formulated by Temple: 'Authority contracting it self (as it seems naturally to do till it ends in a point or single Person)' (*Miscellanea*, 1680, p. 75).

l. 226. '*The Power of Impeachments* therefore in the Commons, seems to be an *Original Inherent Right in the People of* England, *reserv'd to them in the first Institution of the Government by the Law of Nature, and Self-preservation, for the Common Security of their Just Rights and Liberties*' ([Sir

Humphrey Mackworth,] *A Vindication of the Rights of the Commons of England*, [August] 1701, p. 32).

l. 229. Among the unprecedented or lapsed powers which the House of Commons exercised or demanded during the impeachment proceedings were the following: (1) the right to petition the King to remove from his presence and Council for ever the four Lords Partitioners before they were tried; (2) the right to imprison the five Kentish petitioners in the Gate House without bail; (3) the right to demand that the accused lords give 'sufficient security to abide the Judgment of the House of Lords'; (4) the right to appoint the day for the trial; (5) the right to demand that at their trials the accused lords sit outside the Bar, as criminals; (6) the right to exclude the accused lords from sitting as Judges in each other's trials; (7) the right to demand a committee of both Houses to determine trial procedure. It is difficult not to suspect, in all these complex parliamentary manœuvres, the hand of Robert Harley, whose 'unparalled'd Ability in Parliamentary Affairs' is attested by John Toland (*Anglia Libera*, [June] 1701, p. 50).

l. 237. The power of Parliament was traditionally assumed to be 'double': legislative and declarative (of its own rights and privileges). The legislative power, it was agreed, had 'no bounds', but the declarative power was thought to be limited by the common law. Thus Sir Heneage Finch, at the trial of Clarendon in 1667, maintained 'tho' I know not what the *Legislative* power of a parliament cannot do, yet it is not in the power of the Parliament, King, Lords, nor Commons to declare any thing to be Treason, which is not in the Common-Law a felony before' (*The Proceedings in the House of Commons Touching the Impeachment of Edward Late Earl of Clarendon*, [September] 1700, p. 9). Now, however, by addressing the King to remove the accused Whig lords from his presence and Council before they were tried, the Commons was in effect *declaring* them to be guilty. 'Cette conduite irregulière et emportée', as Bonet called it, seemed to usurp both the King's power of choosing his ministers and the Lords' power of trying ministers upon impeachment charges. Yet the Tory pamphleteers were in fact urging the Commons to wield 'the whole Power' ([James Drake,] *The History of the Last Parliament*, 1702, p. 141).

l. 242. The reference is to the manœuvre known as 'tacking', by which the House of Commons enforced enactment of legislation by attaching it to supply bills. The Bill creating the Commission for taking an Account of the forfeited Estates in Ireland in April 1699, the Resumption Bill vesting title to the forfeited estates in thirteen trustees in April 1700, and the Bill empowering the trustees to sell the resumed estates in April 1701, were all tacked to supply bills.

l. 249. Davenant maintained that the very size and importance of the forfeited estates in Ireland had created new responsibilities, which in turn required new powers, for the House of Commons. He argued that 'the

People' had the power to divert the confiscated estates into the public treasury because 'the Ballance of Property, which is the Ballance of Power,' had fallen into their hands (*Essays upon I. The Ballance of Power*, [March] 1701, pp. 234–5). According to John Toland, it was Sir James Harrington who first propounded this 'most dangerous Tenet' which the Tories had embraced: 'THAT *Empire follows the Balance of Property*, whether lodg'd in one, in a few, or in many hands, he was the first that ever made out; and is a noble Discovery' (*The Oceana of James Harrington, Esq; And His Other Works . . . with an Exact Account of His Life Prefix'd by J. Toland*, [August] 1700, p. xviii).

l. 254. Although the Lords Partitioners were acquitted in June 1701, Poussin reported on 7 July: 'Cette affaire, loin d'être finie, sera . . . reprise par les communes à l'ouverture de la nouvelle session, même avec plus de chaleur qu'elles n'en ont euë dans la derniere' (P.R.O. Transcripts, 3 (France) 189, f. 5^{v}). In September Vernon warned the King, who was at Loo, that 'it looks as if great violence were intended next Sessions and that nothing would satisfy but the utter subduing of those they have sett themselves against' (B.M. Add. MS. 40775, vol. v, f. 116).

l. 256. This is another reference to the Commons' address to the King to remove the Lords Partitioners from his presence and Council before they were tried. See p. 49, above, and I. 237 *n.*

l. 266. Herodotus, i. 29; cf. Aristotle, *Constitution of Athens*, 11–12; Plutarch, *Solon*, 25.

l. 284. Cf. Temple, *Miscellanea, The Third Part*, [October] 1701, pp. 13–14: 'No civil or politick Constitutions, can be perfect or secure, whilst they are composed of Men, that are for the most part Passionate, Interessed, Unjust, or Unthinking, but generally and naturally, Restless, and Unquiet; Discontented with the Present, and what they have, Raving after the Future, or something they want, and thereby ever disposed and desirous to change.'

CHAPTER II

l. 12. Thucydides, i. 2.

l. 19. Plutarch, *Theseus*, 24, 35.

l. 32. Plutarch, *Solon*, 1, 13, 15, 18–19. Swift's reservation of a share of the *summum imperium* for 'the People collective' derives not from classical sources but from Locke: 'there remains still in the People a Supream Power to remove or alter the Legislative, when they find the Legislative act contrary to the trust reposed in them' (*Two Treatises of Government*, 1690, pp. 369–70). This was violently opposed by the Tories; cf. I. 16 *n.*

l. 37. *Herodot.* lib. 1. [59] [Swift's marginal note]; cf. Aristotle, *Politica*, 1273^{b}–4^{a}.

l. 92. Of the four lords impeached for high crimes and misdemeanors in 1701, none was specifically accused of 'Bribery'. 'Arbitrary Proceedings' applies to Somers; Article 14 of the charges against him claimed that he had 'made divers arbitrary and illegal Orders, in Subversion of the Laws and Statutes of this Realm . . .; assuming thereby to himself an arbitrary and illegal Power' (*C.J.* xiii. 550). Somers, Montagu, and Russell were all accused of embezzlement in some form. (No articles were ever presented against Portland.) 'Ill Conduct at Sea' refers specifically to Russell. Article 8 of the charges against him alleged that despite 'many Opportunities of taking or destroying the Ships belonging to the *French* King, the said Earl . . . did suffer and permit the said Ships to return safe into their own Harbours [following Russell's victory off La Hougue in May 1692]' (*C.J.* xiii. 521).

l. 96. Miltiades is Edward Russell, Commander-in-chief of the Fleet, 1st Lord of the Admiralty, and Treasurer of the Navy, during the War of the League of Augsburg. His 'famous Victory' off La Hougue in May 1692 was one of the few successes of this war. Russell's alleged failure to exploit this victory was made the subject of a parliamentary inquiry and, although absolved of any blame by the House of Commons, he was forced temporarily to resign his command. When he was impeached in April 1701 this old charge became Article 8 in the proceedings against him. The source of the classical analogue is Cornelius Nepos, *Miltiades*, 4, 7.

l. 108. Aristides is John Somers, Baron Somers of Evesham. 'The mighty Service he had done his Country' included defending the Seven Bishops in 1688 and serving as manager of the Commons' committee which drafted the Declaration of Rights in February 1689. He was Lord Chancellor of England from April 1697 to April 1700. He was also president of the Royal Society (1699–1704), and, as Hawkesworth has noted (iii. 23), 'the general patron of the literati'. His major offence, as Sunderland told the King, was that he was 'the life, the soul, and the spirit of his party' (*Miscellaneous State Papers*, ed. Philip Yorke Hardwicke, 2 vols., 1778, ii. 446). He was impeached on 14 Apr. 1701. The source of the classical analogue is Plutarch, *Aristides*, 6–8.

l. 126. Themistocles also is Edward Russell, whose father was a younger son of Francis Russell, 4th Earl of Bedford. Before his elevation to the peerage as Earl of Orford in May 1697 he served as M.P. for Launceston, Portsmouth, and Cambridgeshire successively. Hawkesworth (ii. 39) was the first to note that for two of the impeached lords Swift uses more than one classical analogue (cf. IV. 66 *n.*). Actually Swift uses Miltiades, Themistocles, and Alcibiades for Russell; Pericles and Alcibiades for Montagu. Sir Walter Scott (iii. 257) was the first to supply a reason for this anomaly: 'six instances are selected from ancient history, to illustrate the four impeachments. . . . There was, perhaps, danger in making the circumstances tally very closely, for the temper of the Commons was for the time too hot to endure argument.' Russell's 'ungovernable temper' was noted even by his friends. After his 'famous Naval Victory' at La Hougue in May 1692 he was 'banished' (relieved of his command), not 'for five Years', but for ten months (January–November 1693). 'Invitations' from 'the *Persian* Court' refers to a bribe of £20,000 which Louis XIV is alleged to have offered Russell before La Hougue to engage him not to fight but to manœuvre. When Russell reported this to the King, William told him to 'Take the money, and beat them' (Mark Noble, *A Biographical History of England*, 3 vols., 1806, i. 189–90). The source of the classical analogue is Plutarch, *Themistocles*, 1, 10–15, 22–24, 31.

l. 140. Pericles is Charles Montagu. Pericles was never impeached, but 'Thucydides and his party kept denouncing [him] for playing fast and loose with the public moneys and annihilating the revenues' (Plutarch, *Pericles*, 14). Pericles diverted public funds into the 'construction of sacred edifices', 'all fully completed in the heyday of a single administration' (ibid. 12–13). Montagu's 'sacred edifices', all fully completed in the hey-day of the Whig junto, were designed to augment, rather than to annihilate, the public revenues. They included the National Debt, the Bank of England, recoinage of the national currency, Exchequer Bills, and a sinking fund known as the General Mortgage. In the second sentence Swift is paraphrasing a resolution of the House of Commons of 16 Feb. 1698. On this occasion the House discovered grants of forfeited lands in Ireland amounting to some £11,000 to one Thomas Railton, who, it was alleged, was a nominee for Charles Montagu. Montagu admitted that the grant had been made for his benefit, and after a long debate a motion that he should withdraw was defeated, 209–97. Before adjournment the house voted a resolution 'That the Honourable *Charles Mountague* Esquire, Chancellor of the Exchequer, for his good Services to this Government, does deserve his Majesty's Favour' (*C.J.* xii. 116). For these services Montagu was raised to the peerage as Baron Halifax of Halifax in December 1700. The source of the classical analogue is Plutarch, *Pericles*, 8–9, 14, 23.

l. 152. 'The cases of Miltiades and Themistocles seem to apply to the Earl of Orford; those of Pericles and Alcibiades to Halifax' (Scott, iii. 257). Actually the case of Alcibiades suggests both Russell and Montagu. Montagu, the friend of Matthew Prior, had indeed been 'noted for . . . Frolicks and Excursions', but it was Russell who was 'recalled . . . and made chief Commander at Sea' in November 1693; cf. II. 126 *n*. The source of the classical analogue is Plutarch, *Alcibiades*, 18–20, 23–27, 33, 35–39.

l. 176. The reference is to two disasters of William's war which occurred during the time of Russell's banishment. In June 1693 a convoy of merchant ships was surprised by the French fleet in Lagos Bay. About 100 Dutch and English vessels worth £1,500,000 were lost and 'the disgrace of it', as Burnet (ii. 116) observed, 'was visible to the whole World'. In another surprise attack only a month later William's troops deployed south of Louvain were routed and suffered 16,000 casualties. The source of the classical analogue is Plutarch, *Nicias*, 15–30.

l. 181. Within a week after his return to England, following the disasters of June–July 1693, William dismissed Nottingham and 'recalled' Russell as 'vice admiral of England, captain general of the narrow seas, and admiral of their majesties fleet' (Luttrell, iii. 221, 223). This action did not, however, answer William's expectations. After the disastrous failure of 'his Lieutenant', Lord Berkeley of Stratton, in an attack on Brest in May 1694 which he opposed, Russell had no more successes at sea and was again forced to resign in December 1697 (John Ehrman, *The Navy in the War of William III*, Cambridge, 1953, pp. 512–16).

l. 201. It was Demosthenes who coined the *word* 'Philippize' (*De Corona*, 176), but it was Plutarch who added to the meaning the insinuation of bribery (*Demosthenes*, 19–20). In the present context, to 'Philippize' is to write or speak as one was paid to do with French gold (see pp. 73–79 above).

l. 206. Phocion is Willem Bentinck, who commanded a regiment of Dutch horse guards during William's march from Tor Bay to London and was created Earl of Portland in April 1689. His 'Skill at Negotiation' was exerted in the Treaties of Partition (1698 and 1700). He was open to attack, therefore, both as a foreigner and as the supposed author of treaties which the Tories claimed had made dangerous and irresponsible concessions to the French (John Tutchin, *The Foreigners*, 1700, p. 10; *Some Reply to a Letter Pretended to be Writ to a Member of Parliament in the Country in Defence of the Treaty of Partition*, [March] 1701, p. 9; P.R.O. Transcripts, 3 (France) 187, f. 77^{v}). He was accordingly impeached on All Fool's Day in 1701, but no articles against him were ever exhibited. The sources of the classical analogue are Plutarch, *Phocion*, 17, 26–27, 32–35 and Diodorus, xviii. 18, 56.

l. 215. Polyperchon suggests John Churchill, Earl of Marlborough, whose 'Hatred to *Phocion* [Portland]' dates back to Portland's discovery of the Jacobite 'plot' for which Marlborough was stripped of his military command and sent to the Tower in May 1692. In June 1698, however, Marlborough was restored to the Privy Council and to his military honours, and appointed 'Governor' to the 9-year-old Duke of Gloucester, heir-apparent to his mother, the Princess Anne. In June 1701 Marlborough joined the Tory minority in the House of Lords in violent protests against dismissing the impeachment charges against Portland and the Whig junto. In the same month he was appointed commander-in-chief of the allied forces in Holland. Bonet reports that he was regarded 'comme un Espion que les Tories ont voulu avoir en Hollande pour les avertir de tout ce qui se passera' (B.M. Add. MS. 30000E, f. 251^{v}, 10 June 1701). The source of the classical analogue is Plutarch, *Phocion*, 32, but the detail, '*Polyperchon* . . . restored those whom *Phocion* had banished', is not in Plutarch. Plutarch says merely: 'Polyperchon was scheming to dispose the city in his own interests and had no hope of succeeding unless Phocion was banished; he was sure moreover that Phocion would be banished if the disenfranchised citizens overwhelmed the administration and the tribunal was again at the mercy of demagogues and public informers.' Diodorus, however, quotes Polyperchon's edict, which says specifically 'we restore those who have been exiled or banished' (xviii. 56). It seems unlikely, therefore, that Swift would introduce a detail from Diodorus into an account which is mainly derived from Plutarch unless he attached some particular significance to this detail. And, while its exact significance may be impossible to recapture now, the general import is clear enough to suggest the conclusion that Swift doubted Marlborough's loyalty to the Revolution Settlement nine years before he began the attacks in the *Examiner*. The name Polyperchon was familiar to many of Swift's readers as one of the conspirators against Alexander in Nathaniel Lee's tragedy, *The Rival Queens*.

l. 232. Cf. I. 226 *n*. Despite this claim so 'confidently' made and repeatedly acknowledged by the House of Lords (*L.J.* xvi. 717, 759; *C.J.* xiii. 637), the right of impeachment was by no means 'inherent' in the House of Commons. The first case was tried in 1376. From 1450 to 1621 there were no impeachments at all (I. Naamani-Tarkow, *Political Science Quarterly*, lviii [1943], 558–9).

l. 238. [Diodorus Siculus,] *18*. [18] [Swift's marginal note].

l. 269. The 'two Men' are Laurence Hyde, Earl of Rochester, Lord Lieutenant of Ireland, and Sidney Godolphin, Lord Godolphin, 1st Lord of the Treasury, who were 'les principaux chefs' of the Tory ministry of 1700–1 (B.M. Add. MS. 17667UU, f. 364^{v}). In a debate of March 1701 Rochester had said that '"All Men ought to speak respectfully of Crown'd Heads," and ... He was seconded in this Complement to the *French* King by another Earl, who said, "The King of *France* was not only to be respected, but to be feared"' (Oldmixon, p. 223). The classical analogue is Polybius, v. 106: 'giving themselves up to the Counsels and Conduct of *Euryclidas* and *Micyon*, and secluding themselves from the Society of the other Cities of *Greece*; what Flatteries, what Decrees of Honours and Praise (led by the Weakness of their Governours) did [the Athenians] heap on the Neighbouring Kings' (Polybius, *The History . . . Translated by Sir H*[*enry*] *S*[*heeres*], 2nd ed., 3 vols. in 2, 1698, ii. 298).

l. 279. *Polyb.* [ii. 41–71, viii. 1, x. 21, xi. 9] [Swift's marginal note].

CHAPTER III

l. 11. *Dionys. Halica.* [Swift's marginal note]. Dionysius nowhere states explicitly that prehistoric Italy was divided into 'petty Commonwealths' similar to Greek city-states. The source of this passage is Temple: '*Greece, Italy*, and *Sicily*, were all divided into small Commonwealths, till swallowed up and made Provinces by that mighty one of *Rome*' (*Miscellanea*, 1680, p. 48).

l. 33. Swift is again contradicting Davenant, who maintained that the greatest threat to the *existing* balance of power in England lay in the encroachment of the Crown upon the rights of the Commons (*Essays upon I. The Ballance of Power*, [March] 1701, p. 100). Swift's contention that the danger lay in the encroachment of the Commons upon the power of King and Lords, besides being historically true, was also, of course, shared by the peers. L'Hermitage reported that 'Il ÿ a longtems que les seigneurs se plaignent, que les communes empietent tous les jours sur leurs prerogatives' (B.M. Add. MS. 17677UU, f. 202).

l. 37. Cf. Dionysius, i. 5: 'Rome . . . produced infinite examples of virtue in men whose superiors, whether for piety or for justice or for life-long self-control or for warlike valour, no city, either Greek or barbarian, has ever produced.' Temple also calls the Romans 'the Noblest Nation that appears upon any Record of Story' (*Miscellanea, The Second Part*, 1690, Essay I, p. 58).

l. 47. Swift reorients the allegory in a Roman setting by suggesting parallels between augury and the rule of English kings 'by the grace of God', and between the Roman *patres* and 'the Barons of *England* . . . after the Conquest'. The classical source is Dionysius, ii. 4–6, 8–10.

l. 54. Goldsmith recalled, rather wistfully, that 'When the great Somers was at the helm, patronage was fashionable among our nobility' (*An Enquiry into the Present State of Polite Learning*, 1759, p. 129).

l. 66. Before June 1701 the conduct of foreign affairs was the exclusive prerogative of the King. Tindal (iv. 223–4) states the case as follows: 'It is certain, that, by our Constitution, all foreign negotiations were trusted intirely to the Crown: That the King was under no obligation by law to communicate such secrets to his Council, or to hear, much less was he obliged to follow, their advice.' Davenant, however, had argued that 'Resolutions of War or Peace are part of the Executive Power' which the King wields 'in trust for the Whole', not by personal prerogative (*Essays upon I. The Ballance of Power*, [March] 1701, pp. 206–7). Defending royal prerogative, Swift points out that there was no *constitutional* requirement of consultation with the House of Commons, that it was only *gratia rei*. The Act of Settlement of June 1701 was in fact 'the first statutory encroachment on royal control of foreign policy' (Ogg, p. 468). The source of the classical analogue is Dionysius, ii. 12, 14.

l. 84. Tarquinius Priscus is Charles I. More than 40 per cent. of English peers in 1640 had been created by Charles. The source of the classical analogue is Dionysius, ii. 57–58; iii. 1, 36, 46, 67.

l. 89. 'Alluding to the great rebellion, and protectorship of Oliver Cromwell' (Scott, iii. 283). The offer of the Crown to Cromwell was made in May 1657. The source of the classical analogue is Dionysius, iii. 72–73; iv. 1, 8, 12.

l. 98. The classical source is Dionysius, iv. 22.

l. 110. Tarquin the Proud is James II. The source of the classical analogue is Dionysius, iv. 40–41, 84.

l. 120. Prior to June 1701 the royal prerogative included the right to remove judges at will. The first draft of the Declaration of Rights in February 1689 included a clause making judges' commissions *quam diu se bene gesserint* (*C.J.* x. 17), which narrowly missed inclusion in the Bill of Rights. The power to dismiss judges was finally transferred from the Crown to Parliament by the Act of Settlement of June 1701 (*C.J.* xiii. 401). The source of the classical analogue is Dionysius, iv. 84; v. 19. The Latin phrase derives from the translation of Gelenius: 'unam in qua diserte cavit nequis Romae gereret magistratum iniussu populi' (*Dionysii Alexandri F. Halicarnassen. Antiquitatum sive Originum Romanarum Libri X. Sigismundo Gelenio interprete*, Basel, 1549, p. 208).

l. 132. '*Tribunes of the People*' are the Tory party leaders. The inviolability of their persons alludes to the parliamentary privilege by which all members enjoyed freedom from arrest for debts during the sitting of parliament and forty days before and after. An act for limiting this privilege, which was outrageously abused, was passed in May 1701 and widely touted by Tory pamphleteers as one of the great achievements of William's 5th Parliament. Bonet explains why it was passed: the Commons, 'craignans la censure de leurs Representatifs qui ne sont pas contens de leur conduite, ont cru devoir se concilier l'amour du Peuple par un Loy qui est en sa faveur' (B.M. Add. MS. 30000E, f. 219). Defoe had already used the phrase 'Tribune of the People' to stigmatize a Tory demagogue in *The True-Born Englishman*, [December] 1700, p. 58. The source of the classical references is Dionysius, v. 53, 63; vi. 87, 89.

l. 141. Coriolanus suggests William's great Tory minister, Thomas Osborne, Earl of Danby, Marquis of Carmarthen, and Duke of Leeds, who had been impeached for bribery in April 1695. The House of Commons had failed to prosecute, however, and the charges against him were dismissed in June 1701, along with those against the Whig junto. The source of the classical analogue is Dionysius, vii. 18, 64–65; ix. 44.

l. 153. The '*conquered Lands*' are the confiscated estates of English and Irish Jacobites which William, whose 'greatest Infirmity', as Defoe said, 'was too much bounty', had granted in regal profusion to his foreign generals and favourites. In 1700 the Commons tacked to a Supply Bill a clause resuming title to the forfeited estates and vesting it in thirteen trustees. William was forced to give assent to this supply-*cum*-resumption Bill in April 1700 to avert a financial panic. See pp. 24–27, above. The source of the classical analogue is Dionysius, viii. 69–70; ix. 37, 51, 59.

l. 162. Appius Claudius Sabinus may be John Thompson, Lord Haversham, whom William appointed Lord of the Admiralty in June 1699. One of his speeches against the supply-*cum*-resumption Bill is reported by L'Hermitage (B.M. Add. MS. 17677UU, f. 202v; Vernon, iii. 4). He also signed a strong protest against the Bill when it finally passed (J. E. Thorold Rogers, *The Protests of the Lords*, 3 vols., Oxford, 1875, i. 140–2). Since Haversham was not impeached—although there were mutterings in the House of Commons about 'bills of supply with bills of attainder tacked to them'—he did not need to die in the high Roman fashion of his prototype. The course of the classical analogue is Dionysius, viii. 71, 73; ix. 42–45, 52–54; x. 32.

l. 176. *Dionys. Halica.* [x. 1, 15, 30, 34, 50] [Swift's marginal note]. Cf. Temple *Miscellanea*, 1680 pp. 54–55: 'in the forms of the old *Roman* State . . . Laws were made, and resolutions taken, *Authoritate Senatus*, and *Jussu populi*. . . . But when the People began to lose the general opinion they had of the *Patricians* . . . They then pretended to share with the Senate in the Magistracy, and bring in *Plebeians* to the Offices of chiefest Power and Dignity. And hereupon began those seditions which so long distempered, and at length ruined that State.'

l. 183. The phrase 'to give way also to Time' affords a striking example of how closely the *Discourse* is tied to contemporary political discussion. L'Hermitage uses the same phrase to explain why the Lords had not resisted the Commons' encroachments upon their privileges: 'Durant la guerre les seigneurs se sont contentes de faire des protestations, *en cedant au tems*, afin de ne pas causer dans des conjunctures si delicates des divisions qui auroient esté prejudiciables, et à la nation et aux affaires generales' (B.M. Add. MS. 17677UU, f. 202; italics added). In this paragraph as a whole, the 'Tribunes' are the Tory leaders in Commons and the 'Consuls' are the ministers, who were, of course, *partes corporis regis* and not responsible to Parliament. Swift is attacking the Commons' attempt to monopolize power and to wield the *summum imperium* unchecked by King or Lords. The source of the classical analogue is Dionysius, x. 34–35, 48–49, 51–52.

l. 192. Cf. I. 106–11. The source of the classical reference is Dionysius, x. 55–60.

l. 204. The classical sources are Dionysius, xi. 53, 61, and Livy, vi. 42.

l. 219. [Polybius,] *Frag. lib. 6.* [51] [Swift's marginal note].

l. 232. *Dionysius Hal.* [ii. 11], *Plutarch*, [*Tiberius Gracchus*, 19–20], *&c.* [Swift's marginal note]. Cf. Appian, *The Civil Wars*, i. 1–2.

l. 257. [Polybius,] *lib. 5.* [Swift's marginal note is in error, the correct reference is vi. 10]. Cf. Polybius, *The History . . . Translated by Sir H*[*enry*] *S*[*heeres*], 2nd ed., 3 vols. in 2, 1698, iii. 14–15: 'every Form of a *Republick* . . . [is] subject to Change, because it easily falls into [that] Vice, to which it has the most Natural Inclination. For as Rust and the Worm, are Natural to Iron and Wood, which do Corrupt and Destroy them, so that if they cannot be Destroyed by things happening from without, they Perish nevertheless by things drawn from themselves. Even so by the Order of Nature, some Vice or other is born in the Form of every State, and always accompanys it, and is at length the occasion of its Ruine'; Temple, *Miscellanea, The Third Part,* [October] 1701, p. 20: 'Could we suppose a Body Politick, framed perfect in its first Conception or Institution, yet it must fall into Decays, not only from the Force of Accidents, but even from the very Rust of Time.'

l. 261. [Polybius,] *Fragm. lib.* 6. [9, 57] [Swift's marginal note]. Cf. Polybius, *The History . . . Translated by Sir H[enry] S[heeres]*, 2nd ed., 3 vols. in 2, 1698, iii. 14, 75: 'if any Republick be Establisht and Augmented according to the Laws of Nature, it is chiefly the *Roman*, and will Change some time or other according to the same Method.' '*The Republic being thus chang'd, it may seem at first to be for the better; and perhaps it may take upon it the Specious and Illustrious Pretence of Liberty; but however, its supposed happy rest cannot continue long, being become subject to the Government of a blind Multitude, which without Dispute is the most Pernicious in the World. In short, having treated of the Establishment of the* Roman Republic, *its flourishing Estate, and its difference with all others, I shall proceed to speak of something else.*'

l. 266. Polybius did in fact 'pursue his conjectures so far' in vi. 9; cf. *The History . . . Translated by Sir H[enry] S[heeres]*, 2nd ed., 3 vols. in 2, 1698, iii. 13: 'For the People . . . having met with a Bold and Couragious Leader . . . change the *Popular* State into one *Furious* and *Violent*, and being United into one Body, they demonstrate their Fury by Murders, Banishments, and by the Division of Lands; till such time they meet with some Body that usurps the Soveraign Rule and Power'; cf. Temple, *Miscellanea*, 1680, p. 49: 'Tyrannies . . . spring naturally out of Popular Governments.' Cf. I. 221 *n*.

l. 271. The source of this reference to the *lex Canuleia*, 445 B.C., is Livy, iv. 1–6. Temple observed a similar development in England (*Miscellanea, The Third Part,* [October] 1701, pp. 78–79).

l. 277. The gradual accession of the plebeian order to the chief offices of state is described in Livy, vi. 42 (consul); vii. 22(censor); iv. 54 (quaestor); viii. 15 (praetor); vi. 17, vii. 1, x. 6–9 (priesthood); vii. 17 (dictator). The Tory pamphleteers were making similar demands: in August 1700 Vernon reported that 'Dr. Davenant is preparing a book against the Spanish treaty. I don't doubt but we shall have many records brought to prove that treaties are not to be made without the consent of Parliament. Some say there is but that, and the disposal of offices by Parliament, to bring us as near a commonwealth as they desire' (Vernon, iii. 132). Toland urged 'That the Advice of the Parliament be taken in appointing the Lord Chancellor, Treasurer, Admiral, or Commissioners for executing these Offices' (*Limitations for the Next Foreign Successor*, 2d ed., 1701, p. 11), and G. Sharp demanded that the House of Commons should appoint all 'the great Officers of the Realm' (*The Claims of the People of England, Essayed,* [July] 1701, pp. 26, 32).

l. 280. Swift probably refers to the *historiette* with which Charles Mordaunt, 3rd Earl of Peterborough, entertained the House of Lords during the bitter debate on the supply-*cum*-resumption Bill in April 1700. 'He compared the House to a man whose affairs are in disorder. Some one proposes that he should take a rich wife. Although the woman is a baggage, the man prefers to take her and live with a demon than to be exposed to the cruel necessities of life. Peterborough thought that the man was a wise one, and that the Lords would do well to follow his example and obtain security even at the expense of so distasteful a burden as a tack' (Bonet, B.M. Add. MS. 30000D, f. 124^{v}, quoted in A. S. Turberville, *The House of Lords in the Reign of William III* (Oxford Historical and Literary Studies, vol. iii), Oxford, 1913, p. 206).

l. 282. The reference is to the Tory attack on another royal prerogative, the power of veto. G. Sharp, for example, argued that, since he had sworn in his coronation oath to grant 'Leges istas quas vulgus elegerit', William could not veto acts of Parliament (*The Claims of the People of England, Essayed*, [July] 1701, pp. 40–41). This is an issue on which Swift later changed his mind. In his autobiographical fragment, written about 1727–9, he repeats this argument of Sharp's with apparent approval (*Prose*, v. 194). The source of the classical analogue is Livy, iii. 55. Cf. Aulus Gellius, xv. 27. 4.

l. 285. *Dionys. lib.* 2. [14] [Swift's marginal note]. Dionysius comments on this 'inversion' as follows: 'in our day the practice is reversed; the senate does not deliberate upon the resolutions passed by the people, but the people have full power over the decrees of the senate; and which of the two customs is better I leave to others to determine.' The Latin phrases derive from the translation of Gelenius: 'qui mos nostra aetate mutatus est. non enim senatus plebis scita, sed plebs senatus consulta suo assensu comprobat' (*Dionysii Alexandri F. Halicarnassen. Antiquitatum sive Originum Romanarum Libri X. Sigismundo Gelenio interprete*, Basel, 1549, p. 64).

l. 288. The source of the classical reference is Diodorus Siculus, xx. 36. Appius Claudius Caecus is, of course, neither the decemvir mentioned in I. 114 *n.* nor the grandson of the decemvir, mentioned in III. 162 *n.*

l. 298. The source of the classical analogue is Plutarch, *Titus Flamininus*, 18. Q. Terentius Culleo, 'who wanted to spite the nobility', forced the censors in 189 B.C. to eject four *patres* from the Senate and to receive into citizenship anyone who offered himself for enrolment.

l. 301. Publius Scipio Africanus and Lucius Scipio stand collectively for the impeached Whig lords whose 'mighty Services' are summarized in II. 254–63. Swift may have recalled Davenant's unguarded admission that 'Innocence has been sometimes oppressed by Faction. The *Scipios*, the two best Men that *Rome* ever bred, were brought to answer for themselves before the People' (*A Discourse upon Grants and Resumptions*, [November

1699, but dated] 1700, sig. [†2]). The source of the classical analogue is Livy, xxxviii. 50–60.

l. 306. 'The Age of the *Gracchi*' is the period of peace following the signing of the Treaty of Ryswick in September 1697. The Gracchi, generically, are the Tories in the House of Commons who successively dismissed William's Dutch Guards in 1699, resumed William's grants in 1700 (III. 153 *n.*), and managed the impeachment proceedings against William's Whig ministers in 1701 (I. 229 *n.*). They included Robert Harley, Sir Edward Seymour, Sir Christopher Musgrave, John Grubham Howe, Sir Bartholomew Shower, Simon Harcourt, and Charles Davenant. It is tempting to narrow down 'the elder *Gracchus*' and his 'younger Brother [who] pursued the same design' to Robert Harley and his younger brother, Edward, the M.P. for Leominster, but there is hardly enough evidence to do so. Robert Harley, however, was one of the managers for the supply-*cum*-resumption Bill, to which Swift alludes next, and Somers had already attacked the two brothers in print, in a book which Swift certainly read (*Jura Populi Anglicani, Or The Subject's Right of Petitioning Set Forth,* [August] 1701, p. viii). In casting the Gracchi as villains, Swift differs sharply from Temple, who characterized them as 'the truest Lovers of their Country', in a book which Swift was preparing for publication when he wrote the *Discourse* (*Miscellanea. The Third Part,* [October] 1701, p. 12). The source of the classical analogue is Plutarch, *Tiberius Gracchus,* 8, 14, 19, and *Caius Gracchus,* 5, 17.

l. 312. This was the private estate of James II, which William granted to his mistress, Elizabeth Villiers, in May 1695 (see pp. 22–23, above). The classical analogue is found in Livy, *Periochae,* 58.

l. 321. The House of Lords resolved on 23 June 1701 that the Commons' high-handed procedure in the impeachment of the Whig lords (I. 229 *n.*) 'manifestly tends to the destruction of the judicature of the lords; to the rendring trials on impeachments impracticable for the future; and to the subverting the constitution of the English government' (Luttrell, v. 64).

l. 327. It is not certain that Swift intended the tribune L. Appuleius Saturninus to represent any contemporary figure. England had already experienced something very similar to the *leges Appuleiae* of 100 B.C. In January 1649 the Rump resolved 'That the People are, under God, the Original of all just Power, [and] that whatsoever is enacted, or declared for Law, by the Commons, in Parliament assembled, hath the Force of Law; and all the People of this Nation are concluded thereby, although the Consent and Concurrence of King, or House of Peers, be not had thereunto' (*C.J.* vi. 111). Swift may simply be indicating the direction which he believed events were taking in 1701: toward the penultimate imbalance, a *Dominatio Plebis.* The source of the classical analogue is Plutarch, *Caius Marius,* 29.

l. 332. Sir Humphrey Mackworth claimed that the right of judicature of the House of Lords was *not* '*an inherent Right by the Law of Nature*' but 'a subsequent *Right by Institution*' (*A Vindication of the Rights of the Commons of England*, [August] 1701, p. 33). Sir Bartholomew Shower went even further and 'treated it in a Speech publickly in the *Middle Temple* Hall, as a down right Usurpation' (*The True Patriot Vindicated*, [August] 1701, *recto*). The source of the classical analogue is Plutarch, *Caius Marius*, 4.

l. 338. The source of the classical reference is Appian, *The Civil Wars*, i. 100.

l. 339. Plutarch, *Caesar*, 13.

l. 366. Swift may have in mind Temple's parable about the ship bound to sea with a great cargo and 'a numerous Crew who have a Share in the Lading', but who refuse to 'stand to their Tackle, hand Sails, or suffer the Pilot to steer as he pleases'. Inevitably 'they must come at last to fall together by the Ears, and so throw one another over-board and leave the Ship in the Direction of the Strongest' (*Miscellanea. The Third Part*, [October] 1701, pp. 90–92).

l. 391. Pompey's *lex de ambitu* refers to An Act for appointing and enabling Commissioners to take, examine, and state, the Publick Accompts of the Kingdom, which received royal assent in January 1691 (*C.J.* x. 536). The origin and nature of the Act is explained by Burnet (ii. 65): 'Some indeed began to complain of a mismanagement of the Publick Money; but the [Danby] Ministry put a stop to that, by moving for a Bill, empowering such, as the parliament should name, to examine into all Acounts, with all particulars relating to them; giving them authority to bring all persons that they should have occasion for, before them, and to tender them an Oath, to discover their knowledge of such things, as they should ask of them. This was like the power of a Court of Inquisition.' Just as the friends of Julius Caesar suspected that Pompey's law was intended to cast suspicion on Caesar (Appian, *The Civil Wars*, ii. 23), so David Ogg has surmised that the Act of 1691 was directed against William: 'The institution of such a commission may have implied suspicion, not so much of the Treasury, as of the Court; for it was through places and pensions that the crown maintained majorities in the House; and it was mainly through this commission that a minority in the Commons was able to direct its opposition to Court measures' (Ogg, p. 341). The names of two candidates for the Commission which the Commons had voted for in June 1701 were struck from the list in the House of Lords: Sir Bartholomew Shower 'for being a lawyer and having other business to do', and Dr. Charles Davenant 'for abusing the church in his last book (*Essays upon I. The Ballance of Power*], which says men were preferred for being socinians' (Vernon, iii. 150). But the Bill was lost when William prorogued Parliament the next day. The source of the other references to Pompey is Plutarch, *Pompey*, 22, 25, 30. Swift's attitude toward this affair is identical with that of Cato, who urged Pompey 'to ignore the past and give his attention to the future,' for it would not be easy to fix the point at which the investigations of past transgressions should stop and *ex post facto* justice is abhorrent to law (Plutarch, *Cato*, 48).

l. 399. Caesar, *The Civil Wars*, i. 1–5.

l. 404. Caesar, *The Civil Wars*, i. 7, 15.

l. 413. Plutarch, *Pompey*, 60–61.

l. 442. Appian, *The Civil Wars*, iii. 50–51, 63–66, 82–93. The chief of 'those Patriots' was Marcus Tullius Cicero, whom Swift, in the first paragraph of Chapter IV, calls one of 'the wisest Men and best Authors of these Times'.

l. 456. Cicero, *Letters to Brutus*, i. 16 (*The Correspondence of M. Tullius Cicero*, ed. Robert Y. Tyrrell and Louis C. Purser, 7 vols., Dublin and London, 1899, vi. 153).

CHAPTER IV

l. 6. Cf. I. 226 *n*.

l. 14. The source of the classical reference is Cicero, *The Republic*, iii. 13: 'But if the people hold the supreme power and everything is administered according to their desires, that is called liberty, but is really licence.'

l. 21. Sir John Fortescue, *De Laudibus Legum Angliae*, 1616, p. 4 (of separately paginated notes).

l. 52. Even Edward Harley acknowledged that the impeachments of 1701 'tended only to expose the personal malice and folly of the impeachers'. But his assurance that his brother, the Speaker, 'endeavoured by all means to prevent . . . this unhappy step' is not confirmed by less partial witnesses (H.M.C. Portland MSS. v. 646). Vernon (iii. 88) mentions Robert Harley's personal grudge against Somers as early as June 1700. Harley was not only a member of the secret committee that managed the impeachments (*C.J.* xiii. 491), but he even pleaded passionately on the floor of the House, 'contre sa prudence ordinaire', as Bonet observed, for Somers's impeachment. In another dispatch Bonet describes Harley's harassing tactics when Somers appeared in the Commons to answer the charges against him (B.M. Add. MS. 30000E, ff. 121, 143). Vernon explained (iii. 144) that 'these heats don't arise upon the subject matter, but are resolutions formed to take any occasion for excluding those they have so great an aversion to from ever coming into power again'.

l. 55. Cf. II. 201 *n*.

l. 57. While Swift was writing, William III was at the Mauritshuis negotiating the Grand Alliance 'for preserving the liberties of Europe, and reducing the exorbitant power of France' (Luttrell, v. 72). War with France had seemed inevitable since November 1700 when Louis XIV tore up the Second Partition Treaty and claimed the entire Spanish inheritance for his second grandson (who was crowned Philip V of Spain). Cf. V. 61 *n.*

l. 66. Cf. II. 95 *n.*, 107 *n.*, 140 *n.*, 206 *n.* 'Though in other passages [cf. II. 126 *n.*], Lord *Orford*'s character is supposed to be drawn under the name of *Themistocles*, yet he seems to be represented by *Miltiades* here, for *Themistocles* was not impeached at all' (Hawkesworth, iii. 60).

l. 74. Cf. Thucydides, viii. 549; Diodorus Siculus, xi. 87; Livy, xxxviii. 60; Plutarch, *Alcibiades*, 25, 32; Temple, *Miscellanea. The Third Part*, [October] 1701, p. 12.

l. 77. Heb. xii. 1.

l. 83. Cf. Temple, *Miscellanea. The Third Part*, [October] 1701, pp. 28–30: 'The Needy, the Ambitious, the Half-witted, the Proud, the Covetous, are ever restless to get into publick Employments. . . . In the mean time, the Noble, the Wise, the Rich, the Modest, those that are easie in their Conditions or their Minds, those who know most of the World and themselves, are not only careless, but often averse from entring into Publick Charges or Employments.'

l. 89. Plato, *The Republic*, vii. 520D–521A.

l. 91. [Xenophon,] *Memorab. lib. 3.* [7] [Swift's marginal note]. Allen cites Temple, *Miscellanea. The Third Part*, [October] 1701, pp. 14, 29.

l. 101. [Diodorus Siculus,] *lib. 11.* [87] [Swift's marginal note].

l. 108. Cf. Bonet: 'La verité est qu'il n'y a aucune accusation importante à alleguer contre ces deux Lords [Somers and Russell]' (B.M. Add. MS. 30000E, f. 233). Poussin observed that the charges against Montagu 'se réduisent à six articles assez faibles' (P.R.O. Transcripts, 3 [France] 188, f. 94). No articles were exhibited against Portland.

l. 114. This old Divine Right slogan (G. N. Clark, *The Seventeenth Century*, 1929, p. 223) took on a new signification when it was appropriated by Tory pamphleteers to justify the encroachments of the House of Commons upon the power of King and Peers. Cf. John Toland, *Anglia Libera*, [June] 1701, p. 26: 'there is not Title equal to their Approbation, which is the only divine Right of all Magistracy, for *the Voice of the People is the Voice of God.*'

l. 115. On 29 Mar. 1701 a motion to impeach Somers was defeated 189–182 (Luttrell, v. 33). Only two weeks later the same motion was carried 198–188 (*C.J.* xiii. 489).

l. 117. Cf. [G. Sharp,] *The Claims of the People of England, Essayed*, [July] 1701, p. 97: 'managing a Party . . . is no better an Art, than packing the Cards or cogging the Dice.'

l. 128. Cf. III. 280 *n.*

l. 129. Cf. [John Toland,] *The Art of Governing by Parties*, [February] 1701, p. 84: '. . . Justice made a mere Property to be bought and sold.'

l. 137. The lords themselves discovered that 'their kind intentions of maintaining a good correspondence with the commons . . . had no other effect, but to introduce greater impositions upon them' (*Parl. Hist.* v. 1220).

l. 174. Swift is contradicting Sir Humphrey Mackworth, *A Vindication of the Rights of the Commons of England*, [August] 1701, p. 30: 'it is not to be imagin'd that a Majority of so numerous a Body of Gentlemen, can be Influenc'd against Reason and Justice.'

l. 182. Allen cites Temple, *Miscellanea. The Third Part*, [October] 1701, pp. 32–33: 'The Practice begins of Knaves upon Fools, of Artificial and Crafty Men, upon the Simple and the Good; these easily follow, and are caught, while the others lay Trains, and pursue a Game, wherein they design no other Share, than of Toil and Danger to their Company, but the Gain and the Quarry, wholly to themselves.'

CHAPTER V

l. 21. Cf. Temple, *Miscellanea. The Second Part*, 1690. Essay I, p, 29: '. . . no more than Life can, beyond the period to which it was destined, by the strength or weakness of the seminal Vertue.'

l. 24. Cf. Polybius, vi. 57: 'There are two things, by which *all Republicks perish, and come to nothing*. The *Ill* which comes from with[out] it, and the *Evil* engendred within them' (*The History . . . Translated by Sir H[enry] S[heeres]*, 2nd ed., 3 vols. in 2, 1698, iii. 74); Temple, *Miscellanea*, 1680, p. 1: 'The Decay and Dissolution of Civil, as well as Natural Bodies, proceeding usually from outward Blows and Accidents, as well as inward Distempers or Infirmities.'

l. 31. John Toland imagined that 'the Commonwealth of *Oceana* having no Factions within, and so not to be conquer'd from without, is therefore an equal, perfect, and immortal Government' (*The Oceana of James Harrington Esq; And His Other Works . . . with an Exact Account of his Life Prefix'd by J. Toland*, [August] 1700, p. xxxix). Dr. Charles Davenant, 'the *State-Physician*', concurred in the prognosis: 'Commonwealths, well founded, would be Eternal' (*Essays Upon I. The Ballance of Power*, [March] 1701, sig. R3r).

l. 43. Cf. *Aesop in Select Fables*, 1698, sig. D5r: '*If there be no* Mysteries in Christianity, *it seems there are some in* Policy; *when* Jacobites *and* Commonwealths men, *who have mutually branded one another with the harshest Names that Malice and Rancour could invent, should now unite in a Design against the present Government, as a common Centre*.'

l. 49. Even 'that pestilent Disease, the Lethargy', as Swift called it in *A Tale of a Tub* (*TT*, p. 49), became a partisan issue in 1701. See p. 30, above. The Whigs complained about the Tories' 'Lethargy' in voting supplies for the impending war, and the Tories complained about the Whigs' 'Lethargy' in prosecuting the impeached lords. 'This State Lethargy', Davenant exclaimed, 'is such an Apoplectick Symptom, as is commonly the Forerunner of Death to the Body Politick' (*Essays upon I. The Ballance of Power*, [March] 1701, p. 1). G. Sharp picked up the cry 'to awaken [his] drowzy Country-men out of this seemingly fatal Lethargy' (*The Claims of the People of England, Essayed*, [July] 1701, p. 6). And as late as January 1702 a Whig pamphlet complained that 'plausible Arguments of *What need we Fight other Mens Quarrels*, and *We are in no Danger*, have lull'd the People into a Lethargy' (*A Modest Defence of the Government*, [January 1702, but dated] 1701, p. 15). The Biblical phrase is from John xi. 4.

l. 51. *Lucr*[etius, *De rerum natura*, v. 107–8] [Swift's marginal note].

l. 61. Cf. IV. 57 *n*. Bonet reported in February 1701 that while Louis XIV was moving 60,000 men into the Lowlands and building landing barges in all the ports facing England, the House of Commons amused itself by hearing evidence of election frauds (B.M. Add. MS. 30000E, f. 61v). In March Louis reimposed the war-time capitation tax. In April he recalled his ambassador, Tallard, from London and in September, upon the death of James II, he recognized James Francis Edward, the pretended Prince of Wales, as James III, King of England, in direct violation of the Treaty of Ryswick.

l. 68. Swift may refer to the anonymous Tory who wrote *Remarks upon The Two Great Questions, Part II*, [January] 1701. Defoe identifies the author of these 'common places' as a 'Creature' of Harley: '"Twas a Creature of your Speakers', and a fawning Dependent upon the Party, who scribling for Favour, had the Impudence to affirm in Print, *That Leagues and Confederacies, Allies and Foreign Treaties were useless and insignificant to England: that we were an Island separated from the rest of the World, independent of any Body: And if all the World Leagu'd against us, if we were true to ourselves we need not care. As to our Trade, our Manufactures had the Command of the World, and wou'd force their way, and our Fleet could protect and continue our Trade in spight of all Mankind; and that the concern we had in the safety of our Neighbours, was only pretence to raise Armies to Enslave us at home*' (*Legion's New Paper*, [November? 1701, but dated] 1702, p. 9).

l. 74. Swift flatly contradicts Temple: 'The Nature of Man seems to be the same in all times and places' (*Miscellanea*, 1680, p. 45).

l. 86. Davenant had conceded that the House of Commons wielded very little power under James I, who forbade them 'to meddle with any thing concerning his Government or deep Matters of State' (*Essays upon I. The Ballance of Power*, [March] 1701, p. 201).

l. 92. 'Thus it appears that the antient Foundation of the English Monarchy was remov'd in the Reign of K. *Henry* the Seventh; and the overbalance of Lands falling from the Lords to the Commons, 'tis evident that the Monarchy has ever since stood, not upon an Aristocratical, but a Popular Foundation' (*A Letter Humbly Addrest to the Most Excellent Father of His Country, the Wise and Virtuous Prince, King William III*, 1698, p. 6); '*Henry VII* . . . made the first material Change in our Constitution, by giving way to Laws whereby the Ballance of Property came to be on the People's side' (Charles Davenant, *Essays upon I. The Ballance of Power*, [March] 1701, pp. 226–7).

l. 98. Cf. Davenant, *Essays upon I. The Ballance of Power*, [March] 1701, p. 227: 'His Son *Henry VIII*, went farther towards altering the ancient Ballance of Property, by putting into the Hands of Laymen the Church Lands'; John Toland, *Anglia Libera*, [June] 1701, p. 19: 'the Overballance of Property (and consequently of Power) fell into the Scale of the Commons, where it seems to be now wholly fixt.'

l. 101. Swift follows Temple (*Miscellanea. The Third Part*, [October] 1701, pp. 46–47) in dating this period of ideal equilibrium some fifty years earlier than Davenant, who puts it 'towards the latter end of King *James* I' (*Essays upon I. The Ballance of Power*, [March] 1701, p. 234).

l. 105. Cf. Temple, *Miscellanea. The Third Part*, [October] 1701, pp. 47–48: 'before the End of [Elizabeth's] Reign, began a new Faction in the State to appear and swell against the establish'd Government of the Church, under pretence of a further Reformation. . . . These Oppinions or Pretences divided the Nation into Parties, so equal in Number or in Strength, by the Weight of the Establisht Government on the one hand, and the popular Humour on the other, as produced those long Miseries, and fatal Revolutions of the Crown and Nation, between 1641 and 1660.'

l. 113. '*Charles* II and *James* II' (Hawkesworth, iii. 73).

l. 118. Cf. Temple, *Miscellanea*, 1680, p. 49: 'the meaner sort of the people . . . running easily from one extream to another'; [William Stephens,] *A Letter Humbly Addresst to the Most Excellent Father of His Country, the Wise and Victorious Prince, King William III*, 1698, p. 17: 'People commonly run out of one extream into another.'

l. 120. By 'Popularity', of course, Swift means 'a *Dominatio Plebis*, or *Tyranny of the People*'. Burnet (ii. 247) makes a similar observation upon the events of 1700: 'we were falling insensibly into a Democracy.'

l. 124. Cf. I. 215 *n*. The House of Commons' refusal to define its powers and privileges was a common source of complaint among Whig writers; cf. *Jus Regium: Or, The King's Right to grant Forfeitures*, [April] 1701, p. 44: ''Tis hard to say what Parliaments cannot do: The Boundaries of their

Power not being fix'd, 'tis difficult to determine when 'tis carry'd beyond the utmost extent of its Tether.' One of the replies to the *Discourse* deplores 'those unthinking, or evil dispos'd Persons, who make such an unreasonable Clamour to have the Rights and Priviledges of the House of Commons settl'd and determin'd' ([James Drake,] *The History of the Last Parliament*, [January] 1702, p. 143).

l. 130. 'Mr. James Harrington, who, in the time of the Commonwealth, published an Utopian scheme of government, entitled, The Commonwealth of Oceana. Several speculative persons, and among others Mr. Henry Neville, embraced his visions as realities, and held a club called the Rota, in Palace Yard, Westminister, to consider of means to make his plan efficient. One article was, that a part of the senate should go out by rote, and become incapable of serving for a certain time' (Scott, iii. 305).

l. 136. The reference is to Jude 13–16, describing the ungodly: 'These are . . . Raging waves of the sea, foaming out their own shame. . . . These are murmurers, complainers, walking after their own lusts; and their mouths speaketh great swelling words, having men's persons in admiration because of advantage.' Cf. Temple, *Miscellanea*, 1680, p. 50: 'the rage of [the] people is like that of the Sea, which once breaking bounds, overflows a Countrey with that suddenness and violence, as leaves no hopes either of flying or resisting, till with the change of tides or winds it returns of it self.'

l. 138. Job xxxviiii. 11.

l. 147. 'Pride the Brewer, Hewson the Cobler, and such other upstarts as the civil war had called into eminence, were summoned to this Upper House by writ' (Scott, iii. 306). The Biblical reference is to Isa. xlv. 9.

l. 157. Cf. IV. 174 *n*.

l. 164. Cf. *A Tale of a Tub*: 'For, the Brain, in its natural Position and State of Serenity, disposeth its Owner to pass his Life in the common Forms, without any Thought of subduing Multitudes to his own *Power*, his *Reasons*, or his *Visions*; and the more he shapes his Understanding by the Pattern of Human Learning, the less he is inclined to form Parties after his particular Notions; because that instructs him in his private Infirmities, as well as in the stubborn Ignorance of the People' (*TT*, p. 171).

l. 191. Cf. *A Tale of a Tub*: 'all the Virtues that have been ever in Mankind, are to be counted upon a few Fingers, but his Follies and Vices are innumerable, and Time adds hourly to the Heap' (*TT*, p. 50).

l. 197. Horace, *Odes*, ii. 1. 6.

l. 203. Cf. *A Tale of a Tub*: 'Let us therefore now conjecture how it comes to pass, that none of these great Prescribers, do ever fail providing themselves and their Notions, with a Number of implicite Disciples. And, I think, the Reason is easie to be assigned: For, there is a peculiar *String* in the Harmony of Human Understanding, which in several Individuals is exactly of the same Tuning. This, if you can dexterously screw up to its right Key, and then strike gently upon it; Whenever you have the Good Fortune to light among those of the same Pitch, they will by a secret necessary Sympathy, strike exactly at the same Time' (*TT*, p. 167); *A Discourse Concerning the Mechanical Operation of the Spirit:* 'Mean while, the Preacher is also at work; He begins a loud Hum, which pierces you quite thro'; This is immediately returned by the Audience, and you find your self prompted to imitate them, by a meer spontaneous Impulse, without knowing what you do' (*TT*, p. 275).

l. 204. Horace, *Epistles*, i. 19. 19.

l. 207. Cf. Polybius, vi. 5: '[Among animals] the most Stout and Robust... Bulls, Stags, Wolves, serve them for Conductors and Leaders; and 'tis most probable that Men at first did the same thing when they were got together, and followed those Leaders who had the most Courage, and possess'd themselves of what they were capable of effecting, which you may justly call Power' (*The History . . . Translated by Sir H*[*enry*] *S*[*heeres*], 2nd ed., 3 vols. in 2, 1698, iii. 8–9).

l. 212. Cf. '[if] being of a Party, is to be the Principal, if not the only Recommendation, then the Hottest Men, who are generally the Worst and Corruptest Members of it, are sure to have the most Power' (Davenant, *A Discourse upon Grants*, [November 1699, but dated] 1700, p. 36); 'All regard of Merit is lost in Persons imploy'd, and those only chosen, that are true to the Party; and all the Talent required, is, to be Hot, to be Heady, to be Violent' (Temple, *Miscellanea. The Third Part*, [October] 1701, pp. 34–35).

l. 227. This cant phrase of the Tory pamphleteers (cf. *The Duke of Anjou's Succession Consider'd*, [January] 1701, p. 55; [John Toland,] *Limitations for the Next Foreign Successor*, 2d ed., 1701, p. 5) had already been noticed in the Whig literature (cf. *The Present Disposition of England Considered*, [January] 1701, p. 11; *Jus Regium: Or, The King's Right to Grant Forfeitures*, [April] 1701, p. 11).

l. 228. Clodius suggests Sir Edward Seymour, 'The Chuffer', whose arrogance and instability had been remarkable over a long career. He was Speaker of the House of Commons in 1673–8 and chief manager of the supply-*cum*-resumption Bill in 1700. A Whig broadside asked 'Whether there ever was a Life more uniform and of a piece, than Sir E—— S——'s! Alike ill-manner'd, ill-natur'd and insolent; alike corrupt, whether in or out of the Chair, whether in or out of Favour; the same Enemy to his Country, when pretending to the Name of Patriot, and when ridiculing it' (*Some Queries, which may deserve Consideration*, [August] 1701, *verso*). In May 1701, while Seymour was serving as chairman of a committee to draw up a Bill for preventing Bribery and Corruption in Boroughs (*C.J.* xiii. 416), letters from one James Buckley were introduced into the hearings revealing that Seymour had promised a new organ for the parish church at Totnes, if he were reelected. Buckley was ordered to be taken into the custody of the Serjeant-at-arms, and imprisoned in the Gate House along with the Kentish petitioners (B.M. Add. MS. 30000E, f. 202v; P.R.O. Transcripts, 3 [France] 188, f. 435). But as a consequence, Seymour had already been identified in print with Juvenal's Clodius: 'But (*Clodius accusat Maechos*) Sir *Edward Seymour* is in pursuit after the Detection of Bribery!' (*Remarks by Way of Answer, Paragraph by Paragraph, to The Character of a Modern Whig*, [September] 1701, p. 26). Swift's source is Plutarch, *Pompey*, 46: 'Among these [popular tribunes] the boldest and vilest was Clodius.' Swift presumably met Seymour in September 1700, when Seymour was lavishly entertained by the lords justices in Dublin Castle (B.M. Add. MS. 30000D, f. 280).

l. 230. Curio suggests Dr. Charles Davenant, whose curious learning was a standing joke: 'he has taken a great deal of pain in hunting for *Knowledge that lies under abundance of Rubbish*' (Davenant's own phrase, quoted in *Jus Regium: Or, The King's Right to Grant Forfeitures*, [April] 1701, p. 17); how Davenant was brought to 'Philippize' is described above, pp. 73–79.

l. 239. Diodorus Siculus, xii. 17. In Diodorus, Charondas is the law-giver of the Thurians, who were successors to the Sybarites (Diodorus, xii. 9–10). Swift may have been influenced to make this slight change by Bentley's 'discovery of another Counterfeit', namely, that '*Charondas* was no THURIAN' (Richard Bentley, *A Dissertation upon the Epistles of Phalaris*, 1699, pp. 345, 363). Montaigne recounts the same story in his essay 'Of Custom': 'The Legislator of the *Thurians* ordain'd, That whosoever would go about either to abolish old Laws, or to establish new, should present himself with a Halter about his Neck to the People; to the end, that if the Innovation he would introduce should not be approv'd by every one, he might immediately be hanged' (Michel de Montaigne, *Essays ... Made English by Charles Cotton*, 3 vols., 3rd ed., 1700, i. 165).

l. 249. Allen cites Temple, *Miscellanea. The Third Part*, [October] 1701, p. 39: 'The first Safety of Princes and States, lies in avoiding all Councils or Designs of Innovation.'

l. 252. Cf. Burnet (i. 268, 382): 'The chief men that promoted this [a parliamentary committee appointed December 1668 for examining the accounts of funds voted for the 2nd Dutch War], were taken off, (as the word then was for corrupting members)'; 'They had taken off the great and leading men'; *A Tale of a Tub*: 'there has been much Thought employ'd of late upon certain Projects for taking off the Force and Edge of those formidable Enquirers.... This is the sole Design in publishing the following Treatise, which I hope will serve for an Interim of some Months to employ those unquiet Spirits' (*TT*, pp. 39–41).

l. 257. The persons who 'began' this distinction were Whigs, during the crisis over the Exclusion Bills in 1679–81. Their purpose was to establish ministerial responsibility. 'For his public acts of state, as distinct from his private deeds, the king needed a minister; and, so long as the king had the initiative, the minister might shelter himself under the cloak of the royal command. It was in order to deprive the minister of this shelter that the Whigs revived the old lawyers' fiction: *The king can do no wrong*. This maxim had at first meant little more than that, for every wrong, the subject has a remedy in the king's courts; it was now applied to matters of state in such a way that the fictive innocence of the king was postulated in order to ensure the responsibility of the minister' (Ogg, p. 506). In 1699–1701, however, the Tories eagerly appropriated this doctrine to themselves, to use as a weapon against the Whig ministers. Bonet had observed that, when Somers appeared in the House of Commons to answer the impeachments charges against him, he justified himself 'au depends du Roy' (B.M. Add. MS. 30000E, f. 143v), and the Tories were willing to 'leave it to the World to judge, who has most Distrust of *His Majesty* . . . those that distinguish betwixt *His Majesty* and His Ministers, those that adhere to the true Maxim of our Government, *That the King can do no Wrong*, or those that to excuse their own Crimes would lay all the Blame on Him' (*The Several Proceedings and Resolutions of The House of Commons in Relation to the Dangers that Threaten England, And the Liberties of Europe, From the late Succession to the Crown of Spain*, [July?] 1701, Preface).

l. 282. Cf. *A Tale of a Tub*: 'all their *Belches* were received for Sacred, the Sourer the better, and swallowed with infinite Consolation by their meager Devotees' (*TT*, p. 154).

l. 289. The 5th Parliament of William III was prorogued on 24 June 1701. Swift must have been writing in July or August.

l. 298. Cf. Davenant's similar observation in *The True Picture of a Modern Whig*, [August] 1701, p. 8. One of the 'Under-Spur-Leathers to the late Ministry' is made to say to the other: 'You had got a good Share of the Mob of your Side, even against a House of Commons, which hardly ever happened before in England.'

l. 300. See pp. 65–66 above.

l. 302. This reaction in the House of Commons to the unfavourable public reception of the imprisonment of the Kentish Petitioners is confirmed by the diplomatic residents in London: 'Le Parlement a été assez intimidé de la requeste presentée au nom de la province de Kent, bien qu'elle ne soit signée que de cent cinquante personnes, toutes du party whigg' (P.R.O. Transcripts, 3 [France] 188, f. 59v); 'on dit qu'il ÿ en a plusieurs, qui ne vont pas plus dans les maisons à café, pour eviter les criailleries et de peur d'estre insultes' (B.M. Add. MS. 17677ww, f. 255v). Defoe made similar claims for the Legion *Memorial*, '*that Paper* which frighted Mr. *P*. and Mr. *H*[*arcour*]*t*, and several others into the Country; *that Paper* which Mr. *Howe*, in a lamentable Tone, told the House, made him, *from the sense of his own Guilt*, afraid' (*Legion's New Paper*, [November? 1701, but dated] 1702, p. 4).

l. 309. Cf. V. 228 *n.*, 230 *n.*

l. 322. It was widely represented that the French could land 20,000 troops anywhere in Kent on a Monday, march on London, hear high mass in St. Paul's on Sunday, and dissolve Parliament the Monday following (*The Apparent Danger of an Invasion*, 1701, p. 3). It was to prevent this that the Kentish Petition urged the Commons to vote supplies so 'that his most sacred Majesty . . . may be enabled powerfully to assist his Allies before it is too late'. Bonet remarked that this was the first occasion 'dont les Annales d'Angleterre fassent mention, où le peuple a demandé d'étre taxé' (B.M. Add. MS. 30000E, f. 346v).

l. 328. As early as March 1689, William complained to Halifax that 'the Commons used him like a dog' (*The Life and Letters of Sir George Savile, Bart., First Marquis of Halifax*, ed. H. C. Foxcroft, 2 vols., 1898, ii. 207). In January 1699, when the Commons refused to allow him to retain the Dutch Guards even after he had made a personal appeal, it was only with difficulty that the King was prevented from abdicating (*Parl. Hist.* v. 1192–6; Ogg, p. 450). And in May 1701, when £100,000 was lopped from the budget for His Majesty's household, John Ellis concluded that the Tory ministry had so little control over their party in the House of Commons that they were not able 'to restrain them from doing unreasonable & Extravagant things only to lessen the king' (B.M. Add. MS. 7074, f. 15). Cf. pp. 22–23, above.

l. 344. This was An Act for preventing of Charge and Expence in the Election of Members to serve in Parliament, which received royal assent on 21 Jan. 1696. The bribing of electors, none the less, continued on an increasingly large scale. One of Harley's henchmen complained in January 1701 that electors were demanding £40–50 for a vote (H.M.C. Portland MSS. iv. 13). Swift, in this 'very unreasonable Paradox', is not defending corrupt elections, but William's influence in elections, for, as Paul de Rapin Thoyras observed, 'Everybody that is in the least acquainted with England, must know how much influence the court has in elections' (*Dissertation sur les Whigs et les Torys*, trans. John Ozell, 1717, p. 42). The King told Burnet that 'he hated it as much as any man could do; But he saw, it was not possible, considering the Corruption of the Age, to avoid it, unless he would endanger the whole' (Burnet, ii. 42).

l. 350. The 'late Parliament' was the 4th of William III, which sat from 6 Dec. 1698 to 19 Dec. 1700 and in which a coalition of 'Wiggs mescontents et Tories' reduced the standing army to the dangerously low level of 7,000, dismissed William's Dutch Guards, and resumed William's grants of forfeited Irish estates.

l. 359. Suetonius, *De vita Caesarum*, I. xix. Swift's memory is faulty. The 'Crisis' was the consular election of 59 B.C. The bribery which Cato justified was that on behalf of the *optimates*' candidate, Marcus Bibulus, against Lucius Lucceius, who had the support of both Pompey and Caesar.

l. 367. Cicero, *Letters to Atticus*, ii. 1. 8 (slightly misquoted); the Teubner text reads: 'tamquam in Platonis *politeía*, non tamquam in Romuli fæce' (*The Correspondence of M. Tullius Cicero*, ed. Robert Y. Tyrrell and Louis C. Purser, 3rd ed., 7 vols., Dublin and London, 1904, i. 249).

l. 386. This was a common complaint; cf. *Now or Never: Or, A Looking-Glass for the Representatives of the People*, [November] 1701, p. 20: 'From *No-body to Some-body* (says a late Author) *is such a Violent stride, that Nature, which hath the Negative Voice, will not give her Royal Assent to it.*'

l. 391. Cf. 'The very Foundations of our Liberties have been struck at, by the Audacious Attempts that some Persons have lately made to Bribe and Corrupt the Buroughs, in their Election of Members for this Parliament [the 5th of William III]' (Davenant, *Essays upon I. The Ballance of Power*, [March] 1701, p. 45).

3. CLASSICAL SOURCES

THE brilliance of the *Discourse* is almost obscured by the effortlessness with which Swift handles his classical sources. His method, the 'way of Allegory', requires him to provide classical analogues for every detail of his story, even for such unimportant details as Danby's Act for appointing Commissioners to examine the Public Accounts in 1691. That he was successful explains, in part at least, why 'The book was greedily bought and read'. The discovery of similitudes in things apparently so unlike—between James II's private estates in Ireland and Attalus's estates in Pontus, and between Danby's Act for appointing Commissioners to examine the Public Accounts in A.D. 1691 and Pompey's *lex de ambitu* in 59 B.C.—qualifies as wit by definition. Davenant had done something like this in *A Discourse upon Grants and Resumptions*, and G. Sharp—a name which sounds suspiciously pseudonymous—had imitated Davenant in *The Claims of the People of England, Essayed*. But no one in '*the Paper-War* in England' had maintained the 'way of Allegory' throughout an entire pamphlet, and this must have fascinated the contemporary reader.

It must have been particularly fascinating for the contemporary reader to pretend that there was a classical analogue for every detail of his political existence: it was like reliving ancient history. This, at any rate, is the illusion which the *Discourse* fosters and it is interesting to notice in passing that there are even classical analogues for reading political pamphlets.[1] But Swift's very success in creating this illusion of reliving the past makes it difficult to imagine how hard it was to put together the

[1] Plutarch, *Tiberius Gracchus*, 8; Cicero, *De divinatione*, ii. 29, 62.

ancient–modern parallels in the first place. The reader is confronted with an extended narrative of Greek and Roman history, for which he is required to supply, in nearly every sentence, the modern instance. The game, of course, is to decipher the allegory, to find the modern instance hidden under, but also conveyed by, the classical analogue. But this game diverts attention away from Swift's difficulty in providing the classical analogue and from his success in meeting the demands of his method.

His success can be measured by a detail in Chapter I. Here Swift is concerned to establish beyond any doubt his First Law, that '*Tyranny* and *Usurpation* . . . are by no means confined to any Number'. So he reels off precedents from Dionysius Halicarnasseus, *Antiquitatum Romanarum*; Plutarch, *Parallel Lives*; Thucydides, *The Peloponnesian War*; and Xenophon, *Hellenica* (or *De Rebus Graecorum*, as Swift cites it in the vulgate), to prove his point that so far from being imposed only by *one* man, tyrannies have in fact been imposed by ten, five, four hundred, thirty, and three thousand men, respectively.[1]

Swift's real mastery of his classical sources, however, can best be demonstrated by the evidence of Chapters II and III. Here his argument requires him to provide *exempla* in support of his conclusion that irresponsible impeachments 'ruined the liberties of Athens and Rome'.[2] This, in turn, demands a wide-ranging survey of both Greek and Roman political history. But instead of following a single source through an entire chapter, or part of a chapter, Swift switches magisterially from one source to another. Thus Chapter II is derived mainly from Plutarch, but in the account of Phocion, Swift does not limit himself to Plutarch's *Life of Phocion*. He adds significant details from Diodorus Siculus to extend, and refine, his allegory.[3] The first half of Chapter III—an account of Roman history from 'the time of *Romulus*' to

[1] I. 90–144.

[2] *Prose*, viii. 119; cf. John M. Bullitt, *Jonathan Swift and the Anatomy of Satire*, Cambridge, U.S.A., 1961, pp. 82–83.

[3] II. 215 *n*.

441 B.C.—is 'chiefly collected out of that exact and diligent Writer *Dionysius Halicarnasseus*' rather than out of Livy,[1] but where his argument requires it, Swift does not hesitate to introduce a corroborative detail from Livy. 'A few Years after, the Commons made further Advances on the Power of the Nobles; demanding among the rest, that the Consulship, which hitherto had only been disposed to the former, should now lie in common to the Pretensions of any *Roman* whatsoever. This, tho' it failed at present, yet afterward obtain'd, and was a mighty Step to the Ruin of the Commonwealth.'[2] This short paragraph derives from two statements of Dionysius (xi. 53 and 61). The last two clauses, however, are not in Dionysius at all, but derive from Livy (vi. 42). Whole paragraphs in Chapter III are similarly made up of fragments from widely scattered sources.[3] The four sentences beginning 'A Law was likewise Enacted',[4] include material from Livy (Book 3), Dionysius, Diodorus Siculus, Plutarch, and Livy again (Book 38).

Even Swift's quotations reveal something of interest. There are four of them in the first part of Chapter III: '*Populi impetratâ veniâ*' . . . '*injussu Populi*' . . . '*Dominatio Plebis*' . . . '*Senatusconsulta*'. . . . The source for this part of the *Discourse* is Dionysius Halicarnasseus, but one of the phrases, '*Dominatio Plebis*', is not from Dionysius at all, but from Polybius. Polybius's word is ὀχλοκρατία, which the first Latin edition simply transliterated as *ochlocratia*. In 1609, however, Isaac Casaubon introduced *dominatum . . . turbe vulgaris*, and it is probably this phrase which Swift renders as *Dominatio Plebis*.[5] Of the three phrases from Dionysius, two—the second and

[1] Swift may have used Dionysius rather than Livy—(1) because Dionysius exaggerates the parallels between Greek and Roman institutions, and (2) because of Dionysius's aristocratic bias in favour of the *optimates* of his own day.

[2] III. 198. [3] III. 232 *n.*, 391 *n.* [4] III. 280.

[5] *Polybij Megalopolitani Historiarum Libri Priores Quinque, Nicolao Perotto Episcopo Sipontino interprete . . . Basileae, per Ioannem Hervagium,* [1549], p. 197; *Polybii Lycortae F. Megalopolitani Historiarum libri qui supersunt. Isaacus Casaubonus ex antiquis libris emendavit, Latine vertit, & commentariis illustravit . . . Parisiis . . . M.DCIX*, p. 452².

fourth above—seem to derive from the Latin translation of Sigmund Gelenius. The first, however, is not from Gelenius at all. Dionysius's phrase is ἐπιτρέψαντος αὐτῇ τοῦ δήμου, which the first Latin translators rendered variously as: *permittente ei populo* (Lapo Birago, 1480); *accepto à populo arbitrio* (Sigismundus Gelenius, 1549); *cum permissum ipsi a populo* (Friedrich Sylburg, 1586); and *quum populus ipsi permisisset* (Aemilius Portus, 1614). Why he rejected Gelenius's phrase, and where (if anywhere) he found the phrase *Populi impetratâ veniâ*, remain mysteries, but it must be clear by this time that Swift did not 'follow' his classical sources; he completely dominated them. Virtuosity such as this reminds us again that Swift wrote with '*his Invention at the Height, and his Reading fresh in his Head*', as he said he did in *A Tale of a Tub*.

Swift was enabled to do this by his long years at Moor Park, where he had access to books, and time to develop 'the excellent habit he had' of making abstracts of what he read. The record of only a small part of what he read at Moor Park has survived. But in 1697, amid much else, he read and made abstracts of Diodorus Siculus; he also read Horace, Cicero's *Epistles*, and Lucretius (three times). In 1698 he read and made abstracts of Thucydides, in Hobbes's translation.[1] All of these works are drawn upon repeatedly in the *Discourse*, and it might be argued that the existence of the *Discourse* presupposes some kind of chronological scheme with abstracts from the different historians in parallel columns.

The use of Hobbes's translation of Thucydides suggests another aspect of Swift's utilization of his classical sources. There can be no doubt about Swift's skill as a classicist. He was *bene* in both Greek and Latin at Trinity College. His Latin commentaries upon Tacitus and Suetonius are preserved in manuscripts in the John

[1] Henry Craik, *The Life of Jonathan Swift*, 2nd ed., 2 vols., 1894, i. 71, n. 2. Lyon's annotated copy of Hawkesworth's *Life* is preserved in the library of the Victoria and Albert Museum.

Rylands Library.[1] But Swift had no interest, or even sympathy, with the purposes of classical scholarship. He was not concerned, as Richard Bentley was, to 'correct' Plutarch; he was only concerned, as Shakespeare had been, to make literature out of Plutarch. For this purpose Thomas North's translation was as good as the *textus receptus* of Henri Estienne. So Swift seems to have used Latin translations of his Greek sources wherever they were available. Of the four Greek historians mentioned in the third paragraph of this chapter, the following editions are listed in the 1745 *Catalogue of Books, The Library of the late Rev. Dr. Swift*:[2]

Dionysii Halicarnassei Opera Graec. Lat. studio Sylburgii Franc. 1586
Plutarchi Opera Graec. Lat. cum notis Doctorum variorum in 2 vol. Par. 1624
Thucydides de Bello Peloponnesiaco, Graec. Lat. studio Laur. Vallae. Cura H. Steph. 1588
Xenophontis Opera Grae.-Lat. cum notis; studio Leunclavij & Porti Paris 1625

All of these are editions with Greek and Latin in parallel columns and it may be inferred that Swift read the Greek historians in Latin translations. The same inference could be drawn from the fact that all quotations from the Greek historians in the *Discourse* are in Latin.

Wherever he could find them, Swift seems also to have used English translations of the classical historians. It is probable, but by no means certain, that he used North's Plutarch.[3] It *is* certain that Swift did *not* use the so-called 'Dryden' translation of 1683, to which Dryden supplied an Epistle Dedicatory and life of Plutarch, but no translations. There is much evidence, however, that Swift used

1 Irvin Ehrenpreis and James L. Clifford, 'Swiftiana in Rylands English MS. 659 and related documents', *Bulletin of the John Rylands Library*, xxxvii (March 1955), 385–8.

2 Pp. 3, 6, 10 (the *Catalogue* is reproduced in Harold Williams, *Dean Swift's Library*, Cambridge, 1932).

3 I. 120 *n*.

two other seventeenth-century English translations in the composition of the *Discourse*. These are *The History of Polybius . . . Translated by Sir H[enry] S[heeres]*, second edition, 1698, and *The Historical Library of Diodorus the Sicilian . . . Made English by G[eorge] Booth*, 1700. Sir Henry Sheeres, the admirer of Elizabeth Pepys, was also a friend of Sir William Temple, and it is possible that Swift met him at Moor Park. Booth's translation of Diodorus Siculus was published three years after Swift had read and made abstracts of Diodorus at Moor Park. Since he could have read Booth's translation only a short time before writing the *Discourse*, his reading of Diodorus must have been '*fresh in his Head*' indeed.

The use of Latin and English translations may have led Swift into an occasional error,[1] but even if it did, this is a fact of no real significance. The *Discourse* is to be judged as a satire—a work of art—not as a work of scholarship. The same allowance must be made for Swift's errors of omission. From the scholarly point of view these are scandalous. To qualify Servius Tullius as his analogue for Oliver Cromwell, who 'wholly applied himself to gratify the Commons', Swift is forced to ignore Dionysius's statement that Servius Tullius actually stripped all power from the *plebs* (iv. 20–21). While Swift assures us that the *decemvirs* 'did immediately usurp arbitrary Power', Dionysius records that for a year the commonwealth was extremely well governed by the *decemvirs* (x. 57). From the paragraph which is quoted above (p. 158) Swift quietly suppresses the amusing sequel of the plebeians' successful struggle to be made eligible for public office: Dionysius tells us that while many plebeians stood for office, none but patricians were elected (xi. 61).

That Swift suppresses contradictory evidence should surprise no one. Unscrupulousness in a scholar is rightly called 'economy' in an artist. What *is* surprising in Swift's handling of his classical sources is his reliance upon Sir William Temple. On several occasions Swift cites

[1] I. 152 *n.*

Dionysius Halicarnasseus or Xenophon in his marginal notes, but actually quotes Sir William Temple in his text.[1] On several other occasions it is impossible to decide whether the immediate source is the classical historian or Temple.[2] In still another case Swift seems unconsciously to include Sir William Temple in the phrase 'the Historians of those Ages'.[3]

The 'facts' of the *Discourse* derive from the classical historians, and to a much lesser extent, from Sir William Temple. The ideas of the *Discourse* derive from Sir William Temple, and to a much lesser extent, from John Locke. In the most striking case of all, Swift tells us that '*The Raging of the Sea*, and *the Madness of the People*, are put together in Holy Writ'. But his memory must have played him false, for it is Sir William Temple who puts together 'the rage of the people' and 'that of the Sea'.[4] While it is merely surprising to encounter Sir William Temple where we expect Polybius or Xenophon, it is positively unsettling to expect an Old Testament prophet and to meet instead the dissolute, sceptical baronet.

[1] III. 11 *n*.; IV. 91 *n*.

[2] III. 37 *n*., 257 *n*., 266 *n*., V. 24 *n*.

[3] IV. 69–74.

[4] V. 136 *n*.

4. FORM AND CONTENT

AMONG the 'Treatises wrote by the same Author', which are advertised on the fly-leaf of *A Tale of a Tub*, is *A modest Defence of the Proceedings of the* Rabble *in all Ages*. It may be helpful for a moment to think of the *Discourse* as this treatise and to ask how '*the Proceedings of the* Rabble' are represented therein.[1]

The *Discourse* opens with the fashionable premise that political power is by its very nature absolute: 'in all Government there is an absolute unlimited Power.' But everywhere else in the *Discourse* Swift's argument requires him to assume that power is limited: when the Commons seize *more* power, King and Lords are left with *less*. Swift further assumes that each of the '*Tres Ordinis Regni*' is constantly 'upon the Scramble for more Power than its own'. This supposition in turn is based upon a truth which Swift accepts as axiomatic: 'So endless and exorbitant are the desires of Men, whether consider'd in their Persons or their States, that they will grasp at all, and can form no Scheme of perfect Happiness with less.'[2] Political power in a constitutional monarchy, therefore,

[1] In 'this present Month of *August*, 1697' it was the intention of the narrator of *A Tale of a Tub* to publish *A modest Defence of the Proceedings of the* Rabble *in all Ages* 'by way of Appendix' to *A Tale of a Tub*. But finding his commonplace book to fill more slowly than he had expected, he was forced to defer publication to 'another Occasion' (*TT*, p. 54). This apparent nonsense finds a kind of oblique confirmation in the claim of the narrator of the *Discourse* that his Greek and Roman *exempla* were collected long before 'the late publick Proceedings . . . gave Occasion to this Discourse' (V. 1–6).

[2] I. 281. Although this idea is one of the basic, unexamined assumptions of Swift's thinking, there are, nevertheless, good classical precedents for it. Dionysius Halicarnasseus observed that 'the desires of the unintelligent mob are insatiable and boundless' (*Antiquitatum Romanarum*, v. 67).

subsists in a state of unstable equilibrium, balanced precariously between the one, the few, and the many. It is with the third estate, the many—and the Commons, their representatives—that Swift, by an outrageous synecdoche, identifies 'the Rabble'.

Thus, '*the Proceedings of the* Rabble *in all Ages*' are simple and predictable. 'The *Many*' tend to upset the balance of power in a state just as effectively as 'the *One*' or 'the *Few*'. And they do so by the same means: by attempting to monopolize power. But monopoly of political power by any one of the three estates equally qualifies as tyranny. 'Tyranny of the People' is a no less real and present danger than tyranny of 'the *One*' or 'the *Few*'.[1] Even without having heard the words, Swift clearly understood the danger of a dictatorship of the proletariat. 'In all Free States', he said, 'the Evil to be avoided is *Tyranny*', but once tyranny is let in, 'from which Door of the three it matters not'.[2] Swift may not have been the first 'strenuus . . . Libertatis Vindicator' to foresee the tyrannizing potential of the majority, but he must have been the first to formulate it as a law: '*Tyranny* and *Usurpation* in a State, are by no means confined to any Number.'[3] And he went on to provide evidence that five, ten, thirty, four hundred, three thousand, or even a majority of 'the People collective', are 'as capable of enslaving the Nation, and of acting all manner of Tyranny and Oppression as it is possible for a single Person to be'.[4]

The difference is that 'the *One*' and 'the *Few*' can wield 'absolute unlimited Power' in a state, but 'the *Many*' cannot. Examples of successful dictatorships and successful oligarchies were everywhere at hand in 1701, but there

[1] Bishop Burnet was similarly apprehensive; in 1700, he complained, 'we were falling insensibly into a Democracy' (Burnet, ii. 247). 'Democracy', of course, was still understood in its Aristotelian sense of degenerate constitutional government (*Politics*, 1279[b]). For each of the 'Three Forms of Government . . . known in the School': monarchy, aristocracy, and constitutional government, there were corresponding corruptions: dictatorship, oligarchy, and democracy.

[2] IV. 175, I. 232.

[3] I. 207.

[4] I. 97.

were no examples of a successful democracy. The House of Commons unquestionably could seize power, as it did during the Civil Wars, but since it cannot wield power, a dictator, who can, invariably intervenes. Paradoxically, therefore, when the people seize *more* power, they end up with *none*.

This conclusion, which constitutes Swift's Second Law, is elaborated in one of the infrequent metaphors in the *Discourse*:

> although most Revolutions of Government in *Greece* and *Rome* began with the Tyranny of the People, yet they generally concluded in that of a Single Person; so that an usurping Populace is its own *Dupe*; a meer Underworker, and a Purchaser in Trust for some single Tyrant, whose State and Power they advance to their own Ruin, with as blind an Instinct, as those Worms that die with weaving magnificent Habits for Beings of a Superior Nature to their own.[1]

The machinery by which the Third Estate could administer 'absolute unlimited Power' simply did not exist in 1701. Nor was it thought desirable, even by all Whigs, that it should exist. A Whig member of parliament in 1701, for example, was instructed by his electors '*To oppose all Instances of making the Legislative Power* Executive'.[2] It was, in fact, these very 'Contests and Dissentions', so deplored by Swift, which finally enabled the legislative power to usurp the executive. In 1701, therefore, Swift seems wholly justified in concluding that monopoly of power by the Third Estate could only devolve into 'Single and Despotick Slavery'.[3] This was also the fear of André Bonet, the most astute of the diplomatic residents in London. Bonet's dispatch of 17 January 1701 corroborates Swift's argument at so many

[1] IV. 178.

[2] *A Letter From Some Electors, To One of their Representatives in Parliament. Shewing The Electors Sentiments, touching the Matters in dispute between the Lords and Commons the last Session of Parliament, in Relation to the Impeachments*, 1701, p. 21.

[3] III. 445.

points that it is worth quoting at length. Members of parliament, Bonet said,

sont guidés par leurs interets particuliers, plutot que par ceux du public; qui ont pour la pluspart des connoissances trés-bornées; qui n'aperçoivent le mal que quand il est present; et n'est jamais satisfait de la constitution de son gouvernement. La Chambre des Communes, parcequ'elle est Maitresse des bourses, a forcé les Rois de leur ceder mille privileges qui favorisent a la verité en un sens le Peuple, mais qui rendent les deliberations importantes a l'Etat de plus en plus difficiles et dangereuses. Non contente de voir ses anciens privileges rétablis, et sa Religion affermie par le secours de S. M. à present Regnante, elle ne cesse dans toutes ses sessions d'ébranler la balance du pouvoir qui a rendu cette Nation heureuse et florissante; de sorte qu'on peut craindre que ce desir d'empieter sur les prerogatives de la Couronne, ou que cette jalousie invéterée qui a été de tout tems entre le Roy et le Peuple, apres avoir produit pendant un tems la conservation des Privileges et le bonheur de cet Etat, n'en produire un jour la perte.[1]

After this, it can be seen that Swift's fears were neither unique nor exaggerated.

In its argument, therefore, the *Discourse* is essentially a cautionary tale applying Swift's Second Law to the events of 1700–1:

. . . whenever it comes to pass, that a popular Assembly . . . already possess'd of more Power, than an equal Balance will allow, shall continue to think they have not enough, but by cramping the Hand that holds the Balance, and by Impeachments or Dissensions with the Nobles, endeavour still for more; I cannot possibly see in the common course of things, how the same Causes can produce different Effects and Consequences among us, than they did in *Greece* and *Rome*.[2]

In its genre, however, the *Discourse* is a satire. It is not, strictly speaking, also an essay, at least in the form that the essay assumed before Addison. Montaigne, who invented the genre, insisted on its tentativeness: 'if my mind were made up', he said, 'I would not essay myself.' But Swift's

[1] B.M. Add. MS. 30000E, ff. 13^{v}–14.

[2] V. 331.

mind was made up. He boasts, in fact, that he had not 'forced one Example, or put it into any other Light than it appeared to me, long before I had Thoughts of producing it'.[1]

What makes the *Discourse* a satire is that it creates a fictional world, like Lilliput or Brobdingnag, which in turn provides standards for a verbal attack on contemporary affairs: 'the late publick Proceedings' of the Tory majority in the House of Commons during the 4th and 5th Parliaments of William III, and of the propagandists who supported them in print. It seems to make no difference that in this case the 'fiction' is true, or at least historical. Swift's Athens and Rome function in precisely the same manner as Lilliput and Brobdingnag: they supply good and bad examples—'a Cloud of Witnesses', as Swift says in a significant Biblical phrase—for implicit contrasts and comparisons with the objects of satire.

If the qualifying *substantia* is the fiction, incidental identifying attributes are the familiar satirical devices: *litotes*, diminution, the dry mock, *occupatio*, 'Blame-by-praise', and 'Praise-by-blame', all of which function in the *Discourse*. One of the most interesting of these devices is reification, the reduction of human products, or relations, to *things*. Thus, in the phrase 'a *few Words* put together, which is called the *Vote*'[2], these '*Words*', constituting a resolution of the House of Commons, are, under the pressure of Swift's scorn, decorticated, deprived of intelligence, and reduced to physical objects. Another example occurs a few lines later: '. . . let us suppose five hundred Men . . . proposing, debating, resolving, voting, according to the meer natural Motions of their own little or much Reason and Understanding; I do allow, that abundance of indigested and abortive, many pernicious and foolish Overtures would arise and float a few Minutes; but then they would die and disappear.'[3] In this case, debates on the floor of the House first become substances, albeit 'indigested and abortive', but then something even less

[1] V. 3. [2] V. 172. [3] V. 179.

than substantial: short-lived, carious gases, having neither form nor content, but tending to expand indefinitely—symbols for the products of parliamentary debate which are not wholly lacking in 'force and humour'.

In the *Discourse*, as in Swift's major satires, the most striking effects are achieved by the most economical means. The basic metaphor is the body politic, which keeps its health so long as there is a Galenical balance of humours. Diseases, however, can attack from without and from within: 'yet, we may manage a sickly Constitution, and preserve a strong one; we may watch and prevent Accidents; we may turn off a great Blow from without, and purge away an ill Humour that is lurking within.'[1] Like so much of the *Discourse*, the outside–inside contrast has a counterpart in Sir William Temple: 'The Decay and Dissolution of Civil, as well as Natural Bodies, proceeding usually from outward Blows and Accidents, as well as inward Distempers or Infirmities.'[2] Almost the only other repeated metaphor in the *Discourse* is that of the vulture, swooping down from a position of superiority to destroy a small rodent, or to dissect a dead carcass, on the ground. The vulture, of course, is France, the real presence of the danger 'from without'.

The tone of '*Assurance* and *self-perswasion* and *concern*, which becomes a Satyrist', has been noticed above.[3] In the *Discourse*, it is built into the very structure of the work. Confidence is conveyed even in the repetition of such locutions as: 'there is hardly a Spot of Ground in *Europe*', 'there is hardly to be found thro' all Nature . . .'[4] It appears in the use of similar, and similarly self-assured, expressions at the end of successive chapters: 'This appears not only from what has been already said . . . but more manifestly from a Passage in *Diodorus*'; 'And to put it past dispute, that this entire Subversion . . . was altogether owing to those Measures which had broke the Balance . . .'[5] Emphasis at critical points is achieved by

[1] V. 21.
[2] *Miscellanea*, 1680, p. 1.
[3] Cf. p. 12 above.
[4] V. 72, 259.
[5] II. 236, III. 432.

simple alliteration: 'Counterpoise to the Power of the People', 'Calmness of the Scene and the Season.'[1] A more subtle device is that which might be called rhetorical *non sequitur*, in which the narrator dismisses as trivial or insignificant something which the reader is likely to feel is the heart of the matter. This kind of irony occurs frequently in *A Tale of a Tub* and *A Discourse concerning the Mechanical Operation of the Spirit*: 'To instance no more; Is not Religion a *Cloak*?' '. . . the *Spirit* being the same in all, it is of no Import through what Vehicle it is convey'd.'[2] One example in the *Discourse* refers to the impeachment of Edward Russell, 1st Earl of Orford, *alias Miltiades*: 'the Consequences of this Proceeding . . . were no other than the untimely Loss of so great and good a Man.'[3]

As this *alias* reveals, in form the *Discourse* is an allegory. Part of the fun of reading it is to savour Swift's ingenuity in finding classical analogues for such *minutiae* of contemporary history as Article VIII of the impeachment proceedings against Russell, or, what is even more difficult, his success in finding the classical analogue which would also supply a wry, ironical comment on the contemporary detail—'Forraign Instances, with Oblique Reflections upon Home', as the author of *The Source of Our Present Fears Discover'd* so nicely phrased it.[4] Swift made certain that the *Discourse* would be read as allegory by constantly interjecting controls. He did not, in other words, leave the reader entirely alone to 'make his Applications as often as he shall think fit'. Instead, he intervenes in the middle of Chapter I to say: 'The

[1] II. 57; III. 240; V. 291. [2] *TT*, pp. 78, 281.

[3] II. 104.

[4] See below, p. 238. Only on one occasion does the *Discourse* confirm Samuel Johnson's judgement that 'allegories drawn to great length will always break'. Momentarily forgetting that one of his purposes was to induce the Commons to quit its prosecution of the Lords Partitioners (I. 253), Swift introduces the Argive rabble murdering the 'Orators of the People . . . in modern Phrase, *Great Speakers in the House*' because they '*withdrew their Impeachments*' (I. 157), Reminding them of other prosecutors who were murdered because they desisted, is a strange way to induce Harley, and the others, to desist.

Orators of the People at *Argos* . . . left off their Accusations, or to speak Intelligibly . . . they *withdrew their Impeachments*. . . . And this last Circumstance, as Cases have lately stood, may perhaps be worth noting.'[1] This is rather heavy-handed, of course, but political satire in the form of allegory cannot afford to be too subtle.

Again, at the beginning of Chapter III, Swift reminds us parenthetically that the period from Romulus to Julius Caesar is 'not many Years longer than from the *Norman* Conquest to our Age',[2] in order to prepare us to see Cromwell in Servius Tullius and James II in Tarquin the Proud. In Chapter IV, where conclusions are drawn, 'one cannot conclude less, than that the Commons in *Greece* and *Rome*, (whatever they may be in other States) were by no means qualified either as Prosecutors or Judges in such matters'.[3] Here the control may have two functions: first, to remind 'the judicious Reader' to make his applications, and second, to forestall retaliatory action in the House of Commons. The Kentish petitioners, after all, had been imprisoned for a much more polite arraignment of the competency of the House.

There is one sense, however, in which the *Discourse* is not *A modest Defence of the Proceedings of the* Rabble *in all Ages*. Its method is the very opposite of that implied in '*A modest Defence*'. It is, in the Aristotelian term reintroduced by Northrop Frye, an 'alazonic' attack on the 'Proceedings' of the Tory majority in the 4th and 5th Parliaments of William III. There are several reasons why an alazonic attack should be more effective than an ironic defence.

In the first place, it relieves Swift of the necessity for defending the four Lords Partitioners. Instead, the emphasis can be shifted squarely on to an attack on the Tory majority for prosecuting them. To defend the Whig ministers might seem to imply that the charges against them were serious. By attacking instead of defending,

[1] I. 157. [2] III. 30. [3] IV. 42.

Swift implies that the charges were utterly frivolous and undertaken solely for party advantage. He is so successful at this, that, when he does retail the actual charges, 'Bribery . . . Embezzlement . . . Misconduct at Sea', all normal reactions to these crimes seem to be inhibited. Swift is helped here, of course, by the allegory. Reading about Montagu's alleged peculations wholly in terms of a remote and Golden Age of Pericles must have made it difficult even for the most high-flying Tory to be properly indignant.

There is another reason for Swift to adopt the method of alazonic attack rather than that of ironic defence. Ironic defence requires a narrator who is a *naïf*, like the Grub-street hack who tells *A Tale of a Tub*. This character, it will be remembered, was 'so entirely satisfied with the whole Present Procedure of human Things' that he was preparing *A Panegyrick upon the World*. The narrator of the *Discourse*, on the contrary, is entirely *dis*satisfied with 'the whole present Procedure of human Things'. It is his 'Reflections upon the late publick Proceedings' which provide the occasion for the *Discourse*.

The narrator of the *Discourse* is a profound scholar, widely read in the classics. If he sounds, on occasion, pompous and serenely self-assured, like Sir William Temple, this is not strange since so many of his ideas derive from Sir William Temple. He understates his 'little Reading' and obviously would like to *appear* modest. But he cannot resist opportunities to hint at how much more he knows than he can commit to paper: 'one Example more among a great Number that might be produced . . .', 'Many Examples might be produced . . .', 'several Instances might be brought from other States . . .', 'I might easily produce many more Examples.'[1] For similar reasons, the narrator finds it impossible to omit from his

[1] I. 155, 309, 316; II. 249. This emphasis on 'Examples' undoubtedly parodies Davenant, whose *Discourse upon Grants and Resumptions* and *Essays upon I. The Ballance of Power* provide 'infinite Examples'. The narrator of the *Discourse*, in fact, is a kind of amalgam of Sir William Temple, Dr. Richard Bentley, and Dr. Charles Davenant.

narrative incidents he knows to be irrelevant. He is equally reluctant to make an unqualified statement or a positive commitment. His favourite locutions are 'it seems to me', 'seems . . . to agree', 'seems to have been'. He exhibits, in short, all of the classic symptoms of the impenitent pedant.

On the positive side, some qualities of the pedantic narrator undoubtedly inspire confidence. He is careful to appeal to none but 'the most ancient and approved *Greek* Authors' and the 'best Authors of those times'.[1] He tries to be objective, impartial, and reasonable. He boasts that he has not 'forced' the evidence. This willingness to be reasonable and conciliatory is important in the rhetorical structure of the *Discourse*. In September 1701 England indeed stood 'more in need of *Emollients* than *Corrosives*'.[2] And the somewhat obtuse but complaisant pedant whom Swift conjures up to narrate the *Discourse* is well conceived to administer the emollients.

The conciliatory tone is established in the first three words, 'It is agreed'—even though what is agreed is a premise which is contradicted everywhere else in the work. In the third sentence the narrator appeals, very reassuringly, to 'the best Legislators of all Ages', and in the fifth sentence he avoids making any commitment on the subject of the origins of government, on which Whig and Tory were sharply divided. Later he propitiates two Tory idols: England's 'Greatness at Sea' and the sanction of '*Divine Appointment*'.[3] Party differences in general are minimized, probably because Swift saw the impeachment proceedings primarily as a contest between the two Houses of Parliament, rather than between the two parties which divided the Houses. The conciliatory tone of the *Discourse* makes a sharp contrast, on the one hand, with the gay, bantering, irresponsible tone of *The True Patriot*

[1] I. 91; III. 227; IV. 13.

[2] *A Vindication of the Rights and Prerogatives of the Right Honourable The House of Lords. Wherein a late Discourse Entitled, A Vindication of the Rights of the Commons of England Is Consider'd*, [September] 1701, p. 21.

[3] II. 127; III. 44.

Vindicated, and, on the other, with the savage violence of *Jura Populi Anglicani*. Its 'middling' tone must have been deliberate. Swift was more sensitive than Davenant to the mood of his readers, for it was observed that the effectiveness of *The True Picture of a Modern Whig* was diminished by its violence: 'l'autheur paroist si passionné, et outre si fort le caractere qu'il en donne, que son livre fait peu d'effet sur l'esprit des gens moderés.'[1] The moderate tone of the *Discourse* has been noted before,[2] but it seems not to have been pointed out that the tone is not consistent throughout the work. There is, in fact, an unmistakable shift in tone at the end of Chapter IV, which corresponds to a major change in the structure of the work.

Like a school exercise, the first four chapters of the *Discourse* elaborate the argument and the last chapter draws the application. The structure may be represented as follows:

Chapter I: Basic premises.
Chapter II: Historical examples of 'Encroachments' of 'the Many' by the method of 'particular Impeachments'.
Chapter III: Historical examples of 'Encroachments' of 'the Many' by the method of 'general Dissentions'.
Chapter IV: Conclusions.
Chapter V: Application.

In Chapters I–IV, where the application to contemporary England is only implicit, the tone is cautious, conciliatory, 'middling'. In Chapter V, however, the narrator is drawn, almost reluctantly, to apply his *exempla* to the contemporary scene: 'I cannot conclude without adding some particular Remarks upon the present Posture of Affairs and Dispositions in this Kingdom.'[3] The cautious pedant

1 B.M. Add. MS. 17677WW, f. 332v.

2 'The *Discourse* . . . lacks the angry violence of a Grubstreet pamphlet' (Allen, p. 11).

3 V. 7.

finally is forced, by the structure of his argument, to commit himself. 'It seems to me' and 'seems . . . to agree' give way to 'I know very well', 'I think it a great Error', and 'Neither can I see any Reason'. 'Towards the end', as Lord Weymouth told Harley, 'there are pretty bold reflections.'[1] By the end of Chapter IV the tone becomes that of a superior being looking down on the antics of a perverse and despicable people:

> it is hard to recollect one Folly, Infirmity or Vice, to which a single Man is subjected, and from which a Body of Commons either collective or represented can be wholly exempt. For, besides that they are composed of Men with all their Infirmities about them; they have also the ill Fortune to be generally led and influenced by the very worst among themselves; I mean, *Popular Orators*, *Tribunes*, or, as they are now stiled, *Great Speakers*, *Leading Men*, and the like. From whence it comes to pass, that in their Results we have sometimes found the same Spirit of Cruelty and Revenge, of Malice and Pride; the same Blindness and Obstinacy, and Unsteadiness; the same ungovernable Rage and Anger; the same Injustice, Sophistry and Fraud, that ever lodged in the Breast of any Individual.[2]

This is a strain which is not heard again until the King of Brobdingnag's more famous indictment of 'the most pernicious Race of little odious Vermin that Nature ever suffered to crawl upon the Surface of the Earth'.

It is probably true, as George Orwell has said, that 'Violence and scurrility are part of the pamphlet tradition'.[3] On the other hand, the perfectly *controlled* violence and scurrility of the *Discourse* is probably the best evidence there is that the *Discourse* is something more than an occasional pamphlet: a calculated rhetorical structure, calculated in advance to produce specific impressions 'sur l'esprit des gens moderés'.

[1] H.M.C. Portland MSS. iv. 25.

[2] IV. 160.

[3] *British Pamphleteers*, ed. George Orwell and Reginald Reynolds, 2 vols., 1948–51, I. 8.

5. PUBLICATION AND RECEPTION

JONATHAN SWIFT was a name almost completely unknown in London in 1701. Very few readers would have recalled him as the editor of *Letters Written by Sir W. Temple, Bart.*, which had appeared late in 1699.[1] Almost no one, fortunately, would have remembered 'The wild excursions of a youthful pen', Swift's Pindaric ode *To the Athenian Society*, which had appeared early in 1692.

On 28 March 1701 the lords justices of Ireland were recalled and ordered to 'repair into the royal presence with all convenient expedition'.[2] The Earl of Berkeley arrived in London on 15 April,[3] accompanied, one would suppose, by his domestic chaplain, the new vicar of Laracor. It is to these exciting weeks in April that Swift attributed the first conception of the *Discourse*:

when, returning with the Earl of Berkeley from Ireland, and falling upon the subject of the five[4] great Lords, who were then impeached for high crimes and misdemeanors, by the House of Commons, I happened to say, that the same manner of proceeding, at least as it appeared to me from the views we received of it in Ireland, had ruined the liberties of Athens and Rome, and that it might be easy to prove it from history. Soon after I went to London; and, in a few weeks, drew up a discourse, under the title of The Contests and Dissentions. . . .[5]

[1] See above, p. 21, *n.* 3.

[2] *Calendar of State Papers Domestic . . . 1700–1702*, ed. Edward Bateson, 1937, p. 282.

[3] B.M. Add. MS. 30000E, f. 149v; Add. MS. 7078, f. 3.

[4] Writing in October 1714, thirteen years after the event, Swift probably confused the *five* Kentish petitioners with the *four* Lords Partitioners who were impeached.

[5] *Memoirs, Relating To That Change which happened in the Queen's Ministry in the Year 1710* (*Prose*, viii. 119).

The little that is known of Swift's activities from April to September of 1701 can be summarized very quickly. He may have visited Moor Park and arranged for Esther Johnson and Rebecca Dingley to remove to Ireland.[1] If the interview with William III described in *A Letter . . . Concerning the Sacramental Test* actually took place, it must have happened in 1701, not 'when I was last in *England*', as Swift asserted in December 1708. It was during this interview, probably on the occasion when the returning lords justices were granted an audience with the King, that Swift told William that 'the highest Tories' in Ireland would make 'tolerable Whigs' in England.[2] But all that it is certain Swift did during these five months is that he arranged for the publication of two books.

In July he inserted an announcement in *The Post Angel*: 'Mr. *Jonathan Swift* is going to publish *Miscellanea*, The Third Part, written by the late Sir *William Temple*'.[3] On 28 July *Miscellanea. The Third Part* was entered in the Stationers Register.[4] Both Temple's *Miscellanea* and Swift's *Discourse* were published in October. The first reference to the *Discourse* appears in *The Flying Post* for 21–23 October: '*Advertisements* To morrow will be published . . ., A Discourse of the Contests and Dissentions between the Nobles and Commons in Athens and Rome, with the Consequences they had upon both those States. Printed for John Nutt, near Stationer's-Hall. Price 1 s.'[5] Both *Miscellanea. The Third Part* and the *Discourse* are mentioned in *The History of the Works of the Learned* for October 1701. The *Discourse* is the last item in a list of 'Books Publish'd this Month and not Abridg'd'.[6] The

[1] *Journal to Stella*, ed. Harold Williams, 2 vols., Oxford, 1948, I. xxviii.

[2] *Prose*, ii. 283. William set out for Holland on 30 June 1701.

[3] *The Post Angel*, ii (July 1701), 64.

[4] *A Transcript of the Registers of the Worshipful Company of Stationers, 1640–1708*, ed. G. E. B. Eyre and C. R. Rivington, 3 vols., 1913–14, iii. 494.

[5] *The Flying Post*, No. 1008, 21–23 Oct. 1701. This reference, although cited in F. Elrington Ball, *Swift's Verse*, 1929, p. 60, seems to have been lost track of by later writers about Swift.

[6] *The History of the Works of the Learned*, iii (October 1701), 639.

Miscellanea is both reviewed and abridged in the October and November issues.

By this time, of course, Swift had returned to Ireland. Perhaps on the very day that Lemuel Gulliver set sail from Blefuscu—24 September 1701, 'at six in the Morning', resolving 'never more to put any Confidence in Princes or Ministers'[1]—Swift departed from London, leaving the manuscript of the *Discourse* in the hands of John Nutt: 'This discourse I sent very privately to the press, with the strictest injunctions to conceal the author, and returned immediately to my residence in Ireland.' The *Discourse* was an overwhelming success: 'The book was greedily bought, and read; and charged some times upon my Lord Sommers, and some times upon the Bishop of Salisbury; the latter of whom told me afterwards, that he was forced to disown it in a very public manner, for fear of an impeachment, wherewith he was threatened.'[2] It was even more 'bought' than Swift imagined, as the recent discovery that there were two editions in 1701 indicates.[3] Furthermore, if Samuel Johnson's sources are correct, the wide sale of the book even provided Swift with a delicious opportunity to persevere in the right: 'paying a visit to some bishop, he heard mention made of the new pamphlet that Burnet had written, replete with political knowledge. When he seemed to doubt Burnet's right to the work, he was told by the Bishop that he was *a young man*; and, still persisting to doubt, that he was *a very positive young man*.'[4] One of the first buyers in London was Thomas Thynne, 1st Viscount Weymouth, a Tory wheel horse, who promptly reported his purchase to Robert Harley: 'Your absence may possibly have deprived you of the sight of a pamphlet about the dissensions of the Nobles and Commons of Athens and Rome, whose author pretends

[1] *Prose*, xi. 61–62.

[2] *Prose*, viii. 119.

[3] R. H. Griffith, 'Swift's "Contests," 1701: two editions', *N & Q*, 192 (22 Mar. 1947), 114–17; H. Teerink, 'Swift's Discourse . . .', *The Library*, 5th Series, iv (December 1949), 201–5.

[4] Samuel Johnson, *Lives of the English Poets*, ed. G. B. Hill, 3 vols., Oxford, 1905, iii. 10.

to much reading and great sincerity, but towards the end there are pretty bold reflections.'[1] It would be interesting to know whether it occurred to Harley that he might find employment for this 'conjured spirit, that would do mischief' if not better employed.

One early allusion to the *Discourse* occurs in a folio half-sheet entitled *A Short Defence of the Last Parliament with a Word of Advice to all Electors for the Ensuing*, published by E. Mallet in November 1701.[2] In this broadside, the author, James Drake, who later wrote an extended rejoinder to the *Discourse*, simply mentions in passing that the Romans became great 'by the exact Distribution of Reward and Punishment': 'This Severity of the Romans was so far from being (what some People call it) Ingratitude, that it was the Preservation of their State.' Swift had indeed called it 'Ingratitude', and he had referred repeatedly to the severities suffered by the Roman senate at the hands of 'a prevalent Populace'.[3]

A Whig pamphlet in December 1701 seems to borrow and develop Swift's point that even if the Tory charges against the Lords Partitioners had been true, the accusations were not in the public interest: 'Was it . . . for the *Publick Good*, that my Lord *Orford*, that prevented a French Invasion, and burnt all their Shipping at *la Hogue*, should be prosecuted to a Fine or Imprisonment for Crimes uncertain . . . ? Was it . . . for the *Publick Good*, to prosecute a Man of my Lord *Sommers*'s publick Merit, Capacity, and Zeal for the Nations Service . . . ?'[4] This

[1] H.M.C. Portland MSS. iv. 25. Harley left London for Brampton during the second week in October and returned about 1 November.

[2] William III dissolved his 5th Parliament on 11 Nov. 1701. *A Short Defence* must have been published shortly afterward, for it is mentioned by Defoe in *Legion's New Paper*, which itself was published before the end of November (*Calendar of State Papers Domestic . . . 1700–1702*, ed. Edward Bateson, 1937, p. 456). *A Short Defence Of the Last Parliament Answer'd Article by Article* was published in December 1701 (*The History of the Works of the Learned*, iii (December 1701), 760].)

[3] II. 136; III. 382.

[4] *The Moderator: Or A View Of The State of the Controversie Betwixt Whigg & Tory, Short Animadversions on The Picture of a Modern Whigg, With a Defence of the Treaty of Partition, and the Impeach'd Lords. A Vindication of His Majesty in*

sounds very much as if it were derived from the *Discourse*: '*to Impeach* Miltiades *after a great Naval Victory, for not pursuing the* Persian *Fleet: To Impeach* Aristides, *the Person most versed among them in the Knowledge and Practice of their Laws, for a blind suspicion. . . .*'[1]

But the most surprising allusion to the *Discourse* occurs in a pamphlet by John Tutchin, who had not yet undertaken *The Observator* and who was enormously resentful of Montagu's failure to provide patronage. The product of Tutchin's resentment was entitled *The Mouse grown a Rat: Or The Story of the City and Country Mouse Newly Transpos'd. In a Discourse Betwixt Bays, Johnson, and Smith.* While it is not really witty, Tutchin's pamphlet contains some things that are like wit, as Congreve claimed for Cibber's *Love's Last Shift.* The reference to the *Discourse* is of the most casual kind, but it is significant because it links together Swift and Defoe for the first time. Tutchin contrasts his own arrest under a warrant signed by the Secretary of State for his poem *The Foreigners*, with the apparent immunity enjoyed by Whig writers:

> We can have your Legion Letters, your Stories of *Rome* and *Athens*, and 100 other Libels against the Parliament, in order to subvert our Constitution, publickly sold and dispersed without any Secretary of State's Warrant against either Authors or Publishers...; when at the same time if a Body happen to make a Ballad reflecting upon a Foreigner, that has run away with more then all the Honest Men in *England* have got since the Revolution, the Author is brought into Jeopardy by Warrants and Presentments.[2]

When Swift returned to London in May 1702, he had only to acknowledge the *Discourse* to establish his reputation. Writing about it even a dozen years later, he was unable to conceal the pride and excitement of success:

> Returning next year for England, and hearing the great approbation this piece had received, (which was the first I ever printed)

Dissolving the late Parliament. By a True English man of no Party, 1702, p. 30. This pamphlet was published in December 1701 (*The History of the Works of the Learned*, iii [December 1701], 760).

[1] IV. 58.

[2] *The Mouse grown a Rat*, 1702, p. 32.

I must confess, the vanity of a young man prevailed with me, to let myself be known for the author: Upon which my Lord Sommers and Hallifax, as well as the Bishop [of Salisbury], desired my acquaintance, with great marks of esteem and professions of kindness: Not to mention the Earl of Sunderland, who had been of my old acquaintance. They lamented that they were not able to serve me since the death of the King, and were very liberal in promising me the greatest preferments I could hope for, if ever it came in their power. I soon grew domestic with Lord Hallifax, and was as often with Lord Sommers, as the formality of his nature (the only unconversable fault he has) made it agreeable to me.[1]

The meeting with Sunderland, whose fall five years before had precipitated some kind of crisis in Swift's life, must have been particularly satisfying. Sunderland was a link between the buried, dependent life at Moor Park and the brilliant new career which was unfolding in London.

Unlike most of Defoe's pamphlets of this period, the *Discourse* was not honoured with a full-scale reply 'Paragraph-by-Paragraph'. Instead, it was answered in passing by three works devoted primarily to other purposes. These were James Drake, *The History of the Last Parliament* (1702), an anonymous pamphlet, *The Source of Our Present Fears Discover'd* (1703), and Charles Leslie, *The New Association. Part II* (1703), excerpts from which are included in the Appendix below.

The next year, in May 1704, Swift finally published *A Tale of a Tub*, with its dedication in 'all Respect and Veneration' to Lord Somers, whose political fortunes were again in the ascendant. Soon it would be impossible for the Whigs to lament 'that they were not able to serve me'. In September 1705, however, Robert Harley bought a copy of *A Tale of a Tub* for four shillings and this casual purchase proved to be more fateful for Swift than the long-delayed and hopeful dedication to Lord Somers.

Having written once, in October 1714, so candidly about the *Discourse*, in *Memoirs, Relating to that Change which happened in the Queen's Ministry in the Year 1710*,

[1] *Prose*, viii. 119.

it is regrettable that Swift ever wrote less candidly about it. But as a result of 'That Change which happened in the Queen's Ministry in the Year 1710' Swift abandoned his Whig patrons, if not his Whig principles, and went to work for Harley as the Tory *chef de propagande*. *The Examiner*, No. 13, the first written by Swift, is dated 2 November 1710. In February 1711, in the midst of printing off the *Discourse* for inclusion in *Miscellanies in Prose and Verse*, Swift cancelled the last paragraph, perhaps because he felt that this flippant defence of corrupt elections was incompatible with his new dignity. By May 1711, when he wrote the *Examiner*, No. 42, Swift had so far changed his mind about the meaning of the *Discourse* that he was able to think of Harley, whom he had originally styled as the villain seducing the Commons into vindictive and irresponsible impeachments, as the hero who 'prevented this growing evil'. The whole passage should be compared with the statements in *Memoirs, Relating To That Change*, which have just been quoted:

> Observing indeed some Time ago, that Seeds of Dissention had been plentifully scattered from a *certain Corner;* and fearing they began to rise and spread, I immediately writ a Paper on the Subject; which I treated with that Warmth, I thought it required: But the Prudence of those at the Helm soon prevented this growing Evil; and at present it seems likely to have no Consequences.[1]

[1] *Prose*, iii. 153.

6. EDITIONS

WHAT appears below is a description of all witnesses to the text of the *Discourse* which appeared *during* Swift's lifetime, and the editions of John Hawkesworth, Thomas Sheridan, John Nichols, Walter Scott, and a few others which were published *after* Swift's death. The complicated relations between these different versions are represented diagrammatically in Figure IV. Substantive versions, which received some degree of Swift's attention, are printed in bold-face type.

1701$^{(1)}$. The *editio princeps* of the *Discourse* is an unpretentious pamphlet published in October 1701 by John Nutt 'near Stationers-Hall' (Teerink *478*). It is wholly innocent of the '*Prefaces, Epistles, Advertisements, Introductions, Prolegomena's, Apparatus's, To-the-Reader's*' and other arts by which the big book is made. Apart from Swift's references to his classical sources, printed in the margin, there is no editorial apparatus. The large number of printer's errors in this edition confirms the impression gained from Swift's account in *Memoirs, Relating to that Change which happened in the Queen's Ministry* that he did not see it through the press.[1] But since it must have been set up from Swift's manuscript, or a fair copy thereof, 1701$^{(1)}$ has been chosen as the copy text for the present edition. As Samuel Johnson reminds us, 'they who had the copy before their eyes were more likely to read it right, than we who read it only by imagination'. The most recent edition of the *Discourse*, published in 1939, is based on 1735$^{(1)}$. Herbert Davis's aim, however, was 'to give in every case the final corrected version of the author',[2]

[1] *Prose*, viii. 119.

[2] *Prose*, xi. 285.

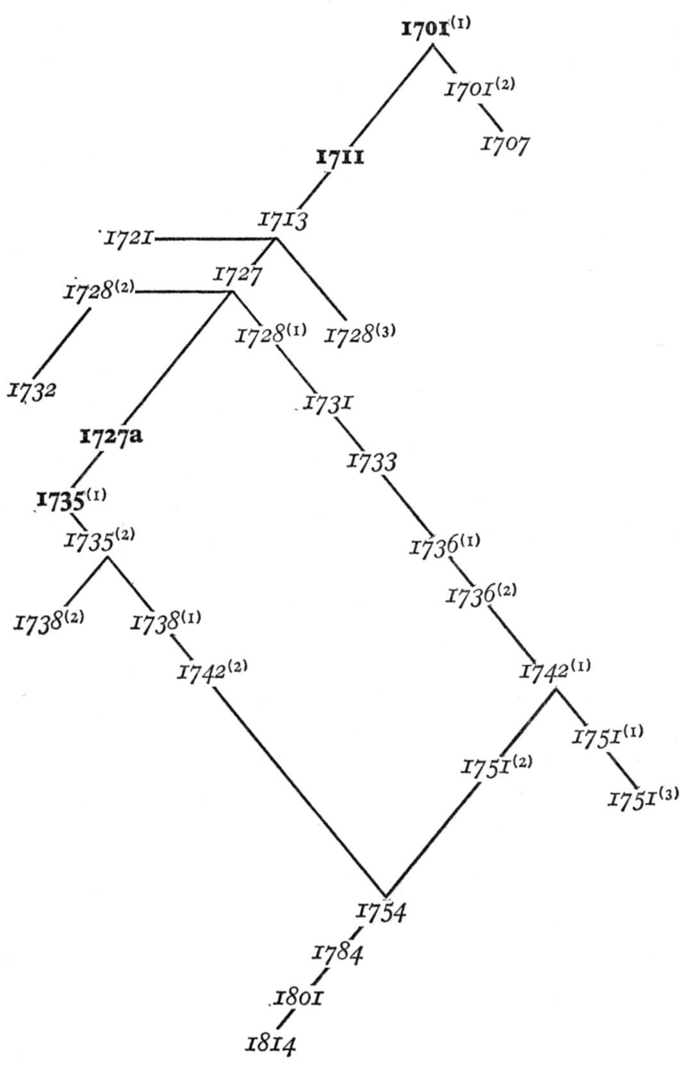
1701(1)
1701(2)
1707
1711
1713
1721
1727
1728(2)
1728(1)
1728(3)
1732
1731
1727a
1733
1735(1)
1735(2)
1736(1)
1736(2)
1738(2)
1738(1)
1742(2)
1742(1)
1751(1)
1751(2)
1751(3)
1754
1784
1801
1814

Figure IV.

whereas the aim of the present edition is to present the *Discourse* in its historical context. This means presenting the text which actually precipitated the replies printed in the Appendix to the present work, or, more accurately, the text which Swift intended to publish in October 1701. This also means restoring to the text a few readings (including the entire last paragraph) which Swift omitted in later revisions, even though this seems to confirm the joint complaint of Pope and Swift, in the *Preface* to *1727*, that it is 'the Editor's Interest to insert, what the Author's Judgment had rejected'.

1701(2). It was R. H. Griffith who discovered that there were actually two editions, or issues, of the *Discourse* published in 1701.[1] Working with copies of the *Discourse* in the University of Texas Library, which he designated as *x*, *y*, and *z*, Griffith was not, however, able to establish the priority of the two editions. The reason for this, as the late Herman Teerink very neatly demonstrated,[2] was that whereas *x* was an example of 1701(1), *y* and *z* (a fragmentary copy) were both made-up copies, embodying elements of 1701(1) and *1701*(2). The evidence supplied by Teerink explains why there are two editions of the *Discourse* in 1701: the decision to print a new edition was taken before the type of the first edition had been completely distributed. Accordingly, the distributed type,[3] together with new marginals throughout, had to be reset, and the result is *1701*(2). The two editions are distinguishable even on the title-page: the two rules are both broken in 1701(1), but unbroken in *1701*(2). In the body of the text *1701*(2) corrects a dozen errors in 1701(1), including

[1] R. H. Griffith, 'Swift's "Contests," 1701: two editions', *N&Q*, cxcii (22 Mar. 1947), 114–17.

[2] Herman Teerink, 'Swift's *Discourse . . . Contests . . . Athens and Rome*, 1701', *The Library*, 5th Series, iv (December 1949), 201–5.

[3] According to Teerink, the type for all of sheet A, pp. 9–10, 12–16 of sheet B, all of sheet C, pp. 25, 28–29, 31 of sheet D, pp. 33, 38, 39 (lines 1–15) of sheet E, and pp. 42 (lines 1–13), 43 of sheet F, had been distributed before 'it appeared that more copies were wanted' (ibid.).

one which establishes the priority of the two editions. Where Swift had written 'may perhaps be worth noting' (I. 166), 1701$^{(1)}$ rendered as 'may perhaps be worth nothing'. Confronted with this nonsense, the compositor of *1701*$^{(2)}$ emended it to 'may perhaps be worth remarking', which at least preserves Swift's meaning. This same example, of course, also demonstrates that *1701*$^{(2)}$ was set up directly from 1701$^{(1)}$ and not from the original manuscript.

1707. The *Discourse* was first anthologized in *A Collection of State Tracts Publish'd on the Occasion of the late Revolution in 1688, and during the Reign of King William III.*[1] This series of three folio volumes published in 1705–7 was apparently a venture of John Darby, who had been stigmatized as 'the common Scandal Printer, *Pillory Darien John Darby* . . . the Third of his Family that has stood in the *Pillory* for Printing *Libels* against the Government, and . . . so Bigotted a *Phanatick Republican*, that nothing can cure his Spleen'.[2] Darby was indeed the publisher of the collected works of Algernon Sidney and James Harrington, and of Defoe's *The True-Born Englishman*,[3] but *A Collection of State Tracts* is neither fanatic nor republican. All of the selections accept the Revolution Settlement, but on issues such as the standing army, which became 'the very test . . . of Whig and Tory' in 1698–9, pamphlets on both sides of the question are included. Thus the Preface to the second volume explains that it was not 'the business of the Publishers to pretend to determine which Party has the strongest Reasons, but to leave everyone to judg for himself'. Volume III, therefore,

[1] This edition is not listed in Teerink. It was first noticed by Robert J. Allen, 'Swift's *Contests and Dissensions* in Boston', *New England Quarterly*, xxix (March 1956), 73, n. 2, and has been included in Arthur H. Scouten's new edition of Teerink (1963).

[2] Richard Kingston, *Impudence, Lying and Forgery, Detected and Chastiz'd*, 1700, pp. 4–5. None of the three volumes of *State Tracts* bear a publisher's imprint, but 'Books sold by J. Darby in Bartholomew-Close' are advertised in Volume III.

[3] *The Post Boy*, No. 907, 28–30 Jan. 1701.

which includes Swift's *Discourse*, *The Present Disposition of England Considered*, attributed to Montagu,[1] and Somers's *Jura Populi Anglicani*, also includes Tory works such as *The Claims of the People of England, Essayed* and *Limitations for the Next Foreign Successor*. The claim of the publisher that the collection is 'carefully and judiciously put together' is also borne out by the care with which the text of the *Discourse* is printed. Nearly two dozen printer's errors in the copy text, *1701*⁽²⁾, are eliminated, and only three or four new ones are introduced. The whole collection is also fitted out with marginal notes and an index.

1711. The *Discourse* was printed next as the first item in the first collected edition of Swift's works, *Miscellanies in Prose and Verse*, published by John Morphew on 27 February 1711 (Teerink *2*). This octavo volume exists in two states: with and without leaves G6 and G7. The reason for this difference was Swift's desire to delete the last paragraph of the *Discourse* with its most 'unreasonable Paradox' in defence of corrupt elections. Only three months before, Swift had undertaken the editorship of the *Examiner* for the Tory ministry of Harley and Bolingbroke. As Herbert Davis conjectures, 'It would have been too dangerous for the *Examiner* to run the risk of being known to have such views on the advantages of bribery in elections' as were expressed in the last paragraph of the *Discourse*.[2] So Swift ordered the last paragraph to be cancelled. 'Consequently', as Teerink explains, 'as was usual in such cases, G6 and G7 were slit halfway from bottom upwards, to tell binders that they were to be cancelled and replaced by the new leaf annexed.'[3] The

[1] Without being mentioned by name, Montagu is insinuated to be the author in *England's Enemies Exposed, and its True Friends and Patriots Defended*, 2nd ed., 1701, pp. 5, 9, 11, 13.

[2] *Prose*, i. 301.

[3] Teerink goes on to tell how he made this discovery: 'This is betrayed by the B.M. copy (838. g. 1) . . . in which the leaves G6 and G7 (slit, but repaired!) have been preserved in their original place, while the cancel A8 (pp. 91 + blank) is still to be found before page 1 of the text' (Teerink, p. 2).

new leaf was A8, which had been left blank in the original state.

Swift's intervention in the press run of *Miscellanies in Prose and Verse* belies his protestations to Stella on 28 February 1711: 'Some bookseller has raked up everything I writ, and published it t'other day in one volume; but I know nothing of it, 'twas without my knowledge or consent: it makes a four shilling book, and is called *Miscellanies in Prose and Verse*. Took pretends he knows nothing of it, but I doubt he is at the bottom.'[1] The truth of the matter, as Stella knew, was that Swift had been planning for years to publish a collection of his verse and prose. On the back of a letter addressed to him in October 1708, which is now lost, he had written down twenty-two 'Subjects for a volume', of which the first was 'Discourse on *Athens* and *Rome*'.[2] It was Swift's intention that Benjamin Tooke, who had published Temple's *Memoirs. Part III* for Swift in 1709, should publish both the volume of miscellanies as well as a fifth edition of *A Tale of a Tub*. Tooke wrote to Swift in July 1710: 'It was very indifferent to me which I proceeded on first, the Tale or the Miscellanies. . . . I think too much time has already been lost in the Miscellanies; therefore, hasten that; And whichever is in the most forwardness, I would begin on first.'[3] Tooke obviously expected Swift to supply him with copy for the miscellany volume, and this confirms the evidence derived from collation that 1711 is set up from a corrected copy of 1701$^{(1)}$. Presumably Swift himself made the corrections. There are about a dozen substantive variants which, according to McKerrow's *dictum*, 'could not reasonably be attributed to an ordinary press-corrector'. 'May perhaps be worth nothing', for example, is restored to 'may perhaps be worth noting'. Why this volume was published by John Morphew, with

[1] Swift, *Journal to Stella*, ed. Harold Williams, 2 vols., Oxford, 1948, i. 203.

[2] John Nichols, *A Supplement to Dr. Swift's Works*, 1779, p. 741.

[3] *Corr.* i. 186. As late as 17 Oct. 1710 Swift told Stella: 'Tooke is going on with my *Miscellany*' (*Journal to Stella*, 1948, i. 62).

Tooke 'at the bottom of it', instead of by Tooke himself, remains a mystery. But Swift was delighted to be able to report to Stella that it sold 'mightily'.

1713. As its title implies, *Miscellanies in Prose and Verse. The Second Edition*, is a page-for-page resetting of 1711. It was actually published in February 1714, the same week in which John Morphew also published Swift's *The Publick Spirit of the Whigs*, which caused him to be taken into custody for publishing a 'false, malicious, and factious Libel'.[1] Since *1713* retains even the most obvious errors of 1711, including the repetition of the last two lines of page 64 as the first two lines of page 65, it is apparent that Swift had nothing to do with it.

1721. Morphew's *Miscellanies* were pirated in 1721 by a Dublin printer named Samuel Fairbrother, whom Swift called 'Fowlbrother' and characterized as 'an arrant rascal in every circumstance'.[2] Fairbrother called his volume, a small octavo, *Miscellanies in Prose and Verse. The Fourth Edition* (Teerink *18*). Actually it is a word-for-word resetting of *1713*.

1727. In its next manifestation, the *Discourse* appeared as the first item in the first volume of the Pope–Swift *Miscellanies in Prose and Verse*, published by Benjamin Motte in June 1727 (Teerink *25*). This project was concerted between Swift and Pope during Swift's visit to Twickenham, May–August 1726, when he was negotiating the publication of *Gulliver's Travels*. Upon his return to Dublin, Swift assured Pope that he was keeping his promise: 'I am mustring as I told you all the little things in verse that I think may be Safely printed, but I give you despotick Power to tear as many as you please.'[3] Pope announced in February 1727 that 'Our Miscellany is now quite printed',[4] but publication was delayed until Swift's

[1] Teerink, 2nd ed., ed. Arthur H. Scouten, Philadelphia, 1963, p. 3; *Prose*, viii, pp. xxi–xxii.

[2] *Corr.* v. 332, 322.

[3] *Corr.* iii. 349.

[4] *Corr.* iii. 380. Sir Harold Williams observed that Pope's 'accompanying

return to England. The Preface to the series was signed by both Pope and Swift at Twickenham and dated 27 May 1727. The first two volumes were published, in octavo, a month later, on 24 June 1727. The contents of the first volume is described in the Preface: 'The Papers that compose the first of these Volumes were printed about sixteen Years ago, to which there are now added two or three small Tracts.'[1] As far as the *Discourse* is concerned Pope seems to have exercised his 'despotick Power' not at all. *1727* is a word-for-word resetting of *1713*. It is the first edition of the *Discourse* to make a consistent effort to normalize the accidentals of the text: to capitalize nouns but not adjectives, to set off appositional phrases in commas, and so forth.

1727e. Five of the numerous printer's errors in the text of *1727* are corrected in an errata list which is included in the first volume (sig. π2v).

1728(1). Despite the shortcomings of the texts, the Pope–Swift *Miscellanies in Prose and Verse* enjoyed such a good sale—Thomas Sheridan said it was 'immense'—that a new edition became necessary early in 1728 (Teerink *25*).[2] Motte was then printing the third volume of the series, called *The Last Volume*, so he was able to double the press run, dating part of it 1727 and the rest 1728. As a result[3] the second edition of the third volume of the series was published eight months before the second edition of the first volume, which did not appear until November 1728.[3]

remarks give a completely erroneous description of the set as it was finally published. He speaks of "this joint volume, in which methinks we look like friends side by side". In the first volume, consisting wholly of prose, the only piece by Pope is the preface, jointly signed by Swift and himself' (*Poems*, I. xx). And Pope himself speaks of the authors of the Preface as 'we' (*Corr.* iv. 393).

[1] *Miscellanies in Prose and Verse. The First Volume*, 1727, sig. A2r. The 'added' tracts are *A Letter to a young Clergyman lately enter'd into Holy Orders* and *Thoughts on Various Subjects*.

[2] Thomas Sheridan, *The Life of the Rev. Dr. Jonathan Swift*, 1784, p. 250.

[3] Teerink, pp. 11–12; R. H. Griffith, *Alexander Pope, a Bibliography*, 2 vols., Austin, Texas, 1922, i. 161–2.

1728(1) is a word-for-word resetting of *1727*. The proof-reading, however, is somewhat better. More than two dozen printer's errors are corrected and only five or six new ones introduced.

1728(2). Having pirated Morphew's *Miscellanies* in 1721, Fairbrother probably did not wait long to capitalize on the success of Motte's *Miscellanies* in 1727. He published two duodecimo volumes of *Miscellanies in Prose and Verse*, dated 1728 and impudently advertised on the title-page as 'The Second Edition' (Teerink *33*). These two volumes included the contents of Motte's first, second, and '*Last*' volumes. The contents of Volume I are the same as Motte's *The First Volume*, with the addition of John Arbuthnot's *The History of John Bull* from *The Second Volume*. The text of *1728*(2) is a word-for-word resetting of *1727*. Like *1728*(1), it corrects more than two dozen printer's errors in *1727* and shows other evidence of careful press work.

1728(3). A second piracy of the *Discourse* in 1728 took the form of an octavo pamphlet published in Boston, Massachusetts. This edition was, in fact, ordered to be published by the newly arrived governor, William Burnet, the son of Swift's *bête noire*, Gilbert Burnet, then the late Bishop of Salisbury. There is further irony in the fact that the pamphlet which the son appropriated to his own defence in 1728 had been widely attributed to the father when it was first published in 1701. How the governor of Massachusetts, the governor's council, and a refractory House of Representatives happened to re-enact the archetypal conflicts described in the *Discourse* has been recounted by Robert J. Allen and need not be repeated here.[1] The text of *1728*(3) is a word-for-word resetting of *1713*.

1731. Although dated 1731, the third edition of Motte's *Miscellanies. The First Volume* was published in October

[1] Robert J. Allen, 'Swift's *Contests and Dissensions* in Boston', *New England Quarterly*, xxix (March 1956), 73–82.

1730 in duodecimo (Teerink *26*). It is a word-for-word resetting of *1728*(1).

1732. A second edition of Fairbrother's piracy of the Pope–Swift *Miscellanies*, advertised on the title-page as 'The Third Edition', appeared in Dublin in 1732 (Teerink *33*). It is another duodecimo edition, a word-for-word resetting of *1728*(2).

1733. The fourth edition of the Pope–Swift *Miscellanies. The First Volume*, another duodecimo volume, was published by Motte in 1733 (Teerink *27*). It is a word-for-word resetting of *1731*.

1727a. According to Sir Harold Williams, the proposal for an authoritative edition of Swift's works originated in the dissatisfaction of Swift's friends with the Pope–Swift *Miscellanies*, where Swift's more important works are jumbled together indiscriminately with those of Pope, Arbuthnot, and Gay, along with his own 'ludicrous and little things' of no consequence.[1] 'Swift's friends', in the Aesopian language which Swift customarily adopted when talking about the publication of his own works, usually means Swift himself. But however it originated, the proposal crystallized, late in 1732, into an undertaking by George Faulkner, a Dublin printer whom Swift had known for several years, to publish Swift's collected works by subscription, 'Beautifully Printed, in Octavo, on a fine Genoa Paper, and neatly Bound' in four volumes. Swift protested, galvanically, and even claimed later that he had had 'no dealings' with Faulkner. But it is no longer possible to doubt that Swift supplied Faulkner with corrected copy for all his works which had appeared in the Pope–Swift *Miscellanies*. The evidence, preserved in the Rothschild collection at Trinity College, Cambridge, is Swift's copy of the 1727 edition, 'with his autograph corrections, additions and comments in pen and pencil',

[1] Williams, p. 45; *Corr.* iv. 342.

designated **1727a** in the present volume.[1] There are 113 of these corrections, and 93 of them were incorporated into Faulkner's text (1735$^{(1)}$).[2] Swift's correspondence indicates that he was at work on this task in July and August 1733.[3] **1727a** is almost certainly not the actual printer's copy from which 1735$^{(1)}$ was set up, but Swift's control copy from which the actual printer's copy was transcribed.[4] The nature of Swift's corrections has been summarized by Sir Harold Williams: '[they] are almost all of a minor nature—mis-spellings, changes in punctuation, substitutions of 'it is' for ''tis', of 'although' for 'tho'', of 'hath' for 'has', together with a few improvements in grammar or phrase.'[5] The substantive 'improvements' also seem to be of a minor nature: *with* for *by*, *leave* for *quit*, and *who* for *that*; and there are barely a dozen of these. Even the changes of a minor nature are not consistently carried out. By no means all of the *'tis*'s, *tho*'s, and *has*'s are converted to their longer forms. Glaring errors are passed over unnoticed. Only one of the five errata noticed in *1727e* are corrected. Where *1727* reads '*Meltiades* . . . liv'd about Ninty Years after', Swift corrected the spelling of *Miltiades*, but overlooked *Ninty*. In the phrase 'in the Time of Marius Saturnius' Swift failed either to correct the spell-

[1] *A Catalogue of Printed Books and Manuscripts, by Jonathan Swift, D.D., Exhibited in the Old Schools in the University of Cambridge. To Commemorate the 200th Anniversary of his Death, October 19, 1745*, Cambridge, 1945, p. 24.

[2] Sir Harold Williams put these figures at 86 and 78 (Williams, p. 77), but since some of Swift's corrections consist simply in converting a comma into a semicolon, and since he frequently neglects to signal the correction with a proof-reader's mark in the margin, it is almost impossible to find all of them.

[3] *Corr.* v. 1, 26.

[4] The evidence for this is the considerable number of emendations made by Swift (e.g. commas inserted after 'For' at III. 156 and III. 169) which he neglected to indicate by proof-reader's marks in the margin. If **1727a** had been used as copy, the compositor would have seen the corrections, but since there were no proof-reader's marks in the margin, the copyist failed to transcribe the corrections into the copy which was sent to the printer. It is presumably this copy that Faulkner mentions in one of his advertisements for 1735$^{(1)}$: 'a Friend in whom the Author much confided . . . had leave to correct his own printed Copies from the Author's most finished Manuscript' (*Corr.* v. 450). In the case of the *Discourse* 'the Author's most finished Manuscript' must have been **1727a**.

[5] Williams, p. 77.

ing of *Saturninus* or to insert the crucial comma after *Marius*. In at least two instances Swift seems to have introduced new errors by his changes.[1] All of this, of course, merely corroborates the impression gained from his letters that Swift was by no means so careful an editor of his works as his much-maligned friend Alexander Pope.

1735$^{(1)}$. George Faulkner, whom Swift called 'the prince of Dublin printers', published the first three volumes of *The Works of J.S, D.D, D.S.P.D.* in November 1734 in octavo (Teerink *41*). The *Discourse* was again accorded the place of honour as the first piece in the first volume. Swift, however, did not decide the order in which the selections were printed. Orrery said that 'the situation and arrangement of each particular piece, in verse and prose, was left entirely to the editor'.[2] Swift did, however, exercise a veto power in this regard; in August 1734 he admitted that he had 'put [Faulkner] under some difficulties by ordering certain things to be struck out after they were printed'.[3] Faulkner's published claim, corroborated by the young Earl of Orrery, that Swift 'was pleased to revise every Proof Sheet',[4] is completely supported by the evidence of collation. In the text of the *Discourse* alone there are some 1275 variants between the copy of **1727a** which Swift supplied to the printer and the **1735**$^{(1)}$ edition which came off the press. Almost all of these variants are accidentals and may be assumed to be the work of the compositor. It is impossible, for example, to imagine that Swift is responsible for the petty and excessive pointing of the following clause: 'under whose Conduct, or Fortune, one Side is, at first, Victorious, and, at last, both are Slaves' (III. 430). But about sixty of these

[1] III. 225 and V. 245.

[2] John Boyle, 5th Earl of Orrery, *Remarks on the Life and Writings of Dr. Jonathan Swift*, 3rd ed., 1752, p. 52.

[3] *Corr.* v. 85.

[4] *Dublin Journal*, No. 1834, 29 September–2 October 1744; Orrery, *Remarks*, 3rd ed., 1752, p. 52: 'every sheet . . . was brought to the Dean for his revisal and correction.' The young Earl of Orrery was a member of the deanery circle in 1733–4 (*Corr.* iv. 381, v. 8).

variants are substantive and must have been introduced by Swift himself on the proofsheets of 1735$^{(1)}$.[1] For it is equally impossible to imagine 'Friends of the Author' making changes like the following: *wanted Time to adjust them* for *could not then give them up* (II. 144); *as almost impossible* for *as impossible* (V. 31); or *the present* for *this* (V. 288). In different ways, these three examples provide further evidence that Swift was not a good polisher of his own work. In one example after another the changes he made on the proofsheets of 1735$^{(1)}$ weaken the original prose of 1701$^{(1)}$. Or perhaps the point is simply that a man of 67 is not a good editor of his own work done at 33.

1735$^{(2)}$. Faulkner's duodecimo edition of *The Works* (Teerink *49*), is a word-for-word resetting of *1735*$^{(1)}$.

1736$^{(1)}$. A fifth edition of the Pope–Swift *Miscellanies. The First Volume*, another duodecimo and the first to which Charles Bathurst's name is joined with Benjamin Motte's on the title-page, was published in 1736 (Teerink *28*). It is a word-for-word resetting of *1733*. After the Dublin edition of *The Works* (1735) had weeded out everything that was not Swift's, it was easy for the London publishers to append a note to the table of contents: '*N.B.* Those Pieces which have not this Mark ☞ ☞ were not wrote by Dean *Swift*', and so to designate Swift's work.

1736$^{(2)}$. The need for another edition of the Pope–Swift *Miscellanies. The First Volume* within a year must reflect an increased interest in Swift aroused by Faulkner's edition of *The Works* (1735), which sold widely in London. The sixth edition is identical with the fifth except that Swift's work is identified with a different mark: ☞★ (Teerink *29*). The text of the *Discourse* is a word-for-word resetting of *1736*$^{(1)}$.

[1] Williams, pp. 87–88. Sir Harold Williams put this figure at 'about fifty', but see p. 192 *n*. 2 above.

1738$^{(1)}$. Faulkner's second octavo edition of *The Works* (Teerink *42*) is a word-for-word resetting, not of 1735$^{(1)}$, as might be expected, but of the first duodecimo edition, *1735*$^{(2)}$.

1738$^{(2)}$. Faulkner's second duodecimo edition of *The Works* (Teerink *50*) is also a word-for-word resetting of *1735*$^{(2)}$.

1742$^{(1)}$. After the death of Benjamin Motte in 1738 his partner and successor, Charles Bathurst, brought out a seventh edition of the Pope–Swift *Miscellanies. Vol. I*, called 'The Fourth Edition Corrected'.[1] This was the first volume of a small octavo collection of Swift's work in 13 volumes (Teerink *66*). The text of the *Discourse*, which continued to occupy first place in the volume, is a word-for-word resetting of *1736*$^{(2)}$.

1742$^{(2)}$. Faulkner's third octavo edition of *The Works* (Teerink *43*) is a word-for-word resetting of *1738*$^{(1)}$. A large-paper copy in the Smith College library was formerly the possession of John Boyle, 5th Earl of Cork and Orrery. The fly-leaf of Volume I is inscribed 'Orrery January 2d. 1741–2. These are the Books from which I extracted my Remarks on the Life and Writings of Doctor Swift', but the annotation of the *Discourse* includes nothing of interest.

1751$^{(1)}$. After Swift's literary career was terminated by a writ *De lunatico inquirendo* in August 1742, Charles Bathurst published in 1747 and 1751 two more editions of the Pope–Swift *Miscellanies. Vol. I*, both in octavo, which he designated, respectively, as 'The Fifth Edition' and 'The Sixth Edition' (Teerink *67* and *68*). The *1751*$^{(1)}$ text of the *Discourse* derives from *1742*$^{(1)}$. The unknown press corrector of *1751*$^{(1)}$ must have been something of

[1] Although *1742*$^{(1)}$ is called 'The Fourth Edition', only two earlier octavo editions of *Miscellanies. The First Volume* are known, *1727* and *1728*$^{(1)}$. The existence of a third octavo edition, therefore, may be surmised.

a classics scholar, for he is the first to give the correct name of Terentius Culleo (III. 298) and he restores the correct spelling of Saturninus (III. 325).

1751$^{(2)}$. Charles Bathurst published a second octavo edition of the Pope–Swift *Miscellanies* in 1751 which he called 'The Fourth Edition Corrected' (Teerink *69*). The text of the *Discourse*, which again appears in the front of Volume I, is collateral with *1751*$^{(1)}$, being derived from *1742*$^{(1)}$.

1751$^{(3)}$. Teerink observed that Charles Bathurst's duodecimo edition of *The Works of Dr. Jonathan Swift* in 1751 is 'noteworthy as a link between the former *Miscellanies* . . . and the following *Works* (Hawkesworth, &c.), in being the first to place *A Tale of a Tub* [Volume I] and *Gulliver's Travels* [Volumes II–III] . . . in front' (Teerink *82*). As a consequence the *Discourse* is relegated to the front of Volume IV. Textually it is *1751*$^{(2)}$ that forms the link between the *Miscellanies* and the later *Works*, for Hawkesworth adopted it as the copy text for *1754*. *1751*$^{(3)}$ is a word-for-word resetting of *1751*$^{(1)}$.

1754. The first editor of the *Discourse* was John Hawkesworth (1715?–73) who forms an interesting link between Swift and Samuel Johnson, with whom he lived 'in great familiarity' in the 1740s and 1750s.[1] From an apprenticed attorney's clerk Hawkesworth rose by his 'considerable literary talent'[2] to be a member of the Ivy Lane Club, Johnson's collaborator in *The Adventurer* (1752–4), and the recipient of a Lambeth LL.D. degree. In 1754 he also began publication of *The Works of Jonathan Swift, D.D. Dean of St. Patrick's, Dublin, Accurately revised in Twelve Volumes, Adorned with Copper-Plates; With Some Account of the Author's Life, and Notes Historical and Explanatory*, in large octavo (Teerink *88*).[3]

1 Hester Lynch Piozzi, *Anecdotes*, ed. S. C. Roberts, Cambridge, 1925, p. 23.
2 *D.N.B.* ix. 205.
3 The octavo edition seems to have preceded the quarto (Teerink *87*).

For the *Discourse*, which is the first work in Volume III, Hawkesworth wrote a short but accurate headnote, explanatory footnotes on tacking, ostracism, and James Harrington, and identified the 'modern Instances' disguised in Aristides, Themistocles, Pericles, and Phocion. He was also the first to notice that Orford is represented by both Themistocles and Miltiades; but, strangely enough, he failed to notice that Orford is actually represented by three classical prototypes (Themistocles, Miltiades, and Alcibiades) and Charles Montagu by two (Pericles and Alcibiades). But there is nothing in Hawkesworth's edition of the *Discourse* to justify Deane Swift's complaint that 'Hawkesworth's edition . . . is the vilest that ever was yet published', any more than there is anything in Faulkner's edition of 1735 to justify Hawkesworth's 'bitter but ignorant and misguided attack' in *The Preface* to Volume I.[1] As John Nichols pointed out in 1779, the faults Hawkesworth cites are typographical errors which 'might easily have been occasioned by the inattention of a printer, though he had the advantage of the Dean's corrected copy' in front of him.[2] The attacks of editors on their predecessors are wholly conventional, like the preliminary flourishes of the matador. The evidence of collation shows Hawkesworth to be particularly disingenuous, since he adopts dozens of 'the *Irish* variations' that he scorns. Nichols, quite properly, concluded that 'a careful collation of the present *English* edition with the *Irish* would be the best method of attaining exactness', and this is exactly what Hawkesworth had done. He chose *1751*⁽²⁾ for his copy text, so that the accidentals of his text are derived from the English editions. But then he introduced substantive variants from the Irish editions *ad lib.*, producing a conflated text which became the source of subsequent editions of the *Discourse* for nearly 200 years. Apart from occasional archaizing—the introduction of 'approacheth' for 'approaches'—Hawkesworth's made-up

[1] Nichols, *Illustrations*, v. 376: *Poems*, i, p. xxxiii.

[2] John Nichols, *A Supplement to Dr. Swift's Works*, 1779, p. v, *n*. g.

text is excellent, and at least one of his emendations (II. 105–6) accidentally restores a reading of **1727a** which failed to be incorporated into **1735**(1).

1784. Thomas Sheridan (1719–88), Swift's next editor, was the third son of Thomas Sheridan of Quilca, county Cavan, one of Swift's closest friends. He was Swift's godson, a scholar at Trinity College, Dublin, an actor, manager of the Theatre Royal in Dublin, the father of Richard Brinsley Sheridan, friend ('Sherry derry') and then enemy ('What! have they given *him* a pension?') of Samuel Johnson, a fanatic believer in the power of orthoepy whose disciples included the young James Boswell, the recipient of honorary degrees from both Oxford and Cambridge, the biographer of Swift, and finally, in 1784, editor of *The Works of the Rev. Dr. Jonathan Swift, Dean of St. Patrick's, Dublin. . . . A New Edition, in Seventeen Volumes*, octavo (Teerink *119*). In this edition the *Discourse* follows *A Tale of a Tub* and *Gulliver's Travels* in Volume II. After the ritualistic attack on all previous editions of Swift as 'thrown together in the most irregular undigested form ever known',[1] Sheridan virtually appropriates Hawkesworth's edition intact. He reprints, without any acknowledgement, Hawkesworth's headnote to the *Discourse* as well as his footnotes on tacking, ostracism, and James Harrington. He omits, however, Hawkesworth's important footnotes identifying the 'modern Instances' of the Athenian characters and pointing out that two Athenians represent the same 'modern'. Sheridan's contribution to the *Discourse* is limited to five footnotes correcting or criticizing Swift's prose style. One of these footnotes is manifestly wrong (at I. 316 Sheridan proposes to alter 'though several Instances might be brought from other States thereof' to 'though several instances thereof, might be brought from other states', ignoring the fact that 'thereof' refers to '*Greece*', not to 'Instances'); and three of them are too petty to mention.

[1] Nichols, *Illustrations*, v. 395.

One of them, however, criticizes Swift for exactly the same kind of locution as Swift himself condemned in Clarendon and Burnet. At I. 275 in Hawkesworth's text Sheridan read: 'to break or overthrow this balance, which every one of the three parties hath continually endeavoured, as opportunities have served; as might appear from the stories of most ages and countries.' Sheridan, accordingly, complained that 'The repetition of the particle, as, at the beginning of two members of a sentence so near each other, has a bad effect', and recommended a change to 'Whenever opportunities offered'.[1] **1701**(1), however, reads 'which might appear', presumably what Swift wrote, and the offensive repetition of 'as' may be attributed to the compositor in John Morphew's shop who set up **1711**. As might be expected, the *1784* text of the *Discourse* is a word-for-word resetting of *1754*.

1801. Swift's third editor was John Nichols (1745–1826), the great antiquarian whose collections are indispensable to the study of the eighteenth century. Nichols, the son of a baker in Islington, was apprenticed to William Bowyer, the printer. Twenty years later, as Bowyer's successor, he became the printer of Samuel Johnson's *Lives of the Poets*, a member of the Essex Head Club, and friend of Horace Walpole, Earl of Orford. Before he died at Islington, in 1826, he had served as editor of the *Gentleman's Magazine*, alderman for Farringdon Without, and Master of the Stationers' Company. His work on Swift began in 1775 when he published an additional volume (XVII) to Hawkesworth's edition of 1754. In 1776 and 1779 he added *A Supplement to Dr. Swift's Works*, which became Volumes XXIV and XXV of Hawkesworth's octavo edition (Volume XIV in the quarto edition). By 1779 he had already projected his own edition of Swift,[2] which finally appeared in 1801 as *The Works of the Rev.*

[1] *The Works*, ed. Thomas Sheridan, 17 vols., 1784, ii. 375 *n*.
[2] H.M.C. Charlemont MSS. i. 347.

Jonathan Swift, D.D., Dean of St. Patrick's, Dublin. Arranged by Thomas Sheridan, A.M. With Notes, Historical and Critical. A New Edition, In Nineteen Volumes; Corrected and Revised by John Nichols, octavo (Teerink *129*). Although Sir Walter Scott admired his 'labour and accuracy', Nichols's work on the *Discourse*, which occupies pages 291–346 of Volume II, is disappointing. He appropriated Hawkesworth's headnote, not, however, without acknowledgement, and added to it only a short note from Lord Orrery's *Remarks*. He also adopted those few footnotes of Hawkesworth which Sheridan had included. Of Sheridan's own 'stylistic' footnotes Nichols omitted the one which was manifestly wrong, but retained the other four, thus unwittingly revealing his ignorance of the text of 1701[(1)]. His text of the *Discourse* is a word-for-word resetting of *1784*.

1814. John Nichols's complaint that Sir Walter Scott, 'by abridging my tedious annotations', had turned lead into gold, is true only to the extent that Scott did indeed undertake an edition of Swift to make money. The success of Scott's edition of Dryden, which appeared in April 1808, encouraged Archibald Constable to offer Scott £1,500 for an edition of Swift. Scott accepted, and in a prospectus dated January 1809 announced that he would provide 'historical explanations and anecdotes' for Swift's political treatises, and that the edition would be ready for publication about Christmas 1810.[1] Scott failed to meet his deadline by three and a half years; the nineteen octavo volumes of *The Works of Jonathan Swift, D.D. Dean of St. Patrick's, Dublin . . .; With Notes, and a Life of the Author, By Walter Scott, Esq.* (Teerink *138*) were not published until July 1814. But Scott completely fulfilled his promise to provide 'historical explanations'. For the *Discourse*, which occupies pages 259–312 of Volume III, he wrote a brilliant new headnote, completely revised

[1] Sir Walter Scott, *The Letters*, ed. Herbert J. C. Grierson, 12 vols., 1932–7, ii. 79–81.

Hawkesworth's notes on tacking, ostracism, and James Harrington, expanded Hawkesworth's notes identifying the '*Athenian* characters', cut out all of Sheridan's fatuous 'corrections', and added half a dozen new notes on a variety of subjects.[1] Scott's only indebtedness to Nichols is for the text of the *Discourse*; *1814* is a word-for-word resetting of *1801*. One of the few occasions on which *1814* corrects *1801* indicates that Scott may have scrutinized the text very carefully. At III. 252, in a long quotation from Polybius, Scott restores the word *as* which had dropped out of Nichols's text. '*And that as Rust eats away Iron, and Worms devour Wood, and both are a sort of Plagues . . .; so with every Form and Scheme of Government. . . .*' This does not seem to be the kind of emendation typical of a press-corrector.

Of the editions described above, the following copies have been collated;

1701(1)	Huntington Library, Halsey copy
1701(2)	Columbia University copy
1707	Yale University copy
1711	Yale University copy
1713	Yale University copy
1727	Smith College copy
1728(1)	Dartmouth College copy
1731	Harvard University copy
1733	Yale University copy
1727a	Trinity College, Cambridge
1735(1)	Yale University copy
1735(2)	University of Pennsylvania copy
1736(1)	Smith College copy
1736(2)	University of Texas copy
1738(1)	Bodleian Library copy
1738(2)	British Museum copy
1742(1)	Yale University copy

[1] Only on two occasions does Scott's accuracy falter: he writes 1701 for 1700 in a footnote on p. 267, and mistakenly assumes that '*Phocion's . . . negotiations*' refers to Portland's involvement in the Treaty of Ryswick, instead of the Second Partition Treaty.

1742(2) Smith College copy
1751(1) Yale University copy
1751(2) University of Pennsylvania copy
1751(3) Yale University copy
1754 Yale University copy
1784 Yale University copy
1801 Yale University copy
1814 Yale University copy

Only substantive variants, occurring in substantive editions, are recorded below and they are recorded in the order in which the editions are described above (piracies, of course, have been excluded).

I. 9 the Legislators] the best Legislators 1735(1)–*1735*(2) *1738*(1)–*1738*(2) *1742*(2) *1754*–*1814*
I. 31 and] or 1701(1)–1711
I. 32 or] and 1735(1)–*1735*(2) *1738*(1)–*1738*(2) *1742*(2)
I. 33 is] are 1701(1)–*1733* *1736*(1)–*1736*(2) *1742*(1) *1751*(1)–*1751*(3)
I. 60 within] with 1701(1)–*1702*(1)
I. 75 with utmost] with the utmost 1735(1)–*1735*(2) *1738*(1)–*1738*(2) *1742*(2) *1754*–*1814*
I. 75 the several Scales] each Scale 1735(1)–*1735*(2) *1738*(1)–*1738*(2) *1742*(2)
I. 84 Institution] Institutions 1701(1)–*1707* 1735(1)–*1735*(2) *1738*(1)–*1738*(2) *1742*(2)
I. 117 Kings] King 1711–*1727* 1727a–*1735*(2) *1738*(1)–*1738*(2) *1742*(2)
I. 120 Age] Ages 1701(1)–*1733* *1736*(1)–*1736*(2) *1742*(1) *1751*(1)–*1751*(3)
I. 147 and that to] and this to 1735(1)–*1735*(2) *1738*(1)–*1738*(2) *1742*(2) *1754*–*1814*
I. 163 Accusations] Accusation 1735(1)–*1735*(2) *1738*(1)–*1738*(2) *1742*(2)
I. 195 for upholding] for the upholding *1727*–*1814*
I. 198 Interest] Interests 1701(1)–*1707*
I. 202–3 conceive] think it an uncontroulable Maxim 1711–*1814*
I. 203 is safer] is always safer 1711–*1814*
I. 204 those] these 1735(1)–*1735*(2) *1738*(1)–*1738*(2) *1742*(2) *1754*–*1814*

I. 204 of one] from one 1735(1)–*1735*(2) *1738*(1)–*1738*(2) *1742*(2) *1754–1814*

I. 215 defect] defects 1711–*1727* 1727a–*1735*(2) *1738*(2)

I. 218 Rights] Privileges 1701(1)–*1707*

I. 219 Privileges] Rights 1701(1)–*1707*

I. 236 started at all before] started before 1727a–*1735*(2) *1738*(1)–*1738*(2) *1742*(2)

I. 273 of Legislators] of the Legislators *1713–1814*

I. 276 every one of] every of 1701(1)–*1733* *1736*(1)–*1736*(2) *1742*(1) *1751*(1)–*1751*(3)

I. 277 which] as 1711–*1814*

I. 290 did at several] did several *1727–1814*

I. 297 But] Yet 1735(1)–*1735*(2) *1738*(1)–*1738*(2) *1742*(2) *1754–1814*

I. 306 Rock they] Rock that they 1735(1)–*1735*(2) *1738*(1)–*1738*(2) *1742*(2) *1754–1814*

I. 312 Dissentions] Dissention 1701(1)

I. 312 Dissentions between] Dissentions in *Greece* and *Rome*, between 1735(1)–*1735*(2) *1738*(1)–*1738*(2) *1742*(2) *1754–1814*

I. 313 them, in *Greece* and *Rome*, wherein] them, wherein 1735(1)–*1735*(2) *1738*(1)–*1738*(2) *1742*(2) *1754–1814*

II. 19 the] that 1701(1)–*1707*

II. 22 confusions] Confusion *1727–1814*

II. 62 being] were 1735(1)–*1735*(2) *1738*(1)–*1738*(2) *1742*(2) *1754–1814*

II. 66 of] or 1701(1)–*1727* 1727a

II. 78 and the Issues] and Issues 1735(1)–*1735*(2) *1738*(1)–*1738*(2) *1742*(2) *1754–1814*

II. 81 justly to apprehend] justly apprehend 1701(1)–*1701*(2)

II. 100 the *Persian* Fleet] the Fleet 1711–*1814*

II. 101 them] the Enemy 1735(1)–*1735*(2) *1738*(1)–*1738*(2) *1742*(2)

II. 101 for] to 1735(1)–*1735*(2) *1738*(1)–*1738*(2) *1742*(2)

II. 105–6 other than] otherwise than by 1701(1)–*1733* *1736*(1)–*1736*(2) *1742*(1) *1751*(1) *1751*(3); more than 1735(1)–*1735*(2) *1738*(1)–*1738*(2) *1742*(2)

II. 112 manner the Chancellor] manner Chancellor *1727–1814*

II. 117 however, they had] they had soon 1735(1)–*1735(2) 1738(1)–1738(2) 1742(2)*
II. 127 that] who 1735(1)–*1735(2) 1738(1)–1738(2) 1742(2)*
II. 144 *could not then give them up*] *could not give them up* 1701(1)–*1707*; wanted Time to adjust them 1735(1)–*1735(2) 1738(1)–1738(2) 1742(2)*
II. 166 Powerful] Popular 1701(1)–*1707*
II. 169 desires] Desire 1735(1)–*1735(2) 1738(1)–1738(2) 1742(2)*
II. 177 his Conditions] his own Conditions 1711–*1814*
II. 203 preserving] recovering 1735(1)–*1735(2) 1738(1)–1738(2) 1742(2) 1754–1814*
II. 211 Negotiation] Negotiations 1711–1727a *1736(1)–1736(2) 1742(1) 1751(1)–1814*
II. 225 are *Popular Assemblies*] have *Popular Assemblies* been 1711–*1814*
II. 226 deserve] deserved 1711–*1814*
II. 235 overthrown] overthrew 1701(1)–*1728(1)* 1727a
II. 244 that great] that this great 1735(1)–*1735(2) 1738(1)–1738(2) 1742(2)*
II. 251 upon] on 1727–*1814*
II. 278 by] with 1727a–*1735(1) 1738(1)–1738(2) 1742(2)*

III. 19 those] these 1701(1)–*1701(2)*
III. 25 Principle] Principles 1711–*1736(2) 1738(2)–1742(1) 1751(1)–1784*
III. 37 Stage of the World] Stage 1701(1)–*1707*
III. 61 Those] These 1735(1)–*1735(2) 1738(1)–1738(2) 1742(2)*
III. 127 quit] leave 1727a–*1735(2) 1738(1)–1738(2) 1742(2) 1754–1814*
III. 140 Dissensions] Dissention *1727*–1727a
III. 146 began] begun 1735(1)–*1735(2) 1738(1)–1738(2) 1742(2)*
III. 164 but disdaining] but he disdaining 1735(1)–*1735(2) 1738(1)–1738(2) 1742(2)*
III. 173 obtain'd] obtain 1701(1)–*1707*
III. 184 and to the] and the 1735(1)–*1735(2) 1738(1)–1738(2) 1742(2)*
III. 225 adhered] adhere *1727* to adhere 1727a
III. 260 from popular] from the popular *1713–1814*
III. 268 for] of 1701(1)–*1701(2)*
III. 293 the entire destruction] the destruction 1711–*1814*

III. 325 *Saturninus*] *Saturnius* *1727–1728*(1) **1727a**; *Saturnus* *1731–1733* *1736*(1)–*1736*(2) *1742*(1) *1751*(2)–*1751*(3)

III. 332 *ancient and inherent*] *ancient inherent* *1727–1814*

III. 333 perfect] absolute **1735**(1)–*1735*(2) *1738*(1)–*1738*(2) *1742*(2) *1754–1814*

III. 346 Accounts] Account *1713–1814*

III. 352 Offices] Office **1711–1727a** *1736*(1)–*1736*(2) *1742*(1) *1751*(1) *1751*(3)

III. 392 are] were **1701**(1)–*1701*(2)

III. 395 of introducing] to introduce **1735**(1)–*1735*(2) *1738*(1)–*1738*(2) *1742*(2)

III. 399 For he] He **1735**(1)–*1735*(2) *1738*(1)–*1738*(2) *1742*(2)

III. 420 become] became **1711**–*1731* **1727a**–*1735*(2) *1738*(1)–*1738*(2) *1742*(2)

III. 422 that] who **1727a**–*1735*(2) *1738*(1)–*1738*(2) *1742*(2)

III. 423 Armies just ready] Armies ready **1711**–*1814*

IV. 9 was] lay **1735**(1)–*1735*(2) *1738*(1)–*1738*(2) *1742*(2) *1754–1814*

IV. 32 was] were **1735**(1)–*1735*(2) *1738*(1)–*1738*(2) *1742*(2)

IV. 38 Impeaching] Impeachment **1735**(1)–*1814*

IV. 42 one] we **1735**(1)–*1735*(2) *1738*(1)–*1738*(2) *1742*(2) *1754–1814*

IV. 46 have reserved] reserve **1735**(1)–*1735*(2) *1738*(1)– *1738*(2) *1742*(2)

IV. 62 *expounded*] *expound* *1713–1814*

IV. 64 *Paultry*] *inconsiderable* **1735**(1)–*1735*(2) *1738*(1)–*1738*(2) *1742*(2) *1754–1814*

IV. 67 Discouragement] Discouragements **1701**(1)–*1731* **1727a**

IV. 74 Persecutors] Prosecutors **1735**(1)–*1735*(2) *1738*(1)–*1738*(2) *1742*(2)

IV. 85 one] a Man **1735**(1)–*1735*(2) *1738*(1)–*1738*(2) *1742*(2) *1754–1814*

IV. 97 or] and *1713–1728*(1) **1727a–1735**(1)

IV. 98 had] possessed **1735**(1)–*1735*(2) *1738*(1)–*1738*(2) *1742*(2) *1754–1814*

IV. 115 not of the] not the **1735**(1)–*1735*(2) *1738*(1)–*1738*(2) *1742*(2)

IV. 125 or] and **1735**(1)–*1735*(2) *1738*(1)–*1738*(2) *1742*(2)

IV. 146 no Course] no other Course **1735**(1)–*1735*(2) *1738*(1)–*1738*(2) *1742*(2) *1754–1814*

IV. 146 but] than 1735$^{(1)}$–*1735*$^{(2)}$ *1738*$^{(1)}$–*1738*$^{(2)}$ *1742*$^{(2)}$ *1754–1814*

V. 16 those] these 1735$^{(1)}$–*1735*$^{(2)}$ *1738*$^{(1)}$–*1738*$^{(2)}$ *1742*$^{(2)}$

V. 31 as impossible] as almost impossible 1735$^{(1)}$–*1735*$^{(2)}$ *1738*$^{(1)}$–*1738*$^{(2)}$ *1742*$^{(2)}$

V. 105 and] who 1735$^{(1)}$–*1735*$^{(2)}$ *1738*$^{(1)}$–*1738*$^{(2)}$ *1742*$^{(2)}$

V. 112 Thirty] Forty 1701$^{(1)}$–*1707*

V. 178 Method] Methods 1711–*1814*

V. 192 Corruptions] Corruption 1701$^{(1)}$–*1707*

V. 203 is so apt] is apt 1701$^{(1)}$–*1707*

V. 223 of the Herd] of Herd 1701$^{(1)}$–*1701*$^{(2)}$

V. 240 to] from 1727a–*1735*$^{(2)}$ *1738*$^{(1)}$–*1738*$^{(2)}$ *1742*$^{(2)}$ *1754–1814*

V. 244–5 that he provided] as he provided 1727a; as to provide 1735$^{(1)}$–*1735*$^{(2)}$ *1738*$^{(1)}$–*1738*$^{(2)}$ *1742*$^{(2)}$

V. 255 Ambition, or] Ambition, their Vanity, or 1735$^{(1)}$–*1735*$^{(2)}$ *1738*$^{(1)}$–*1738*$^{(2)}$ *1742*$^{(2)}$

V. 257 *Politick*] *political* 1735$^{(1)}$–*1735*$^{(2)}$ *1738*$^{(1)}$–*1738*$^{(2)}$ *1742*$^{(2)}$

V. 288 this] the present 1735$^{(1)}$–*1735*$^{(2)}$ *1738*$^{(1)}$–*1738*$^{(2)}$ *1742*$^{(2)}$ *1754–1814*

V. 291–2 the native sedateness] the sedateness 1735$^{(1)}$–*1735*$^{(2)}$ *1738*$^{(1)}$–*1738*$^{(2)}$ *1742*$^{(2)}$

V. 305 to] for 1701$^{(1)}$–*1707*

V. 315 to] for 1711–*1733* *1736*$^{(1)}$–*1736*$^{(2)}$ *1742*$^{(1)}$ *1751*$^{(1)}$–*1751*$^{(3)}$; against 1727a–*1735*$^{(2)}$ *1738*$^{(1)}$–*1738*$^{(2)}$ *1742*$^{(2)}$ *1754–1814*

V. 324 Sense] Experience 1711–*1814*

V. 331 may] will 1735$^{(1)}$–*1735*$^{(2)}$ *1738*$^{(1)}$–*1738*$^{(2)}$ *1742*$^{(2)}$ *1754–1814*

V. 339 than] from what 1711–*1814*

APPENDIX

A. James Drake, *The History of the Last Parliament* (1702)

B. *The Source of Our Present Fears Discover'd* (1703)

C. Charles Leslie, *The New Association: Part II* (1703)

A. James Drake, *The History of the Last Parliament* (1702)[1]

Drake's animadversions on the *Discourse* occur in that portion of his book, pages 29–131, in which he defends the Act of Settlement, passed by the 5th Parliament in May 1701. One article of this act, providing 'That no Pardon under the Great Seal of *England*, be pleadable to an Impeachment by the Commons in Parliament', had been included to forestall a possible pardon for Somers. Drake's defence of this article led him to reconsider the impeachment and mock-trial of the four Lords Partitioners and, finally, 'because of a fancy'd Similitude, that some Persons think they have found to some late Cases at Home', to reinterpret the impeachments of Themistocles, Aristides, Pericles, and Phocion. Thus without ever mentioning Swift or his book, Drake provides a clever and mocking reply to the second chapter of the *Discourse*.

In the next part of his book, pages 132–53, Drake goes on to defend the House of Commons for imprisoning the Kentish petitioners, and since this also includes references to the *Discourse*, part of it has been included as well.

[103] . . . The way of Trial by *Impeachment*, is taken from the *Romans*, amongst whom, in the purest times of their Commonwealth, it was in frequent use. This way of bringing Offenders to Judgment, was taken against such, as the ordinary Jurisdiction of the *Prætor*,

[1] Published no later than March 1702 (*Bibliotheca Annua*, iii. 30). Drake's authorship is established in Anthony Hammond's autobiographical fragment: '24 June [1701] this Parliament rose. . . . This is the Parliament, of which the History of the last Session is writ by Dr. Drake, who was assisted by me in that Work, and afterwards dedicated it to me' (Bodleian, MS. Rawl. A.245, f. 67v). The Epistle Dedicatory to Anthony Hammond appears for the first time in the second edition of *The History* (1702).

and other Magistrates, did not reach; either because the Nature of the Crime was such, as was beside their Cognizance, or the Quality, Power, and Authority of the Person, set him above their Enquiry. In such Cases the *Tribunes* of the *People*, the *Quæstors*, or the *Aediles*, or other Publick Magistrate, Impeach'd 'em to the *People*, who were the Supream *Judges*, from whom [104] there lay *no Appeal*; and exhibited *Articles*.

These Articles usually contain'd Matters of *Publick Grievance*; as *Conspiracies against the State*, *Male-Administration during Office*, *Misapplication of the Publick Treasure*, *Wrong Appropriation of the Forfeited*, *or Conquer'd Lands*, *Invasion of the Rights and Liberties of the People*, *Pernicious Counsel*, &c. And according to the special Nature of the Crime, they Impeach'd of *Treason*, or *Misdemeanor*, and their Judgments extended to Life, *Confiscation of Goods and Estate*, or *Fine* only. In short, whatever Disaster, whatever Miscarriages, whatever Grievances the *Romans* felt; the Person, thro' whose Fault these Evils arose, very rarely escap'd Judgment, but by Flight, or Death. And herein seems to have consisted the main Strength of the *Roman Commonwealth*, that all Services done to the Publick, met with Honour and Reward, and all Offences against it, with certain Punishment, which no Plea of past Services or Merits cou'd avoid. I doubt not, but such Proceedings here at this time, wou'd be call'd Hardships, unjustifiable Severities, and terms on which no Man [105] wou'd serve the Publick; yet they were the very Foundation of the *Roman* Liberty, Virtue, and Discipline, which produc'd such a wonderful Succession of brave and great Men, and together with which all these things decay'd and expired. Tho' the Persons so Impeach'd, were sometimes the most Illustrious for their Quality, the Merits of their Families, and their own proper Services, in cases of the greatest danger; tho' the Senate thought themselves bound in the strongest Obligations to employ all their Power and Interest in their Favour, and the People confess'd themselves deeply indebted to 'em; yet such was the awe of an accusation on the behalf of the Publick, that they durst not interpose their Authority to stifle any such Complaint, or move for any Arrest of Judgment, otherwise than by Solicitation and Supplication, to prevail with the Accusers to let the Prosecution drop, or with the People for a favourable Sentence; of which I shall offer a few of the most remarkable Instances, both for the Quality and high Deserts of the Persons themselves, or their Families, and the lightness of the Crimes objected to 'em, which [106] will sufficiently evince, what is here laid down.

While the *Commonwealth* was yet in its Infancy, being but 18 Years old, and the *Tribunate* scarce out of its Cradle, but of three Years; a Dearth arose, occasion'd by the Lands lying fallow the Year before, upon the score of Domestick Differences. To remedy this Evil, the *Senate* had purchas'd vast Quantities of Corn with the Publick Money, from the Neighbouring Countries; and it was debated amongst 'em, at what rates it should be retail'd out to the People. *Cnaeus Martius* was a Nobleman of the first Rank; who besides his Quality, had his own particular Services, which were great and glorious, to value himself upon; the taking of *Corioli* by his particular Valour, (whence he was Sirnam'd *Coriolanus*) and thereby putting an end to a difficult War, was an Action of such lustre, that the Historian tells us, it quite eclips'd the Glory of the *Consul*. Yet this Man in the Pride of his Glory, while his Merits were yet fresh in the Peoples Memories, attempting to oppress the *Commons*, was Impeach'd by the Tribunes, *for advising the* Senate *to starve the* Commons *into a* [107] *Complyance with their Demands, and to deny 'em Corn, till they consented to suppress the Office of* Tribunes *of the* Commons. The *Nobility* exerted their utmost Authority, and used all their Art in his behalf, united in the *Senate*, and severally out of it; they threatned and solicited their *Tenants*, *Clients*, and *Dependants*, to stop the *Prosecution*, but all in vain. When they found that impossible, the whole *Senate* condescended in a Body, to supplicate the *People* for his *Pardon*, and prevail'd as little. He was forc'd to fly, and not appearing on the appointed Day, was condemn'd tho' absent.

Titus Menenius was impeach'd by the *Tribunes* for suffering *Cremera*, a *Roman* Garrison to be taken without attempting to relieve it, when he was Consul and lay with an Army not far from it. Here the Senate again interpos'd as heartily as before for *Coriolanus*, and, thro' the Value the People had for the Memory of his Father *Menenius Agrippa*, succeeded somewhat better. For they prevail'd with the *Tribunes* to moderate the Prosecution, and instead of trying him for Life, as was at first intended, the matter ended in [108] a Fine. However the Grief of this Disgrace cost him his Life.

His Misfortune stood his Successor *Spurius Servilius* in good stead. He was impeach'd by the *Tribunes* for having endanger'd the Army under his Command as Consul, and suffer'd a Repulse with great Loss in a rash Attempt to force the Enemies Camp. But the fatal Issue of *Menenius*'s Disgrace had made such an Impression upon the People, that they suffer'd *Servilius* to come off.

Appius Claudius, a violent Asserter of the Authority of the *Nobility* against the *Tribunes* and *Commons*, was impeach'd by the *Tribunes* for *obstructing the* Agrarian *Law*, *and abetting and maintaining those*, *that had gotten possession of the Publick Lands*. He appear'd, and made his Defence, and the further Proceedings being adjourn'd for a short time, before the Trial came on again, he died.

Cæso Quintius, the Flower of the *Roman Nobility*, for extraordinary Endowments both of Body and Mind; who had himself, as had also his Father *Lucius Quintius Cincinnatus*, divers times reliev'd and sav'd the *Roman Commonwealth*, by his own particular Valour and [109] Conduct, was impeach'd by *Aulus Virginius*, of Capital Crimes. The Charge was, *That he had by* Arms *and* Violence *oppos'd and hinder'd the* Tribunes *from passing a Law to* restrain *the* Power *of the* Consuls; *That he had often by* Blows *and evil Treatment*, *driven the* Tribunes, *and* People *out of the* Forum; *That he had struck down one Man with a* Blow *of his* Fist, *whereof he was since* Dead. Neither the Authority of the Senate, the numerous and meritorious Services of himself and Family, nor the Prayers of his Father then abundantly the most illustrious Person, and most deserving of the *Commonwealth* in all *Rome*, avail'd any thing. The People were deaf to all Entreaties, and Arguments in his Favour. The utmost, that cou'd be obtain'd, was to suffer him to be Bail'd upon excessive great Security. This made him withdraw, and live in voluntary Exile. This was so far from mollifying his Judges, that not appearing, he was condemn'd, and the Cautionary Sum levied with such cruel Rigour upon his Father, that he was forc'd to sell all his Goods, and go to live like a Banish'd Man, in an obscure Cottage [on] a Farm of 4 Acres beyond [110] the *Tyber*: And tho' the Evidence *against Cæso*, as to the Manslaughter, *Marcus Volscius* was afterwards convicted of having given false Testimony against him, and Banish'd for it by the *Quæstors*; yet it does not appear, that he was ever suffer'd to return home.

Titus Romulius, and *Caius Veturius*, Consuls, having obtain'd a great Victory, and with it as great a Booty, at a Time when the Publick Treasure was very low; instead of dividing the Spoil among the Soldiers, according to the usual custom, sold all, and put the Money into the Treasury. For this they were both *Impeach'd*, *Condemn'd*, and *Fin'd*.

A Dead Body being dug up in the House of *Publius Sextius*, a Noble Man, he was Impeach'd by *Caius Julius*, one of the *Decemviri*; and the Historian takes a notice of it very particular, and very much to the Honour of the *Decemviri. He did* (says he) *depart from his Right, and abate of the Authority of his Office, to add something to the liberty of the People, contenting himself to become Prosecutor before them in a Cause where the Law allow'd him to be Judge.*

[111] *Appius Claudius*, and *Spurius Oppius*, two of the *Decemviri*, for continuing to exercise their Authority after the limited term of their Office, were impeach'd by the Tribunes, and cast into Prison, and died there by their own Hands. Their Estates were confiscated. The rest of their Colleagues by voluntary Exile avoided Judgment, but their Estates also were confiscated.

Marcus Claudius, for laying false claim to the Daughter of *Virginius*, as Born his Slave, was Impeach'd, Tried for Life and Condemn'd. But the Severity of his Punishment was remitted, and he was Banish'd.

Marcus Posthumius, and *Titus Quintius*, Consuls, were Impeach'd, and Tried for having lost a Battle to the *Veij; Posthumius* was Convicted, and Fin'd, *Quintius* Acquitted.

Agrippa Menenius, Titus Clelius Siculus, and *Marcus Ebutius Helva*, were made Triumvirs, in Order to lead a Colony to *Ardea*. They did so. But in the Distribution of the Lands, having not acted to the Satisfaction of the People of *Rome*, they were Impeach'd. To avoid the force of the Impeachment, they Enroll'd [112] themselves in the Colony, and settl'd there.

But not to be troublesome with too many Instances, of which the *Roman* History is full, I shall close with *Marcus Furius Camillus*. This Man was not only the most Fortunate, but the best Man that ever *Rome* bred, taking him in all Capacities as a Great Soldier, and a Wise Magistrate. He had by his own particular Conduct, gain'd a Great and a Glorious Victory over the *Veij*, besides a Prodigious Booty, which by the Laws and Usage of *Rome* should have been distributed to the Army. But *Camillus*, considering the Poverty of the Treasury, and the Exigencies of the Publick, presuming upon his Merits, made bold to stretch his Authority, and dispensing with the Law on that occasion, sold all the Booty, and put the Money into the Treasury. For this, when he return'd, he was Impeach'd, for having exceeded his Commission against the Law. And tho' he had acted to the best of his Judgment, (perhaps not Erroneously) for the good of the Publick, and was not accus'd of having reserv'd any thing to his own private use, yet he was forc'd to fly his [113] Country to save his Head, and continued in Exile 'till the Calamities of *Rome* made him again absolutely necessary for its preservation.

Such Severities as these, in so corrupt an Age, and so loose an Administration as ours, would, no doubt, be reckon'd intolerable. Almost every one in Publick Trust, takes as great Liberties, and commits as great Outrages, as any of the aforementioned Illustrious Persons; but, their Vertues, and Merits, which should plead their excuse, we are at a loss to find. Should we then prosecute their Offences, with the same Rigour, it is to be fear'd, we should soon have but a thin Ministry. Yet to this exactness, in calling to account their great Men, was the Preservation of their Liberty and Constitution, from Domestick Invasions and Encroachments, mainly owing. It kept their great Men from presuming, upon the Merits of their Services, to usurp upon the Rights of their fellow Citizens: And aw'd the Ambitious, from attempting, by gradual Incroachments, any thing against the Liberties of the People. For these Examples, and such as these, gave 'em frequent Convictions, that the People were [114] Jealous of their Rights, and Resolute in the defence of 'em, and that they wou'd suffer no Man, upon any pretext whatsoever, to abuse his Trust, affront the People, dispense with their Rights, or assume more Authority than they had given him, and to entertain at the same time hopes of Impunity.

This Observation wou'd be still better confirm'd, had we room in this place to examine what was the consequence of the after remissness of the same People in this Point. After the Destruction of *Carthage*, the People of *Rome* was so Intoxicated with the Greatness of their Empire, and the Merits of *Scipio Africanus*, that when he was call'd to Account, by the Tribunes, for divers Arbitrary and Illegal Actions by him committed, during the time of his Command, he, instead of answering to the Matters laid to his Charge, presuming upon his own Merits, and the Favour of the People, Harangu'd 'em on his own Services, and the Greatness of their Deliverance, thro' his Means, and after the Harangue, without making any direct answer to the Accusation brought against him, rose abruptly, and Invited the People, who [115] follow'd him with Acclamations, to go to the *Capitol*, and give thanks to the Gods for the Success of their Arms. This Affront to the *Tribunitial* Authority, and the Indulgence of the *Romans*, tho' to so Great a Man and in Matters of small Importance, bating the Contempt of the Magistrates, was however of fatal consequence to their Liberty. For tho' *Scipio* himself was a Man of that great Temperance and Moderation, that he made no other ill use of his Popularity and Greatness with the People; yet it taught those that came after him, what advantages might be made of such a Reputation and Interest, to an Ambitious Man. From that time the Authority of the *Tribunes* vanish'd; and with it, the whole Security of the Liberties of the People, who lay open, from that time forward, to the Ambition and Intrigues of their designing Great Men, against whom they had no Protectors. For every succeeding Captain profited of this Example, despis'd Authority, and scorn'd to be call'd to an Account.

This gave Spirit to the Ambition, and Birth to the Designs of *Marius*, *Sylla*, *Crassus*, *Pompey*, and *Caesar*; whose In-[116] trigues and Quarrels, put the Commonwealth into long and terrible Convulsions; cost her the Lives of all her best and bravest Men, and ended at last in an entire dissolution of the Commonwealth it self, and of all the Civil Rights and Liberties of the People. This destructive consequence had their unwary Indulgence to one Great Man, to whom they had otherwise the highest Obligations possible, in Contempt of their own Authority.

This may serve as a sufficient Lesson to all free States, That there must be no Balancing of the Services and Offences of Great Men, especially in derogation to their own Authority. For that will beget in 'em such an habitual Expectation and Confidence of Impunity, that they will look upon themselves as Injur'd, whenever their Principals shall dare narrowly to inspect their Conduct. This will naturally make 'em Loose and Wanton in the Administration of Publick Affairs, and Inspire Men of an Active Daring Spirit, with Ambition, and a perverse desire of grasping more Power than may be consistent with the Safety and Security of the People who Employ 'em.

[117] I know some Men will be apt to think that I refine too nicely on these Matters; and having been us'd to hear of other Causes of the Dissolution of the *Roman* Commonwealth, will think I strain this Point too far, in ascribing so much to this Action of *Scipio*. I grant there are other concurrent Causes, which 'tis not to my present purpose to take notice of here. But I dare affirm, That none of 'em had more Influence in producing the great Troubles and Revolutions that follow'd in that State, than the debauching the Bravest and Noblest Spirits among 'em, with Notions of Impunity, and a Contempt of that Authority which was their only Curb. From that time they flung off all Awe and Reverence for those Magistrates, and gave a loose to their Ambition, which kindl'd a Flame which cou'd never be extinguish'd, but with the Commonwealth it self.

Among the *Athenians*, who were also a Brave and Wise People, this Practice of Impeachments was no less frequent, and no less esteem'd than among the *Romans*. They likewise thought it the Security of their Government, from Do-[118]mestick Incroachments and Usurpations, and the only Check upon their Aspiring Citizens. Their Government, indeed, was not of so strong a Constitution as the *Roman*, and therefore as they knew themselves more Obnoxious to the Attempts and Intrigues of designing Men, so were the People also more prone to Jealousie and Suspicion, which might not always be over well grounded. However this diffident Temper was perhaps the greatest Security of their State, and tho' it might sometimes expose 'em to the Censure of Ingratitude, it protected 'em a long time from the danger of a Tyranny, to which the Frame of their Government seem'd to lay 'em almost naked and unfortify'd, but for this Practice and Humour.

I shall confine my self to Three or Four Instances of their Exercise of this sort of Judicature, which I prefer to the rest, because of a fancy'd Similitude, that some Persons think they have found to some late Cases at Home, tho' I can't yet discover wherein lies the Parallel.

[119] We shall first produce *Themistocles*: He was a Man of singular Parts and Abilities, both of Mind and Body, of great Courage and Sagacity, but withal exceedingly Ambitious. He affected Popularity, and had from a mean Extraction and Fortune, by his many and great Services to the *Greeks* in general, and to the *Athenians* in particular, made himself the most considerable Man for Power and Reputation, not only in *Athens*, but in all *Greece*. But presuming too much upon his Merits and Interest, and falling into Intrigues, which rendred him suspected of affecting a Tyranny, he was Banish'd. During his Exile, his Friend *Pausanias* being Convicted of Treason, some Letters and Papers were seiz'd about him which imported at least the Privity of *Themistocles*; whereupon he was Impeach'd of Treason, in the Name of all the *Greeks*. Great Endeavours were us'd to take, and bring him to Tryal; to avoid which, he fled into *Persia*, and ended his Life in Exile at *Magnesia*.

The next was *Aristides*, a Man of great Reputation for his Probity, and good Services. But among his many Vertues, he had two great Blemishes, which [120] brought him for a short time into Disgrace. One was, That Envying the Power and Popularity of *Themistocles*, he descended to bandy Factions, and often times to oppose such Counsels as he knew to be wholesome, and profitable for the State, only because his Rival made the motion, whose Reputation he labour'd to sacrifice at the expence of the Publick. The other was, That affecting an Interest, and Authority amongst the People, he drew to himself the Distribution of Justice, and the decision of all Controversies, and Suits, without any Authority for so doing, in Derogation to the Publick Courts of Justice. This his Adversary *Themistocles* laid hold on, and Impeach'd him for it as an Act of Majesty, which plainly shew'd a design of usurping the Soveraignty of the State. For this he was Banish'd; but after three Years, he was recall'd home, and spent the remainder of his Days with Honour, and Authority in his own Country.

However, this short Disgrace, so far cur'd both him, and *Themistocles*, that tho' their private Animosity and Hatred continued, yet they came to a more honest accord for the Service of the Publick [121] ever after. Some Authors say, That he was Impeach'd and Condemn'd for Bribery and Corruption; and *Plutarch* himself, makes him confess, That while he was Treasurer, tho' he did not Rob the Publick himself, yet he knowingly suffer'd his under Officers to do it, and Conniv'd at their Spoil, and Plunder of the Publick Revenue, without giving 'em any Check, or Disturbance in their Frauds, during the time of his Office. It's true, he gave 'em a severe Reprimand for it afterwards, but the best Defence that can be made for him in that Case, is, That he did a very ill thing, to say a good one, and countenanc'd Corruption, during the whole time of his Ministry, only for an Ostentatious Opportunity of reproving it afterwards. It is not improbable that as much as the *Athenians* valu'd good Sayings, the Publick might think they paid too dear for this. However it may be a good Light to us, how some Men among us now come by their great Interest.

Pericles shall be the next. He was a Man of a Noble Family, of an Ambitious daring Spirit, a ready Wit, and a good Speaker in Publick. He aim'd ear-[122]ly at Preferment and Grandeur; which he pursu'd rather by Intrigue, Address, and Management, than by open and fair Services; not but that after he arriv'd at Power, he shew'd himself capable of those also. Knowing the fondness of the *Athenians*, for Pomp, and Show, to make himself Popular, he affected an extraordinary Magnificence, and entertain'd the People with Plays, and Musick Prizes, and contrary to his Natural Humor, which was Haughty and Reserv'd, he descended to Court the Common People. After he had attain'd to Power, he return'd again to his Natural Temper, and grew Haughty and Reserv'd, keeping the Commons at a distance, and huffing those, whom he had us'd before to Wheedle and Cajole. He was Lavishly profuse, in expending the Publick Treasure. In the height of his Ministry he appear'd but now and then, managing those Points that were least Popular and most Invidious by his Instruments, of which number, *Ephialtes*, who broke the Power of the *Areopagites* (who were the Senate of *Athens*) and thereby destroy'd the Constitution, and unbridl'd the Fury and Folly of the Mob, was one. For not be-[123]ing qualify'd himself, to be a Member of that Council, whom he thought to favour more his Rival *Cimon*, whose Honour, Authority, and Real Services, he Envy'd without being able to come up to 'em, he made use of his Power and Interest with the Common People so far, that he Embroil'd and Perplex'd 'em so, thro' the Management of his Creature *Ephialtes*, that he expos'd 'em to the Insults of the Rabble, and effectually defeated all their Power, and by the same Arts procur'd an Ostracism against *Cimon*, the Bravest and most deserving Citizen they had, tho' in his own Distress, he was forc'd to procure him to be recall'd, in hopes of making his own Peace.

These Ambitious, Underhand, and Extravagant Practices, at length Incensed the whole City against him: And then he was requir'd to bring in his Accounts, and Impeach'd for Wasting and Squandring the Publick Treasure.

To avoid the force of this Impeachment, not being able to make up his Accounts, he engag'd the *Athenians* in a Ruinous War. However that did not [124] hinder, but that himself was Disgrac'd, Fin'd, and Discharg'd from all places of Trust.

Phocion the last I shall mention, was in the beginning, and a great part of his time, a successful General, and an able Minister; but in the latter part of his time he went over to *Philip* of *Macedon*, *Alexander* and *Antipater*, whose Interests he successively defended for some Years, and with as much zeal perswaded the *Athenians* to submit to the *Macedonians*, as he had before fought their Battles against others. And after some Years struggle with *Demosthenes* and others, he prevail'd so far as to get 'em expell'd the City, and a *Macedonian* Garrison and Laws from *Antipater*, to be receiv'd into it, which compleated their Ruine. This rendred him suspected and hated by his fellow Citizens, by whom he was at length sentenc'd to Death, and Executed.

I shall only Remark further, That these four Great Men, last cited, were not without their Faults.

The First lay under shrewd Suspicions, not without some Proof of his being engag'd in a Design of Inslaving his [125] own Country, and all *Greece*, for which he fled from Justice.

The Second, had sometimes apparently given up the Interests of his Country, but being in the main a good Man, his Correction was but light, and he was soon Restor'd to his former Power, and Dignity.

The Third, for his own Self-Ends, and to bring about his own Ambitious Purposes, manifestly broke and Dissolv'd the Constitution of their Government; and at last to conceal his own Evil Practices and Intrigues, and to avoid Justice, involv'd the State in a Miserable War, which laid the Foundation of their Ruine.

And the last, Engag'd obstinately in an Interest plainly destructive of the Liberty of his Country, and through his own Power and Credit, gave the finishing stroke to it.

Upon the Balance of the whole Account, the *Athenians* will not, perhaps, appear guilty of so much Ingratitude towards these Great Men, whose Actions, when narrowly inspected, will most of 'em be found to have proceeded from other Causes, than a true Love of their [126] Country, and whose hard Fates are plainly owing to their own Immoderate Ambition, which engag'd 'em in Feuds to the destruction of one another, in which whosoever got the better, the People were generally severe Sufferers.

It is observable upon the whole, that in *Rome* the Contests in the purer times of their Commonwealth, lay betwixt the Bodies of the Nobility and Commonalty in general, and then the Dispute was, Whether the Commons shou'd be Ridden at all, or not. In *Athens* they were betwixt one *Demagogue* and another, or betwixt their *Demagogues*, and their *Tyrants*, and was not so much, whether they should be Ridden at all: For that was usually their Case; But who should Ride 'em. By which the Miserable People, were almost perpetually harrass'd with Factions, and Domestic Broils. However they reap'd this Benefit from these Impeachments, that they let their Riders know, That if they did not sit Easie upon 'em, it was in their Power to give 'em a fall at any time, which made their Nobles, and Great Men observant of the Bounds prescrib'd to 'em, who otherwise perhaps wou'd have acknow-[127]ledg'd none. And in effect neither of these States retain'd any great show of Liberty any longer than they maintain'd to the People a Power of Punishing Offenders against the Publick of what Quality soever.

Those that Argue against such a Power in the Commonalty of any Nation, usually urge against 'em Inconstancy and Ingratitude: But that is a false Charge. For tho' Bodies of Men are not exempt from Passion, Prejudice, or Mistake, yet they are less liable to any of 'em, than a single Person, or a small Number, and always act upon a Principle of Common Security, and Interest; and tho' they may be sometimes mistaken, or misled into a wrong Judgment, through the Craft, or Malice of Evil Persons; yet are they not so liable to be Seduc'd, or Corrupted, as single Persons, or small Numbers, who may more easily be deceiv'd, and act with a more Uniform View of Interest, Malice, or Revenge. Those that make this Objection,[1] usually instance in the Judgments of *Athens* and *Rome*. But were I to produce the History of any one Private Tribunal in the World, for as many Months as these Ob-[128]jectors take in Years,[2] I would not question but to shew Errors and Corruptions ten times as many, and as foul, as are laid to the Charge of those two Commonwealths.

But whether the fore-cited Judgments were just, or not, is nothing to the present Controversie, unless any Person could shew us a sort of Tribunal, that shou'd be less liable to Mistakes, Corruptions, and Partialities, than that of a whole Nation.

But I might fairly urge further, That the Constitution of our Tribunal, is yet more equal and fair to the Persons Accus'd, than any other hitherto Contriv'd in the World. For of the Three Estates, two of 'em, which make the entire Body of the People, usually enter the Composition of it. And if the whole People may not be trusted to do Justice upon one another, it will be impossible to find any Practicable and Equal Method of doing it. For if it be thought unreasonable to Commit the Life or Fortune of any Member, or part of the People to the Judgment of the whole, it wou'd be absurd to think that the Rights, Liberties and all of the whole, shou'd be permit-[129]ted to any part of that whole, which part of that whole wou'd thereby become Superior to the whole, which would have no power to defend it self, but through the permission of that part. The Commons therefore of *England* ought to be very Watchful, that they part not under any pretence whatsoever with the Right of Impeachment, which is their only Legal Security against any Attempts or Invasions upon the Liberties and Properties of the whole People, which they cannot be said to have taken sufficient care of, while any means remain to defeat the Tryal of Persons Impeach'd by a House of Commons, or to Ward off the Punishment of Offenders when Convicted. And therefore the Parliament have made a Meritorious step in defence of our Liberties, in the Clause

[1] IV. 160–3. [2] II. 46.

last recited. And those who through Clamour, Menaces, or Artificial Contrivances, endeavour to obstruct their Exercise of that Power, whether through Malice, Partiality, or Corruption, are no less than Invaders, and Betrayers of the Rights, and Liberties of the People of *England*, and have further to Answer for the Guilt of all those that through Ignorance and their Perswasions [130] and Example, are misled into the like pernicious Practices. . . .

[132] While the Parliament were thus honourably Imploy'd in securing our Constitution from being Overthrown by Attempts from Abroad, they were so continually Alarm'd with Petitions and Complaints of Undue Returns, and Corrupt Elections, that they were justly sensible that we were in no less danger of being Undermin'd at Home. They were rightly apprehensive that such sort of Merchants look'd upon their House only as a place of Traffick, and that they bought only in Order to sell, and that if they did not immediately strike a Bargain for us, it was only because they wanted a Chapman or expected a better Market. They were convinc'd that this Trade had long been driven, but that the Nation was never so openly Stock-Jobb'd as now. They saw, that if they suffer'd these Practices to be continued much longer, no Man wou'd be able to call his Freehold his own, but that all the Free Estates in *England*, wou'd become the Merchandize of a number of small Boroughs, most of whose Inhabitants had none of their own to dispose of. Some Remedies had heretofore been provided, against this growing Evil, but Experience shew'd [133] 'em ineffectual. And the Defect seem'd to lie in their Lenity and Mildness to such sort of Offenders. But the Law having provided no further Punishment, than Imprisonment by Order of the House, which the constant Course and Practice of Parliaments has warranted, they contented themselves with the Commitment of those that had given, and those that receiv'd Bribes upon the score of Electing any Member to serve in Parliament, most of whom were in a short time, upon a due sense and acknowledgment of their Fault, and Submission to the House, set at Liberty, after a Reproof of their past Transgression, and an Admonition to avoid the like Crime for the future.

Those Corrupt Practices struck at the Root of our Constitution; and while they were unadverted upon, it was in vain to expect, that the true Interest of the Nation, should be much regarded in our Publick Councils. This Evil was grown so familiar, that in divers Corporations, Men were Chosen, whose Faces had never been seen there, and their Names scarce heard of 'till the Bargain came to be driven. Societies, and Companies, set up Men at the Charge of their Com-[134]mon Stock, and Private Persons, who had any Point to drive at, spar'd no Expence to procure themselves, or their Creatures, or both to be Elected. It is easie to guess what sort of Representatives these wou'd prove, who came thither only as Solicitors of particular Affairs, and perhaps resolv'd to Sacrifice all the rest to those few Points they aim'd at. This was the ready way, not only to the Subversion of our Constitution, but even to the Enslaving the Nation it self. For by this means, that Power which was intrusted with some Men for the Universal Good and Security of the Nation, was converted to separate Self-ends, and perhaps employ'd against the Interest of the Publick. For Ambitious Intriguing Men having the Command of so many Votes, wou'd naturally link together, and by Confederacy, support those By-interests, against any Opposition they might expect to meet with from those Gentlemen who sought only the Welfare of the Publick, and what might in their Opinion conduce to it. By this means, Votes became a sort of Monopoly, and some Men cou'd Truck, and Contract for Votes, as re-[135]gularly as they do for Troops in Swisserland.

But these Abuses, it seems, had taken too deep Root, and were too powerfully countenanc'd to be remedied with ease. For no sooner did the Commons begin, by purging their House of these Corruptors, and by examining their Agents, and the Brib'd Electors, to endeavour at a Reformation, but a certain Numerous Party, who have heretofore boasted much of their Purity, fell into Terrible Convulsions, and they, who once thought all Power too little for a House of Commons, now thought the least Exercise of it too much.

No sooner did the Commons begin to exercise that Power which the People had intrusted 'em with, to the Reformation of these Notorious Practices, than some People who had heretofore been great Assertors of the Power and Authority of the House of Commons, made it a Question, Whether they had any at all, or not? They found, perhaps, themselves, and divers Zealots of their Party, Obnoxious to the Enquiry of the Commons, and therefore were for pulling down a Power, [136] before which, they could not stand Justify'd.

To this purpose all their Engines were employ'd to Batter the Power of the House of Commons, under pretence that they were not intrusted with the whole Power of the Commons of *England*. But those that Argue at that rate, ought to shew what that reserv'd Power is, which the Collective Body of the Commons is possess'd of, and has not permitted the exercise of to the Body Representative. The Right of Legislature, which gives a Power of tying up every individual to certain restrain'd Conditions, and of submitting him to Pains and Forfeitures in Case of a Breach of any of those Conditions, is certainly the highest Exercise of Power. Yet this is deliver'd up to 'em, without Reserve, the Power of Impeachment, Raising of Money by Assessment, or otherwise, and in short, all the Powers that a People can be suppos'd to have over themselves, have constantly been exercis'd by their Representatives, with allowance.

Nor, indeed, can it be otherwise. For in a Country so large as this, it is impossible to assemble the Collective Body of [137] the People, so as to know their Sense, or have their Assent or Dissent, to any Proposition whatsoever, otherwise than by Convening their Representatives. Nor did the Nation ever make any formal Declaration of their Sense any other way. For however Tumultuous and Troublesome the Times were, tho' Men put themselves into Arms, and stood upon their Guard, yet they never came to any Resolution for themselves, till they had Assembled their Deputies to declare for 'em, whose Judgment they always abode by, 'till a further Opportunity at least of rectifying any Mistakes by another Assembly.

Either therefore the Collective Body of the Commons have no Power or Right to repel Injuries, or Chastise Affronts offer'd to 'em, or that Power is Lodg'd in the House of Commons, their Representatives, since it is impracticable for 'em to Exercise it themselves. If they have no such Right, but must look to another Power not Delegated by them for Redress, they are then no longer Free, but have a Dependance on that Power that can grant or deny 'em that Redress, and consequently are Vassals to that Power. [138] But, this is more than the Adversaries of the late House of Commons pretend to maintain. For while they wou'd beat down the Power of the House, they exalt that of the Commons in general, and endeavour to let loose their Jurisdiction, in order only to make it impracticable.

These large Notions of the Power of the People Collective, and these narrow ones of their Body Representative, have been broach'd by the same Persons, whose design was, while they own'd it in Words, to reject it in Effect; and while they Recogniz'd the Right of the People, to destroy the Exercise of it. There is another drift that some Men have in it, which is to deceive us in the Sense of the People, and by the help of a Corrupt, but Indefatigable Party, to pawm upon us, Mercenary Noise and Clamour, for the general Voice and Consent of the People.

But this is plainly the struggle of a few Men, back'd by a Faction, that find their Interest declining in the Nation, and therefore wou'd take away from the House of Commons, the Power of inspecting their Practice, and punishing their Insolences. They wou'd reduce the Power of the House of Commons, lower than [139] that of the meanest Court of Judicature, only that they might have it in their Power to insult it with Safety; and tho' they resolve all Power into the Collective Body of the People, yet they wou'd allow none to the Representative. But if the Collective Body has any Power over its own particular Members, it is undoubtedly in Cases that concern the whole Body. And if they have such a Power, they have undoubtedly a Right of exercising it. This must be done either by the whole Collective Body, or by Persons deputed or delegated by them for that purpose. By the whole Body it cannot, for they are too numerous to be Assembl'd, or to have their Suffrages orderly taken, and consequently it must devolve upon their Deputies, or sink. This Power must be very small, and in effect none, if it will not extend to the Punishing of an Affront offer'd to their Authority, a Priviledge which the meanest Officer in the State enjoys.

It is absurd to maintain, That the Commons of *England*, are one of the Three Sovereign Estates Independant of either, or both the other two, (any other-[140]wise than as all together constitute our Government) and yet that they shou'd have no Right, or Power to Defend and Protect their Priviledges and Representatives from the Invasions and Insults of their own private Members, or any Persons whatsoever. And it is as absurd to acknowledge, That they have such a Right, and yet to deny 'em the only means of exercising it.

Those that Argue against the Power of the House, generally allow all Power to be Originally in the People; but they urge, That this Power is not committed at large to their Representatives; That the Punishment of all Offences, whether against the Publick, or Private Persons, is left to the Laws; and that the Laws have not made any Provision of Power for the House of Commons to Commit such Commoners, as are not Members of their House; and that consequently, all such Commitments are an Usurpation upon, and a Violation of the Liberties of the People. But these Gentlemen, when they deny that the Commons have intrusted their Representatives with their whole Power, ought to shew us what Limitations their Principals had set to their [141] Power, and what Branches of it they have reserv'd to themselves, in exclusion to their Representatives. This none of 'em ever undertook to do, and therefore it will be lawful for us to presume, that they have the whole Power, 'till some Body shall shew us where our Mistake lies. As for the Redress which the Law affords, it was intended for reparation of Wrongs and Injuries offer'd by one Private Person to another, or by one, or more, to the King, or whole Constitution in general, of which the Laws, the execution whereof was put into the King's Hands, were Judges. But it was never intended that either of the Courts of Parliament shou'd be oblig'd to sue to the King's Courts their Inferiors, for Reparation of any Injuries or Affronts put upon themselves. Of this, the silence of the Laws in all Cases Parliamentary, is a Demonstrative Argument, that the Houses themselves were the only Proper, and Competent Judges of their own Rights and Priviledges, and were Invested with a Power sufficient to Repel and Punish all Injuries and Affronts offer'd to themselves while Sitting. It is not to be imagin'd, that if they needed the Protection of [142] Laws, the whole Body Representative of the People, wou'd have been left unguarded by 'em, while the separate Interest and Concern of every Individual Man, was so carefully fenc'd about. But it was always allow'd, that the Houses had in themselves a Power Declarative of their own Rights and Priviledges, and were enabled by their Principals, to protect and defend 'em. And therefore it had been an Injury to the whole People, whose these Rights were, if they had condescended to Circumscribe 'em by Written Laws.[1]

The Injury and Indignity of such a Proceeding, had been threefold.

First, It is inconceivable that any one Parliament cou'd have given so entire a View of the Rights of the People, as not to have Omitted many things, Essential to their well being, and thereby for the future to have precluded 'em from such Rights at least as far as any such Act of theirs cou'd have been valid.

Secondly, They must have submitted those Rights which were Originally inherent in, and inseparable from the People to the Arbitration of the two other Estates, whose consent wou'd thereby [143] have become Requisite to their Establishment, a hazard they ought never to be expos'd to, and of which they had no need.

Thirdly, Had they brought their whole Priviledges under such an Establishment, they had thereby brought themselves under Vassalage to *Westminster-Hall*, and must have had recourse to an Inferiour Court, subordinate to, and dependant on another of the Estates, to determine whether they were Injur'd or Affronted, and to sue as

[1] V. 121–5.

Private Men for that Relief, which by their Original and Constitution they cou'd give themselves, which were an Injury irreparable, and an Indignity unanswerable to their Principals.

From hence we are furnish'd with a plain Answer to those unthinking, or evil dispos'd Persons, who make such an unreasonable Clamour to have the Rights and Priviledges of the House of Commons settl'd, and determin'd, which we have shewn in the first place to be impracticable, and in the next to be a Breach of Trust of the highest Nature in the Representatives, were it feazible. It is evident therefore from the little care which the Law has taken of the Rights [144] and Priviledges of the Collective Body of the People in general, that the Exercise and Vindication of those Rights was left wholly to their Representatives, who must therefore be suppos'd to be endu'd with a sufficient Authority to protect 'em, and to Repress, and Correct all Insolencies and Affronts offer'd to 'em. If therefore they had Conniv'd at the Corrupt Practices before mention'd, which tended so manifestly to the Subversion of our Civil Rights and Constitution, they had been Traitors to their Country, which had committed the Exercise and Protection of 'em to their Charge. And no Man that acknowledges their Power, can think they have been Rigorous or Severe in the Execution of it, when they contented themselves to punish Crimes of so high a Nature, and so Pernicious Consequences with a short Imprisonment, a Submission, and a Reprimand.

But if they have Power to punish any underhand secret Practices against the Liberties and Rights of the People, it is past question, that they have the same Authority in case of open Affront and Contempt, whether it be offer'd by way of Petition, Remonstrance, Libel, Per-[145]sonal Insult, or Menace. This, if those Gentlemen of *Kent* knew, who presented the *Maidstone* Address to the late Parliament, they made a very bold Experiment of the Temper, and Courage of that Parliament, when they ventur'd to be the Bearers, and Vouchers of a Petition, conceiv'd in Terms so Insolent and Affronting. And the Commons had been wanting in their Duty to the People, whose Representatives they are, if they had tamely put up such an Insult upon their Authority, without shewing their Resentment, and thereby deterring others from following an Example of so dangerous consequence.

But there were at that time a Party of Men, who knew they had offended, and therefore fear'd, and consequently wish'd the Destruction of the Power of the House of Commons. They knew there was no way so ready to effect this, as (if possible) to divide the Sentiments of the People concerning their Proceedings. In order to it, they stirr'd up divers Turbulent, and evil designing Men, to set on foot Libels under the Name of Petitions, wherein the Proceedings of the House shou'd be Arraign'd in Sawcy Language, [146] that if the House should not Resent such Treatment, it might be an Incouragement to a Factious Party, who were beforehand prepared, to follow the Example, and to Libel 'em, by way of Petition, all over *England*: Or if they did exert their Authority on that occasion, they might have an Opportunity of Clamouring against 'em, as if they intended Arbitrarily and Tyrannically to take from the Subject the Liberty of Petitioning. The Natural Consequence of such Practices as these, are Obvious, that they tend to inflame and exasperate the People against their Representatives, and by Surprize, and false Representations to make 'em Accessary to the Destruction of their own Rights and Authority. Such Practices as these, deserve the severest Chastisement, but the Commons who have always been very tender of the Subject in the exercise of their Power, proceeded no further against 'em, than by committing those Persons who appear'd with, and avow'd that Petition, and thereby made themselves the most visible Authors and Abetters of it.

[147] This Lenity of theirs was so far from giving a Check to these Vile Practices, that the Party embolden'd thereby, openly Courted, Caress'd, and Treated the Offenders, as if they had extraordinarily signaliz'd themselves as true *English* Men, and good Patriots. Crowds of Defenders started up, who under pretence of maintaining the Freeholders Right of Petitioning, Assaulted the Power of Parliaments in general, and affronted the particular Members of the Parliament then Sitting. Their pretence was, That all Freeholders have a Right of Petitioning, and that no Indecency, or want of Respect in the Phrase and Expression, was a sufficient reason, why the Petition shou'd be rejected, or any Punishment inflicted on the Petitioners; which, as they alledge, the House has upon no Account, any Right or Authority to inflict.

B. *The Source of Our Present Fears Discover'd* (1703)[1]

The Source of Our Present Fears Discover'd is a kind of group-analysis of some fifteen Whig pamphlets. 'I shall insist', the author explained, 'mainly on those Proofs, which [Drake] was denied time to produce . . . which are the Printed ones.' These 'Dangerous Pamphlets' included *The Free State of Noland*, an anonymous republican utopia 'extracted from *Harington's Oceana*', of which the first edition was published in 1696; Blackmore's *Short History of the Last Parliament*, 1699; *The Present Disposition of England Considered*, 1701, which was widely attributed to Montagu; Defoe's Legion *Memorial* and *The History of the Kentish Petition*, both published in 1701; *Jura Populi Anglicani: Or The Subject's Right of Petitioning*, 1701, attributed to Somers; and John Toland's *Reasons for Addressing His Majesty to invite into England their Highnesses, the Electress Dowager and the Electoral Prince of Hannover*, 1702. The author's insistence that these works provide evidence of a Whig conspiracy to '*new Model*' the government is totally unconvincing and is, in fact, belied by his own admission: 'Whether any of these Authors, the first excepted, did really wish a th[o]rough change in our Constitution, I will not directly determine: But considering the Doctrines they advanced . . . there is just reason to suspect it.'[2]

Of the fifteen works suspected, no more than a few sentences are devoted to any but Swift's. But to his, no less than thirty pages, nearly a third of the volume, are allocated. Like so many others, the author of *The Source of Our Present Fears Discover'd* assumed that the *Discourse*

[1] In an advertisement in a folio half-sheet by Tom Brown entitled *The Last Observator: Or, The Devil in Mourning* ('Come, honest Country-man, what News dost bring?'), *The Source of Our Present Fears Discover'd* is said to be 'written by the *Author of the History of the Last Parliament*', i.e. James Drake. There was a second edition, printed for B. Bragg, in 1706.

[2] *The Source of Our Present Fears Discover'd*, 1703, pp. 29–30.

had been written by Bishop Burnet. In the excerpts which appear below, the original marginal notes are reproduced as footnotes.

[47] . . . But least all this should not suffice, as indeed it did not, out comes a doubty Piece written as is suspected by one not unacquainted with a certain Ecclesiasti-[48]cal writer of an other *House* and order.[1] This *Author*, whether out of Ostentation to shew his Political Reading and Capacity, or to lead his unlearned *Reader* out of his way, or perhaps both, takes a very solemn Progress through *Greece* and *Italy*, and with all the Pomp and Parade of an affected Learning, and far fetch'd strain'd Precedents, endeavours to charge all the Corruptions of *Rome* and *Athens* upon our Country; I shall not say his, least in that I should do him wrong.

By the Liberty this Gentleman indulges to himself in his *Historical Account* of the differences between the *Nobles* and *Commons* of *Rome* and *Athens*, it is easie to guess not only of which side he is at Home, but likewise who is his Casuist, he has acted so fully up to the License granted by a particular Friend of his, to those that write *History* for a *Party*.

[49] It is said by a certain Reverend Historian,[2] *That an Historian who* favours *his* own side, *is to be forgiven, tho' he put a little* too much *Life* in his *Colours, when he sets out the* best *side of his Party, and the worst of those from whom he differs; and if he but* slightly *touches the* failures *of* his *Friends, and* severely aggravates *those of the* other *side; and that tho' in* this *he departs from the Laws of an* Exact *Historian, yet* this *Bias is so* Natural, *that if it* Lessens *the Credit of the Writer, yet it doth* not blacken *him.*

It is indeed a great Liberty which this Casuist allows, and this Author has taken; but it is not much to be wonder'd at. For if Common Fame be not the verryest Lyar in the World, the Divine has not been much more scrupulous than the Historian; and the *Fides Evangelica* has been as freely dealt with as the *Fides Historica.* These Authors keep pace with one another like Friends; and the Discourse is written with all the Latitude of an Exposition. For the Author proffits so well by a great Example, that one third part of our Constitution is treated with no more Reverence, than if it were but one Article in Thirty nine, and the great [50] Body of our

1 *A Discourse of the Contests and Dissensions between the Nobles and the Commons in Athens and Rome, &c.*

2 [Gilbert Burnet,] *Reflect. on Monsieur Varillas his History,* [1686], p.[5].

Legislators are laid upon an unmannerly Level, with the Mob of *Athens* and *Rome*.

To take a view of the Design and Principles of this Author, it will be requisite to look a little into his Introductory and Conclusive Chapters. First, he endeavours to settle a wrong notion of a *Ballance* in *Civil* Power,[1] and having granted, That *in all Governments there is an absolute and unlimited Power, which naturally and originally seems to be placed in the whole Body, whereever the Executive part of it lies*, Where to Lodge this Executive Power, he seems at first to be in some doubt, But soon concludes[2] from the Principles of *Nature* and *Common Reason* (as he pretends) that a *single* Hand is the fittest. Now what sort of Government he means to recommend, is hitherto uncertain; because he does not define what, or how much he means by the *Executive* Power; nor whether he is willing to Prescribe and Limit it according to the known Laws and Present Constitution of *England*. But he is talking yet of Government in general, without any of those Restrictions which particular Countries have thought fit to prescribe for them-[51]selves; and therefore he must be understood of Power in the largest extent, which he Lodges in a *single* Hand, and is what has been called *Tyranny* in the strictest sense, which is now a days called *Absolute Monarchy*, or by terms Synonimous, *Arbitary* or *Despotick Power*.

'Tis true, he mentions Two other forms of Government, a *great Council* or *Senate* of *Nobles*, and the Government by the *Collected* or *Represented Body of the People:* But these he does not Recommend, as either so Natural or Convenient as the first, yet of the two he prefers the former. This is so manifest an Arraignment of the *Constitution* of *England*, that to avoid the Censure of Aiming at the *Subversion* of our Constitution he thinks fit to divide Power in the *Last Resort* amongst all the three former: But, what he means by the Power in the *Last Resort*, he explains no more than he did in the foregoing Page, how far he would extend the *Executive* Power. Yet he tells us, That it will be an Eternal Rule among all free People, That *there is a Ballance of Power to be carefully held by ev'ry State with it self, as well as among several States with each other.*[3]

[52] What he means by ev'ry State *Ballancing* of Power with it self, is hard to be understood: For if it be not Nonsense, it is very unintelligible Sense. Ev'ry State considered in the Aggregate as such, is as much an Individual, how many Members soever it may consist of, as a single Person can be: And therefore to talk of

[1] *Discourse*, I. 1–4. [2] *Discourse*, I. 30–34. [3] *Discourse*, I. 58–61.

Ballancing Power with it self, which implies dividing the Power, is as absurd, as to propose it to a single Person.

If he had said that ev'ry State, consisting of distinct Members, with distinct and separate Powers, ought so to divide those Powers, and so to maintain the Distribution of 'em, that they might remain so far equilibrated, as that one Branch of the Constitution might not be able to oppress the Rest, he had delivered something intelligible. But, [that] this was not his meaning appears evidently from the Description of a *Ballance*, which he immediately subjoyns. *It supposes* (says he) *three things. First, the Part which is held together, with the* Hand *that holds it, and then the* two Scales, *with what is weighed therein.*[1]

By this Notion of a Ballance, it is plain that the whole Power is in the *hand* that holds the Ballance; and that the Powers weigh'd [53] in the *Scales*, are no more than dead weights to be dispersed or tumbled backwards and forwards at the Pleasure and Discretion of the *Weigher*.

If this be the Scheme of Government which he has contriv'd for us (if it should prevail) we might have the most *Arbitrary Despotick* Government in the World; nay, and must have, if it should please the person, or persons into whose hands he would put the Ballance. For what is it that gives any single Man the power of *Tyrannizing* over any Countrey? Surely not the Strength and Force of the single person of the Prince, but the Means of using one part of the people, to serve as Instruments to obtain his ends and purposes upon all the Rest. And what is this more than holding and turning the Ballance (according to our Authors Phrase) as he pleases? which tho' some may do with more Moderation and Tenderness towards their People, than others, yet all that are possess'd of the holding the Ballance, may use with equal Liberty, if they think themselves equally secure.

This is the Condition which we have been strugling for Many Years so hard to prevent, the very Fear of which produced the late Revolution, and cost so many Mil-[54]lions. For if, under Pretence of *Ballancing* the State, it shall be left in the power of any one part to raise or depress the Rest at Discretion, that part is Absolute that has such a power, of what Number of persons soever it may consist. For what does the Notion of *Arbitrary* or *Despotick* power include more, than an Ability to alter and change the Measures in a State at pleasure, and to give weight where there is none, or take it away where there is; which he that holds the *Ballance* between a pair of

[1] *Discourse,* I. 64–67.

Scales is suppos'd able to do? Otherwise a passive *Beam* might serve as well as any *Ballancer* of 'em all. When this *Ballancing* power is exercis'd with *Injustice*, *Violence*, *Oppression* and *Cruelty*, it is called *Tyranny* in the modern Sense of the Word: For, according to the Ancientest Usage of it, it is a Word of no ill Signification.

But this Notion of a Ballance, absolutely destroys that of a free Estate. For the Notion of a Free Estate supposes a Harmony and Symmetry of Parts, Constantly and Regularly Co-operating to the same Ends and Purposes, any one of which parts being Check't, are disorder'd, the Action of the whole Machine is disturb'd, if not destroy'd. But a Ballance supposes such a constant [55] Opposition and Contranitency between the constituent parts of it, without any Spring of Motion in it self, as must necessarily keep it in a State of perpetual inactivity, without *External* Violence.

But his Way of inferring the Necessity of such a Ballance, is yet more absurd, and out of the Way of Reason, than his Notion. For he finds it agreed among the Politicians, that it is necessary for the Preservation of Kingdoms, and States independant and distinct from one another, that a Ballance be maintain'd among 'em, least the greater and more powerful should swallow up the Less; and therefore he concludes it equally good Policy for ev'ry State to erect such a Ballance, likewise within it self. But the Absurdity of this Notion will appear more manifestly, from the very Reason for which such a Ballance is so much desir'd. For the Interest of all Countries, not under the same Government, being separate, and usually opposite to each other, so that no one of 'em can Enterprise any thing, which may not either Immediately, or in the Consequence, turn to the disadvantage and hurt of some other, it is their mutual interest to keep the several Powers suspended, and under an incapacity for Action; so long at least, as [56] they shall be so Equilibrated, as that each Party shall have equal Reason to fear the mischievous Consequences of any Disturbance that may arise amongst 'em. But tho' this may be the Interest of all, consider'd together, it is not of any of 'em separately, when ever their own Fortune, or Prudence shall present 'em with an opportunity to break that Ballance, so as that their own may be the heavier Scale: For it is certainly for their Interest and Security, to have the Ballance incline to their own side. But this Consideration reaches not the several Members of the same Individual State, whose Interest cannot be oppos'd to each other, without manifest Ruine to the whole; and therefore there can be no Ballancing where all must necessarily lye in the same Scale.

This may suffice to give us a Taste of this Authors *Politicks* or his *Morals*: For if he fell into this Errour thro' want of Judgment, he has spent his time in Reading and Writing to little purpose, if he went into it through Design, he has spent it to very ill Purpose. When I considered the Impertinency of his Instances on one hand, and the Malice of his Applications on the Other, I knew not whether to Judge him more unskilfull [57] or perverse, and am at a Loss, what to make of him. But that perhaps is no more, than some that converse with him nearer, have been a long time.

After this the Author falls into an odd, Extravagant Fit of Raving, and talks wildly about the FEW and the MANY, without Coherence, or Pertinent Applications, for several Pages together. But this is one of his Learned Fits, and what is wanting in Argument is made up abundantly in Quotation. And here it may not be amiss, once for all, to give the Reader notice, that he is not to expect both at a time, from this Author.

However not to slight his pains, we will consider briefly how far his Instances suit his purpose. The drift of all his Reasonings (if the Logicians will forgive me for calling Absurdities so) is to shew the Preferrableness of a Government, by one or a few Persons, to a Government by many; that is, of an Absolute Monarchy, or an Aristocracy, to a Democracy, or a mixt Government, such as ours at present is: For these two, are the only forms of Government by many, as he seems to understand the word.

In order to prove this, he rakes up all the Enormities that he can find in the [58] Ancient *Roman* and *Greek* Histories, to have been committed by any number of Confederated Usurpers, and endeavours by Application, to draw an odious Parallel between those Usurpers and our House of Commons. But tho' it may not be Lawful to question the Judgment of one so deep Read in Politicks, yet he may allow me to condemn his Luck, in the choice of his Instances. For most of 'em bear hard, where he least intended they should; and not one of the Rest any way affects that Honourable Body against whom they are apparently pointed.

The first is of the *Decemviri* at *Rome*, who were created on purpose, to Draw up, and Compile a Body of Laws, by which the Rights of the Nobility and Commons might be equally provided for, and secur'd; and that they might meet with no Interruption, the supreme and sole Authority was lodged in them without Appeal, and the Power of all Magistrates was for that year superceded. But whatever was the misbehaviour of those Men (which was indeed very great) they bore no manner of Resemblance to the Body Collective or Representative of any People. For as *Livy* takes notice, tho' the Commons did insist to have some of their Order admitted [59] in to the number, yet the Senate stood it out obstinately, and the People at length yielded the Point to 'em. The Historian does not say by whom those first *Decemviri* were Nominated or Chosen: But they do not seem to have been at the Peoples Choice, by the Persons chosen, whereof Three were particularly obnoxious to the Commons; *Appius Claudius*, the Bitterest and most Implacable Enemy to the Commons in all *Rome*; *Publius Sextius*, who had given 'em a fresh disobligation, in Carrying the Point of Excluding the Commons from a share in the *Decemvirate*, into the *Senate*, against the Consent of his fellow Consul; and *Titus Romulius*, who had but Two years before been Condemn'd and Fin'd by the People upon an Impeachment. These Men we may be sure were upon that score not grateful to the People, and consequently not Chosen by 'em, and 'tis more than probable that none of the rest were; and therefore they were so far from being the *Representatives* of the *People*, that excepting their extraordinary Powers, they seem'd to have been no more than a Committee of the House of Lords.

The next that take their turn are the *Ephori* of *Sparta*: These were a sort of [60] Bench of Justices instituted by King *Theopompus*, who was a Prince so far from our Author's Ballancing principle, and thinking it necessary to have the turning of the Scales as he pleas'd, that he Erected this sort of Court of Judicature, on purpose to be a check to any Extraordinary Exercise of Prerogative; and when he was Reproach'd by his Wife, as having given up his own Authority, he told her, that he was so far from that, that he had only secured the continuance of it. But whether He or his Wife, or our Discourser be in the right, I shall refer the Reader back to History to judge, because the Instance is nothing at all to the purpose, these Judges bearing no Resemblance to any Legal Body or Assembly of Men amongst us. But if there be any Argument Couch'd under it, it is this: The *Ephori* were a check upon the Regal Power at *Sparta*, the *Ephori* became Tyrants, therefore all checks upon Regal Power must become Tyrants. I shall not trouble my self to Expound or Expose, for I think as some Men use 'em, there is no great difference in sense between those two words; nor shall I affront the Reader so far as to Interpret to 'em such plain Doctrines.

[61] The next Step is to *Athens*, and there we find the People discontented upon a long Series of Misfortunes; But the Discourser

takes no Notice of the Reason of that Discontent, which was the Mismanagement and Insolence of some of those who he calls their *Nobles*. In this Fit, instead of an *Archon*, they erected a high Commission, or Council of Four Hundred; and when they did not find that Relief which they expected from that Form, they broke it again. Now what would this Author infer from all this? *Athens* was a Perfect Democracy, and it was certainly the Right of the Collective Body of the People there, to Cast their Government into what Form they pleas'd: And this alteration was not more wonderful and not in the least more injurious to any Body than for our Kings, instead of making a Lord Treasurer, to put the Treasury into Commission. They did as we have done, make the Experiment, and after finding the Mischief of it, return'd to the old Form again. This Instance reaches the Constitution of our House of *Commons* as little as any of the former, except that the Number approach'd as much nearer, and then all the Inference that can be drawn from it, is, that if Four [62] Hundred Men could be Tyrants, Five Hundred and thirteen needs must; any other Conclusion than that is nothing to his purpose.

The rest of his Instances are so loose, so *mal a Propos*, that it would be as Impertinent as tedious to follow him through, especially since to Examine and display 'em at large.

For this Reason I shall pass over slightly his Thirty or Three Thousand Tyrants at *Athens*, and his *Dominatio Plebis*, or (as he has pleas'd to Translate it) *Tyranny of the Commons* at *Carthage*.The First was a Government Imposed by a Conquerer, and therefore had little Regard or Tenderness for the People, but acted as Arbitrarily as if they had his Ballance in their Hands; and if they did not come quite up to *Nero* and *Caligula* in Mischief, it was, Because the Passions of a Number of Men, who pretend to act by any Rule, amongst whom Debates will Naturally arise, have thereby time to settle, and are not so Frolicksome, or so sudden as those of a single Man may be, who in a fit of Humour, or Anger, may do those Rash Things which an Hours time makes 'em repent of, when too late. The latter is a gross Mistake or something worse, for the State of *Carthage* [63] was Ruin'd by the Faction of *Hanno*, out of Envy to *Hannibal*, who had first rescued the Commons from the oppressure of the Nobles (if he will have those Invidious Phrases) and set the Government at Home upon a more equal Foot, and had by the Favour of the People, and his own Great Conduct, in behalf of his Country, bidden fair for the Empire of the World, yet was at last, by the Tricks and Intreagues of one Rascally Statesman and his Faction, defeated and his Country intirely Ruin'd and Subverted when no other Humane Power seemed able to encounter 'em without that Help. I hope no Part of that Instance Reaches us by way of Parallel; but if it does, I doubt the Weight of it will fall where he least intended it.

But least a House of Commons shou'd not be thought capable of the most inhumane Villainies that Mankind abhors, the Orators of *Argos* are brought upon the Stage. And why? Because (as the Discourser says) they were the Occasion that Sixteen Hundred of the Nobles were Murder'd at once.

But least the Reader shou'd not be able to apply this Instance to his Purpose, he takes Care to give 'em a suffici-[64]ent Direction in these Words, Whether you will stile them in Modern Phrase, *great Speakers in the House*, or only in General *Representatives* of the *People Collective*; but it seems their Orators far'd no better themselves, than those whom they accused; they had raised a Spirit they could not lay, and the Mobb tore them in Pieces too. But why? Because (as our Discourser has it) They withdrew their Impeachments. Whether this be a Lesson to our *House* of *Commons*, I shall leave the Members of that Honourable House to Judge; and I shall only observe upon the whole, that in all their Instances, there is a very villainous Misrepresentation of Fact, and a more foul Application. But my Design confining me to the Intention and Aim only of this Discourse, I have not Enlarg'd so much upon Particulars as I might have done; but do Accept of the Challenge in the Title Page of his Book,

Si tibi Vera videtur
dede Manus; Et si falsa est accingere contra.

If he thinks fit to Vindicate, I'll promise him more than I am bound to, to use him like a Gentleman, and take no [65] other Notice of him, than as Author of that Pamphlet; and shall be glad by a Reply, to find him willing to have the Matter fairly, and at large discuss'd; unless he shall give me fresh Provocation to Treat him otherwise.

His Conclusions are not all of a Piece, and do not equally follow from his Positions.

In the First, I agree with him, that a mix'd Government is not of *Gothick* Invention, but has Place in Nature and Reason. And in Favour of this Position, I shall venture so much farther than the

Discourser, as to affirm, That since the *Theocracy* of the *Jews*, no Form of Government that I have read of, can stand in Competition with it. And because he seems so much more fond of Authority than Reason, I will, out of many, fling him in one, that I hope he will have no Opportunity to pervert. *Tacitus*, who was almost as great a *Politician*, and something more Faithful an Historian than our Discourser, says, *Nationes & Urbes Populus aut Primores, aut Singuli regunt, Dilecta ex his & Constituta Reipublicae forma laudari facilius, quam evenire potest.*[1] By which it seems, that *Tacitus*, thought such a Con-[66]stitution as ours, more to be wish'd, than hop'd for; and he had Reason on his side. For whatever our Discourser may fancy, he had never seen nor read of any such Constitution; and was far enough from dreaming of any such Ballance as our Author has invented, to quallifie the Happiness of such a Government, as meer strength of Reason told him, was in it self most Excellent, And 'tis plain, that tho' he never had the Felicity to experience such a Government, that if he had, he would have imploy'd all his Reason (of which, perhaps he was as great a Master as the Ballancer) to have preserv'd it; not to have destroy'd it by false Notions, and Unjust, Malicious Suggestions.

His next Conclusion is false: For if such a Ballance at home, as he has immagined, be utterly inconsistent with the Liberty of a Free Estate (which I think is already demonstrated) then they who oppose it, 'are the mighty Patriots, and as much in the true Interest of their Country, as they can affect to be thought':[2] And on the Contrary, those that, with this Author, Labour to Erect such a Ballance here, ought to be looked upon as Subverters of our Constitution, and the [67] most dangerous sort of Enemies that it can have. But the Ballancer thought he had found an opportunity to misrepresent the Members of the House of Commons; and tho' both his Reasonings, and his Facts were false, yet he would not let it slip, without inferring the worst that Malice was able to impose, or Ignorance to receive.

His Third Inference is the Summ and Substance of his whole Work, and what in all, that has preceded, and in all that follows, he drives solely at.

But this Position is in its own Nature so absolutely destructive of all Free Government, especially that of *England*, That he cares not to come at it, without a great many Doublings, and Turnings, to avoid a close Persuit. However, the Reader shall have it in his own

[1] *Lib.* 4.

[2] *Discourse*, I. 197–9.

Words. *This makes appear, the Error of those who conceive, That Power is safer lodg'd in many Hands, than in One.*[1] This is Doctrine that may perhaps deserve Thanks from the Government in *Turky, Muscovy*, or *France;* but in *England*, requires a severe Chastisement.

The Rest of this Book is spent in Forraign Instances, with Oblique Reflections upon Home, to give the Nice, [68] and unwary, an unsavory Relish of our Constitution; and is written with the Craft of a Fox, who (as the Woodmen tell us), will lay his own Ordure in a Badger's Nest, on Purpose to stink the cleanly Creature out of his Habitation, and to take Possession of it himself.

His next Three Chapters, are spent entirely in Railing at Impeachments, and Representing that Power as too dangerous to be trusted in the *House* of *Commons*. But all that he has said there, even to his particular Instances, and all that I think him capable of saying on the Argument, is already sufficiently, and I believe designedly answer'd in the History of the last Sessions of Parliament: to which from Page 44, to Page 155, I Referr the curious Reader, and doubt not but he will find there that Satisfaction, as to the Reasonableness and Use, which neither the Reason nor the Compass of my Design will allow me to give him here: And therefore I shall only take Notice, that the drift and aim of these Three Chapters, is to wrest from the *Commons* the Power of *Impeachment*, by persuading the People, that they have not Discretion to use it, and that it is useless and dangerous [69] in their Hands. The Discourser may Rail as much as he pleases; but if any *Popular Orator*, either of *Athens* or *Argos*, or the most Factious Tribune of *Rome*, did ever in quiet Times make an Attempt of such pernicious Consequence to the Government under which he lived, as the Discourser has now done, I will be content to see his Ballance erected, and the holding of it put into his Hands, which most that know him would think (as I do) the greatest Misfortune that could befall their Country or themselves.

From these Instances, how wide soever from the Truth, and how loosely and incoherently soever put together, he draws the following Inferences.

First, That 'no Multitude, whether Collective or Represented, has been at any time very Nice in observing the Distinction, between Liberty and Licentiousness.'[2]

Secondly, That 'the Commons have been perpetually mistaken in the Merits of the Causes and the Persons, as well as in the Consequences of Impeachments, upon the Peace of the Estate, and

[1] *Discourse,* I. 202–4.

[2] *Discourse,* IV. 13–16.

therefore were by no Means qualify'd, either as Prosecutors or Judges in such Matters.'[1] 'Tis true, he [70] endeavours to qualifie this Assertion, by pretending to level it more particularly at *Athens* and *Rome*, and to abate something of the Universality of it, by inserting this Parenthesis (*whatever they may be in other States.*) But 'tis plain, he meant to comprehend the *Commons* of *England*, and their *Representatives* in *Parliament* in this Disabling Clause, by Excluding them from *Prosecuting*, which is the peculiar Right of the People of *England*, who pretend not to be Judges in Cases of Impeachments as the *Commons* of *Athens* and *Rome* did, who, on the other Hand, never were *Prosecutors* in such Cases.

Thirdly, 'That the *Commons* think themselves concern'd in Point of Honour, to condemn whatever Person they Impeach, let the Articles be never so frivolous, or the Surmises never so weak, on which they are to proceed in their Proofs.'[2]

Fourthly, That 'the Body of *Commons*, either Collective, or Represented, has the ill Fortune to be generally Led, and Influenced by the very worst among themselves.'[3]

Fifthly, That 'ev'ry Man that is chosen to Represent his Country in Parliament, [71] turns Fool or Mad-man: Or as he expresses it, That there is hardly to be found through all Nature, a greater Difference between Two Things, than there is between a Representing Commoner, in the Function of his Publick Calling, and the same Person, when he Acts in the Common Offices of Life; When he has got near the Walls of his Assembly, he assumes, and affects an intire Set of very different Airs, he conceives himself a Being of a Superiour Nature to those without; and Acting in a Sphere, where the Vulgar Methods for the Conduct of Humane Life, can be of no Use. He is Listed in a Party, where he neither knows the Temper nor the Designs, nor perhaps the Person of his Leader; and has neither Opinions, nor Thoughts, nor Actions, nor Talk, that he can call his own; but all is convey'd to him by his Leader, as Wind is through an Organ.'[4] This is the Character he gives of a *Representing Commoner*, without Exception, or Restriction; which if he can clear, both from Folly and Madness, then I'll be contented to wear the Cap and Bells; if he can not, then that *August* Assembly must, or which, I believe to be most just, this Dogmatizer [72] ought, with something additional, to Grace his Neck or Shoulders.

Sixthly, That 'Buying and Selling of Elections for Members to

[1] *Discourse*, IV. 39–45.
[2] *Discourse*, IV. 104–8.
[3] *Discourse*, IV. 164–5, 167–9.
[4] *Discourse*, V. 259–63, 270–7, 280–2.

serve in Parliament, is a Practice that ought to be Protected and Incouraged.'[1]

And Lastly, He Summs up all with this Use and Application, 'that this Aversion of the People to the late Proceedings of the *Commons*, is an Accident, that if it last a while, might be improv'd to good Uses.'[2]

And here I think I may dismiss him in some of his own Words; which, with a very little alteration, may be as true in my Mouth, as they were false in his : That 'I am not conscious, that I have forced one Inference, or put it into any other Light, than it appear'd to me, long before I had Thoughts of producing it.'[3]

And therefore, I shall only crave leave, to Summ up the Design and Tendency of this pernitious Libel, in a few plain Positions.

First, That the Author had a Design to subvert our Constitution and Establish'd Government, by endeavouring to introduce a Ballance which was inconsistent with it.

[73] Secondly, That in comparing the Methods of Trial by Impeachments amongst us, with that in Use at *Athens* and *Rome*, and charging the injustice of their Judgments upon us; he is guilty of a very foul Mis-representation, and has, to the utmost of his Power, maliciously overthrown the great Bulwark of the Liberties of the People.

Thirdly, By Representing the Collective Body of the People, as a Giddy, Violent, unjust Rabble, unfit for the Exercise of any Power, he does consequently, endeavour to deprive 'em of that Share in the Government, which by our Constitution they ought to have.

And Lastly, That by Characterizing a *House of Commons*, as such, as Consisting of all Fools and Madmen; he has done his utmost to Destroy the very Being of a *House of Commons;* and that by his Comparisons with the *Decemviri*, the *Ephori*, the *Tribunes*, the *Tyrants* of *Athens*, and the *Orators* of *Argos*; he has attempted to Blemish the most Eminent Members of that Honorable House, with the Odious Character of *Seditious Mutineers*, *Traytors*, *Tyrants and Murderers;* and thereby, as far as he could Instigated [74] and Inflamed the Mob, to abuse, evil Treat, and *de Wit* their Persons.

The several Articles of this Charge are already prov'd upon him beyond Contradiction; And therefore I would advise him, if he means to escape the Censure which is due to his undertaking, to keep

1 *Discourse*, V. 396–9.
2 *Discourse*, V. 312–14.
3 *Discourse*, V. 4–6.

himself effectually concealed; or if he can't do that, to plead, that when he wrote and publish'd this Libel, his Brains were under the Dominion of the Moon, and under that Charitable Construction, I recommend him to the Care of Dr. *Tyson*, the sober Diet and seasonable, tho' sharp Discipline of whose Colledge, may Conduce very much to the bettering both of his Mind and Manners.[1]

But if after all he must needs justify, he ought to do it according to his own Motion, after *Charondas* his way, with a Halter about his Neck, and I that am no Prophet can foretel that he will meet with his Fate, and dye by a Law of his own making; however I would advise him not to be any more severe upon *Oliver*'s Lords for the Vileness of their Clay. For however Just the Reflection may be from other Persons, yet if he shou'd step forth and shew his [75] own Face, 'tis possible the Comparison may be little to his Advantage.

By this time it is more than probable that the Reader may be tired as well as convinc'd, by so tedious a Proof of a plain Proposition: But the Insolence and Clamour of a certain Party, by whom the very Libels here arraign'd, and innumerable others of the Like Nature, were Contriv'd, Commended, Countenanced, and Industriously Dispers'd over all the Kingdom, have been of late so very provoking, and there appears so little Probability of laying that Restless Spirit, by meer Connivance or Oblivion, that tho' a private Man might, and ought to forgive personal Injuries, when he thinks it conducive to the Publick Peace, yet ev'ry Man is bound in Duty, as far as he is able, to display and disappoint such Designs, as may at one time or other prove Fatal to it.

For this Reason it is, that I have entred so particularly into the Proof of what the Author of the *History of the last Sessions of Parliament*, has only hinted in his Preface; and I believe after what has been here produced, that no Man will doubt whether there was a Design against our Constitution; and am also persuaded, [76] that ev'ry Impartial Man will see, that open Attempts were made to procure an Insurrection of the Mob upon that *House of Commons*, of which he writes; and considering that no other Provocation was given, than an endeavour to Rectify some Abuses of which the Nation at that time Complained very generally, and very loudly; and to call those, whom they thought the Principal Offenders, to account, and how dangerously Ill used the *Commons* were for it, the Author had

[1] [Edward Tyson, M.D., was physician of Bethlehem Hospital from 1684 to 1703 (John Stow, *A Survey of the Cities of London and Westminster*, ed. John Strype, 1720, Book I, p. 195).]

Reason to say, that the Managers of that Intreague did endeavour *to have given us a new Model of Government of their own Projection, and so to have procured to themselves a lasting Impunity, and to have mounted their own Beast the Rabble, and driven the sober Part of the Nation like Cattle before 'em.*[1]

I shall only now ask the Reader, whether he finds any thing asserted in that Paragraph, which I have not shewn not only sufficient Ground for, but full proof of? And I can assure him, that I have not used one Instance which the Author in that Preface did not so sufficiently referr to, as to lead me to the Particular Proofs, without further help. If any Man thinks what I have here produc'd, not sufficient, [77] let him make his Exceptions Publick, and I'll Promise him Satisfaction, as Ample and as Publick as he can desire. In the mean Time, let no Man be surpriz'd at the Vehement Clamour, and violent Railing of a certain Party. *Tacitus* has given the Reason of such Noises in Three Words, *Acriores quia iniquae.* They have nothing to cover the Foulness of their Designs, and the Injustice of their Accusations; but the Confidence with which they boast themselves, and the Violence wherewith they Attack better Men.

C. CHARLES LESLIE, *The New Association: Part II* (1703)

ON 1 December 1702, three days after the House of Commons, without a division, had passed a Bill for preventing occasional Conformity, Defoe published his most celebrated pamphlet, *The Shortest-Way with the Dissenters*, '*personating* some of these *Violent Church-men*' like Sacheverell and Leslie, and with a title mimicking two of Leslie's earlier pamphlets, *A Short and Easie Method with the Deists*, 1698, and *A Short and Easie Method with the Jews*, 1699. Years later Defoe could recall 'Innumerable Testimonies . . . of the Pleasure with which the [High Church] Party Embrac'd the Proposal of sending all the Dissenters Ministers to the Gallows, and the Galleys—Of having all their Meeting-Houses Demolish'd, and

[1] Pref. to the History, &c.

being let loose upon their People, to Plunder and Destroy them'.[1] But at the time he found himself more involved with the perils than with the triumphs of irony. A warrant for his arrest was signed by the Secretary of State, Daniel Finch, Earl of Nottingham, on 3 January 1703. On 28 February Defoe rushed into print *A Brief Explanation of a late Pamphlet, Entituled, The Shortest Way with the Dissenters*, insisting that he had had no intention of influencing pending legislation, but was merely employing 'an *Irony not unusual*' to answer such books as *The New Association*.[2] But even this explanation came too late, for Defoe had been indicted at the Old Bailey for libel four days before, and was eventually to stand in the pillory for this crime.

Reverberations of the scream that went up, when the high-flyers discovered that they had been bitten by *The Shortest-Way with the Dissenters*, are still audible in the title of Leslie's reply, the Supplement to which is dated 23 March 1703:

The New Association. Part II. With farther Improvements, As Another and Later Scots Presbyterian-Covenant, Besides that mention'd in the Former Part. And the Proceedings of that Party since. An Answer to some Objections in the Pretended D. Foe's Explication, [and] In the Reflections upon the Shortest Way.[3] With Remarks upon Both. Also an Account of several other Pamphlets, which carry on, and plainly Discover the Design to Undermine and Blow-up the Present Church and Government. Particularly The

[1] Daniel Defoe, *Review*, ii (11 Aug. 1705), 277–8. Leslie testified that he had 'heard one, and then another of the *Church-Party* guess'd at for the *Author*' of *The Shortest-Way with the Dissenters* (*The New Association. Part II*, 1703, p. 6).

[2] [Daniel Defoe,] *A Brief Explanation of a Late Pamphlet, Entituled, The Shortest Way with the Dissenters*, [n.t.p., n.d.], p. 2.

[3] This was an anonymous pamphlet, *Reflections upon a Late Scandalous and Malicious Pamphlet Entitul'd, The Shortest Way with the Dissenters; or Proposals for the Establishment of the Church. To which the said Pamphlet is prefix'd entire by it self*, 1703. Leslie attributes it to 'another of the same *Faction*' as Defoe, whom he identifies as 'Milton's *Amanuensis*' (*The New Association. Part II*, 1703, pp. 6, 7). 'Milton's *Amanuensis*' suggests John Phillips (1631–1706). If this attribution is correct, it provides evidence that others than high-flying Tories were bitten by Defoe's irony, for *Reflections upon a Late Scandalous and Malicious Pamphlet* is a bitter attack on *The Shortest-Way* interpreted literally, as if it had been written by a non-juror.

Discovery of a certain Secret History, Not yet Publish'd. With a Short Account of the Original of Government. Compar'd with the Schemes of the Republicans and Whigs.[1]

Swift's *Discourse* is the first of the '*other Pamphlets*' designed to '*Blow-up the Present Church and Government*' which Leslie considers.

Like the anonymous author of *The Source of Our Present Fears Discover'd*, Leslie is intent to frighten his readers with the threat of a vast conspiracy to overthrow the Establishment and set up a Presbyterian commonwealth. His methods, however, are much more sophisticated. He recounts an admitted lie, 'Though no body believes it', knowing that his readers will remember and repeat the lie but forget the disclaimer. He describes the most innocent proceedings in the most sinister terms, even managing to make a formal protestation of loyalty to the Crown appear to conceal a treasonable intent. He is master of the unsubstantiated claim, the casual innuendo, the vague insinuation, the horrific analogy with events of 1641, and the half-formulated accusation: 'They are *Resolv'd*—' and 'we know what we are to Expect.'

Leslie's main targets are Defoe and Gilbert Burnet, surreptitious extracts of whose unpublished *History of His Own Time* Leslie had somehow managed to see. Swift's *Discourse*—attributed to Burnet—is mentioned only in passing in the body of *The New Association. Part II.* But it unquestionably supplied the point of departure for the Supplement, called 'A Short Account of the Original of Government', which, as Leslie Stephen has remarked, is 'a first and very rough sketch of Leslie's political philosophy, afterwards elaborated in *The Rehearsal*'. So what

[1] On account of an error in Falconer Madan, 'A Bibliography of Sacheverell', *Bibliographer*, iii (April 1883), 138, this work has been attributed to Sacheverell (e.g. *Prose*, iv. p. xxiv), but Leslie's authorship was accepted by Thomas Hearne in 1705 (*Remarks and Collections*, 11 vols., Oxford, 1885–1921, i. 10) and is established beyond any doubt in *Notes and Queries*, 7th Series, ii (17 July 1886), 45, and ii (14 Aug. 1886), 135. The pamphlet was advertised in Defoe's *Review*, i (11 Mar. 1704), 32.

appears below is a short passage, pages 27–28, from the body of *The New Association. Part II*, and pages 10–14 of the separately paginated Supplement. The marginal notes of the original text are reproduced here as footnotes.

[27] . . . This *Publick Liberty* is the *Word* and *Cry* of the *Party*. But when you Ask them what they *Mean* by it, or where they wou'd *Fix* it? They cannot tell. They all Agree that it is in a *Common-Wealth-Frame*, against *Monarchy*, which is their *Aversion*: But then, Is this *Common-Wealth* to be Founded upon the *Power* of the *People*? Yes, yes, that is Agreed on all hands. So far we go on Smoothly; But are not the *People* to be *Represented* by *Members* of their own *Election*? and is not a *House* of *Commons* so *Chosen*, Virtually the *People*, and the whole *Power* of the *People* lodg'd with them? Here they Begin to *Boggle*! For there have been *Houses* of *Commons* that have not Pleas'd them. And we have seen them set up *Legion* against the *Commons*, Nay, Appeal to the *Lords* from them. And they whose former *Measures of Obedience* were all Center'd in the *House* of *Commons*, as the only true *Representative* of the *People*, Now, face about, and Compare them to the *Tyranny* of the *Decemviri* at *Rome*, of the *Ephori* at *Sparta*, of the *Council* of *Four hundred* at *Athens*, of the *Commons* at *Carthage*, and whatever can render them *Odious* to the *People*.

Now, *No Multitude, either Represented or Collective, has been at any time very Nice in observing the Distinction, between Liberty and Licentiousness.*[1]

[28] *The Commons have been perpetually Mistaken in the merits of the Causes and the Persons, as well as in the Consequences of Impeachments, upon the Peace of the State; and therefore were by no Means Qualify'd either as Prosecutors or Judges in such Matters.*[2]

The Commons think themselves concern'd in Point of Honour, to Condemn whatever Person they Impeach, however Frivolous the Articles were upon which they began; or however Weak the Surmises whereon they were to Proceed in their Proofs.[3]

The Body of Commons, either Collective, or Represented, have the ill Fortune to be generally Led and Influenc'd by the very Worst among themselves.[4]

1 *A Discourse of the Contests and Dissentions between the Nobles and Commons in* Athens *and* Rome, *&c.*, IV. 13–16.

2 *Discourse*, IV. 39–45.

3 *Discourse*, IV. 104–8.

4 *Discourse*, IV. 164–5, 167–9.

There is hardly to be found thro' all Nature a greater Difference between two Things, than there is between a Representing Commoner, in the Function of his Publick Calling, and the same Person, when he Acts in the Common Office of Life: When he has got Near the Walls of his Assembly, he assumes and Affects an intire Sett of very different Airs; he conceives himself a Being of a Superiour Nature to those without; and Acting in a Sphere, where the Vulgar Methods for the Conduct of Human Life, can be of no Use. He is Listed in a Party, where he neither knows the Temper, nor the Designs, nor perhaps the Person of his Leader; and has neither Opinions, nor Thoughts, nor Actions, nor Talk, that he can call his own; but all is Convey'd to him by his Leader, as Wind is through an Organ.[1]

Now, methinks, there cannot [be] a Clearer Conviction to any Man, that has the Power of *Thinking* left, of the *Folly* and *Inconsistency* of his own *Schemes*, than to see himself forc'd to *Tack about*, and *Over-turn* every *Stone* he had Laid in his *Foundation*!

Where wou'd these Men have the *Centre* of *Government* plac'd? Indeed they know not. They wou'd have it *Fixed* no where. But *Fleeting* and *Rolling* about, just as their *Fancies* Alter'd, or to serve any *Present Occasion* or *Design* they have in hand.

This is the *Publick Liberty* they Plead for. And for not Understanding of this, the *Bishops* are not fit to *Vote* in *Parliaments*; and the *Clergy* are a *Sett* of *Men* we ought to have in Utter *Aversion*! . . .

[10] . . . The Great *Patron* of *Liberty* beforemention'd, says, *That the Saying,* VOX POPULI, VOX DEI, *ought to be Understood of the Universal Bent and Current of a People; Not of the bare Majority of a few* REPRESENTATIVES; *which is often Procur'd by little Arts, and great Industry and Application; wherein those who Engage in the Pursuits of Malice and Revenge, are much more Sedulous than such as wou'd Prevent them.*[2]

But now, How shall this *Universal Bent* and *Current* of the *People* be known, since it must not be taken from their *Representatives*?

Why, from a *Mobb* or *Legion*, set up by any *Party*, to *Whoop* and *Hallow*! And this is *Vox Populi*, and so *Vox Dei*! Let them shew any other way. Wou'd they send Men about to *Poll* the whole *Nation*?

The *Senslesness* of such *Schemes* is *Nauseous*. But if it were not *Destructive* too, we cou'd Bear it the Better.

In the very same Breath, with that before-quoted, he sets it down

[1] *Discourse*, V. 259–63, 270–7, 280–2.
[2] *Discourse*, IV. 113–20.

as a Rule, *Never to give way to Popular Clamours.*[1] Where are we now? Where now is the *Vox Populi*? These Men cannot speak *Consistently* three *Lines* together! Their *Brains* are turn'd. They know not what themselves wou'd be at.

[11] He is very Angry at the *Power* of the *Commons*; and Advises *That the most August Assembly of the Commons wou'd please to form a* PANDECT *of their own Power and Privileges.*[2] Which yet he tells us is Impossible. *When* (says he) *a Child grows Easie and Content by being Humour'd; And when a Lover becomes Satisfy'd by small Compliances, without further Pursuits.* [That's my Man! This was like thy Self!] *There expect to find Popular Assemblies Content with small Concessions. If there cou'd one single Example be brought from the whole Compass of History, of any one Popular Assembly, who after beginning to Contend for Power, ever sat down Quietly with a certain Share. Or, if one Instance cou'd be Produc'd of a Popular Assembly, that ever knew, or Propos'd, or Declar'd what Share of Power was their Due, then might there be some Hopes, that it were a Matter to be Adjusted*, &c.[3]

But if there be no *Hopes* of it; If it be a Matter which they themselves do not *know* (as he says) and so cannot *Declare* it; Why wou'd this Gentleman *Propose* it? It must be only a *Sarcasm* upon *That most August Assembly* of the *Commons*, as he *Ironically* calls them. Upon which I leave them to *Animadvert.*

I have now only to do with his *Schemes* and *Ballancings*. What Remedy do's he Propose for this? Why thus: *That they to whom the rest of the Ballance is Entrusted, shou'd never give way so far to Popular Clamours, as to make the least Breach in the Constitution, through which a Million of Abuses and Encroachments will certainly, in time force their way.*[4]

Ah! *Doctor*, *Doctor*, Was this *Always* your *Doctrine*? Are you come to see it at last? And yet never *Mend!*

But who are they that hold the rest of the *Ballance*? This must be either the *Crown*, or the *Lords*, or *Both*. And they must *Never give way* to the *Popular Clamours* of the *Commons*. And this will hold the *Ballance* even.

But you say, That the *Commons* are never *Satisfy'd*. That they will not be *Content* with a *Share* in the *Ballance*. Nay, That they do not *know* what their own *Share* is. How then shall they *Ballance* it? Is it not Possible, in so *Nice* a Case as this, That the several *Parties*

[1] *Discourse*, IV. 148–9.
[2] *Discourse*, V. 121–3.
[3] *Discourse*, IV. 133–44.
[4] *Discourse*, IV. 147–51.

who held this *Ballance*, may Differ in Opinion (even tho' *Wise* and *Good Men*) as to one Anothers *Share*? And is there no *Umpire*? None who has *Authority* to *Compose* and *Settle* this Matter? Then there is no *Remedy*, but that they go to *Cuffs* about it, and Engage the *Nation* in a *Civil War*.

But all *Power* is *One*, and *Indivisible*, whether in the Hands of *One* or *Many*. And *Several* Independent *Powers*, in the same *Government*, is *Anarchy* and *Confusion*. And is set up by None but who are Laying *Seed-plots* for *Rebellion*, or who are *Besotted* in their *Understandings*.

Let me Imitate a little of this Author's *Rhetorick* and *Fancy*. When CHILDREN *Agree in* SCRAMBLING *for* APPLES; *And Jealous* LOVERS *about their* MISTRESS; *then expect to find* RIVALS *for* POWER *Agree in each other's* SHARE *of the* BALLANCE!

[12] But he tells us of one *Sort* of these *Rivals*, who are the *Fiercest* of any in their *Pursuits* (tho' of late he has found Reason to have a Better Opinion of them) who, *About the middle of Queen* Elizabeth's *Reign*, *or soon after*, *Arose in* England, *under the Name of* PURITAN, *and began to grow Popular*, *by Molding up their new Schemes of Religion with Republican Principles in Government; And gaining upon the* Prerogative *as well as the* NOBLES, *under several denominations*, *for the space of about Sixty Years*, *did at last Overthrow the Constitution; And according to the Usual Course of such Revolutions*, *did Introduce a* Tyranny, *first of the People*, *and then of a single Person.*[1]

This is a very Instructive Passage. And wou'd give one Cause to Enquire, what Reason the *Author* has since found out (except his being ever *In-consistent* with *Himself*) to Struggle so hard for letting the same *Faction* still have a *Share* in the *Ballance* of *Power*!

Has he not seen in his own time (and Himself a great *Manager* in it) the very same Thing done, by the very same *Faction*, in all the Particulars he has before Describ'd?

But he shou'd Explain to Us, How there can be a *Tyranny* (as he says) of the *People*, as well as of a *Single Person*? What is now become of our *Schemes*? Can the *People* be *Tyrants* over *Themselves*! Then it is time to look to it. For that must be a Terrible *Tyranny*! As much more than that of a *Single Person*, as they are more in *Number* than *He*. Or a *Legion* of *Devils* worse than *One*. Who shall hold the *Ballance* of *Power* betwixt the *People* and the *People*? Or, come in with them for a *Share*?

[1] *Discourse*, V. 98–110.

This was so Obvious to him, That he wou'd Exclude the *People* from the *Choice* of their *Representatives* in *Parliament*. How then shou'd it be done? Why let the *Faction* (who are *Wiser Men*) even *Bribe* Downright, and Buy *Votes* where they can. This he Expresly *Justifies*, and *Argues* for it. He says, *That according to the present Turn and Disposition of Men in our Nation, it were a less Abuse to Bribe Elections, than leave them to the Discretion of the Chusers. That the Talents which Qualify a Man for the Service of his Country in Parliament, are very different from those which give him a Dexterity at making his Court to the People; and do not often meet in the same Subject. Then for the Moral Part, the Difference is Inconsiderable; And whoever Practices upon the Weakness and Vanity of the People, is Guilty of an Immoral Action, as much as if he did it upon their Avarice. Besides, the two Trees may be Judg'd by their Fruits. The former produces a Sett of Popular Men, fond of their own Merits and Abilities, their Opinions, and their Eloquence; Whereas the Bribing of Elections seems to be at Worst, but an ill means of keeping things upon the old foot* [that is, in the hands of the Faction] *by leaving the Defence of our Properties, Chiefly in the hands of those who will be the greatest Sufferers, whenever they are endanger'd* [that is, who had Enrich'd themselves by Cheating the Publick, and wou'd be the greatest Sufferers, if brought [13] to Account.] *It is easie to Observe in the Late and Present Parliament, that several Boroughs and some Counties have been Represented by Persons, who little thought to have had such Hopes before* [These were Persons he suppos'd not so well Affected to the Late Government.] *And how far this may proceed, when such a way* [that is, the Freedom of Elections] *is laid open for the Exercise and Encouragement of Popular Arts, one may best Judge from the Consequences that the same Causes produc'd both in* Athens *and* Rome. *For let Speculative Men Reason, or rather Refine as they please; it will ever be true among us, that as long as Men Engage in the Publick Service, upon Private ends, and whilst all Pretences to a Sincere Roman Love of our Country, are look'd upon as an Affectation, a Foppery, or a Disguise; (which has been a good while our Case, and is likely to continue so;) it will be safer to Trust our Property and Constitution in the hands of such, who have Pay'd for their Elections, than of those who have obtain'd them by Servile Flatteries of the People.*[1] Thus that Worthy Author.

And he tells (*ib.*) That he foresaw the Danger to their Constitution, *When the Act pass'd, some Years ago, against Bribing of Elections.*

[1] *Discourse*, V. 356–8, 368–99.

For which Reason he was against it, as since for *Occasional Conformity*.

But, as this is the *Bitterest* thing cou'd be said against the *Revolution*, as if it did not Proceed upon the General *Bent* and *Inclination* of the *People*; but only *Voted* by a Company of *Brib'd* Men; And cou'd stand no longer than the *People* were still *debarr'd* from the *Freedom* of their *Elections*.

So, on the other hand, it is a Total *overthrow* of all the *Scheme* of Founding *Government* upon the *Election* of the *People*, Whose *Weakness* and *Vanity* is such (as this *Author* says) as only fit to be *Practis'd* upon by *Cunning* Men; so that it were *Better* (and he thinks it as *Moral* too) to Trust to whom any *Faction* shall *Bribe*, than to leave it to the *Choice* of the *People*!

And yet He, and every one of the *Faction*, pretend to know the Minds of the *People* as *Bravely* as if they had Consulted *every Man* in the *Nation*; and, upon every *Turn*, they *Appeal* to that, and *Frighten* us with it. This *Author*, speaking of the *House* of *Commons*, says, p. [124] *That they have been Authors of a New and Wonderful Thing in* England, *which is*, *for a House of Commons to lose the Universal Favour of the Numbers they Represent*. Which is as *Bold* and *Malicious*, as it is *False*; most of the same *Members* being again *Chosen*. But it was by their *Arts* of *Imposing* upon the *Weakness* and *Vanity* of the *People*! And their not taking the more *Laudable* way of *Bribing*!

And this is one way of the *Faction* their *Practising* upon the *Weakness* and *Vanity* of the *People*, to give out Lewd *Lyes*, that they may be *Believ'd* by some. Which is but a sort of an *Occasional Conformity*!

And it is not to be thought strange, That these Men shou'd be for *Occasional Conformity*, who have none but *Occasional Thoughts*, and *Occasional Principles*, to *Comply* with every *Turn* of *Faction* or *Interest*, for their own Ends. [14] Like the *Vicar* of *Brey*, who kept his *Living* in all the *Turns* of the *Reigns* of *Edw*. vi, Q. *Mary*, and Q. *Eliz*. without Changing of his *Principle*; for his *Principle* was, as he said, to be *Vicar* of *Brey*, till he cou'd get a Better *Preferment*! What! wou'd he suffer himself to be *Ruin'd*, for the *Iniquities* of other Men! Therefore he never stood out for a *Re-Cantation Sermon* (which was the Custom then, and may be again) but when Q. *Mary* came in, he took for his Text, *State super vias Antiquas*; And bade Men be of the *Religion* of their *Fathers*. But when Q. *Eliz*. Ascended the *Throne*, then his *Text* was, *Cantate Domino Canticum Novum*. Now, *Sing a New Song*.

How many of these *New Songs* have we heard from these Men, from this same Renowned *Author*, the *Cock* of the *Party*; And that within the Compass of a very few years? For the *King*, and Against him! For *Passive Obedience*, and Against it! Against the *Deposing-Doctrine*, and For it! For the *Power* of the *People*, and Against it! For the *House* of *Commons*, and as *Violently* Against it! Against the *Lords*, and Now as much as For them! &c.

Here is *Occasional Conformity* in Abundance! These Men leave no *Principle*, no *Constitution*, no *Thing* in the World *Certain*, but *Un-Certainty*! They are the *Antipodes* to all *Government*, *Method*, or *Settlement*! They are *Harrington's Rota*, perfect *Babel* and *Confusion*! Fitted to *Pull down* every thing; but to *Build up* Nothing! There can be no *Peace* or *Quietness* where they Live, and have any *Power*! When they had the *Whole* in their own hands, they cou'd not *Agree* among *Themselves* (nor ever *Will*, they *Cannot*, having no *Foundation*) but *Divided*, and *Sub-divided*, into New *Schemes*, New *Governments*, New *Constitutions*, every Day! And now they wou'd feign *Try* it *once* more! But these are *Costly Experiments*, and may Draw out the *Hearts-Blood* of the *Nation;* which cannot long Subsist, under many such *Paroxisms*. . . .

INDEX

PRINTED IN GREAT BRITAIN
AT THE UNIVERSITY PRESS, OXFORD
BY VIVIAN RIDLER
PRINTER TO THE UNIVERSITY